DATE DUE

The Kids Market

Myths and Realities

The Kids Market
Myths and Realities

James U. McNeal, Ph.D.

PMP

PARAMOUNT MARKET PUBLISHING

Paramount Market Publishing, Inc.
120 West State Street, Suite 403
Ithaca, NY 14850
www.paramountbooks.com
Telephone: 607-275-8100; 888-787-8100   Facsimile: 607-275-8101

Publisher: James Madden
Editorial Director: Doris Walsh
Project Editor: Diane Crispell

This publication is designed to provide accurate and authoritative information in regard to the subject matter covered. It is sold with the understanding that the publisher is not engaged in rendering legal, accounting, or
other professional services. If legal advice or other expert assistance is required, the services of a competent professional should be sought.

Library of Congress Catalog Number:

Cataloging in Publication Data available
McNeal, James, U. 1931–
The Kids Market

ISBN 0-9671439-1-8

Book design and composition: Anne Kilgore, Paperwork
Index by Robert Kibbee

Contents

Myth: *"Children are not grateful when they are given things."*

Reality: Children may not show their gratitude like adults, but they tell us that they like those who give them things, and they are fondest of the biggest giver.

Myth: *"Children would rather have a free bicycle than a free baseball."*

Reality: It depends on the time. If the children have to wait 100 UPCs for the bicycle and 5 UPCs for the baseball, most of the time they will opt for the baseball.

Myth: *"Public relations is not an alternative to advertising when it comes to the kids market."*

Reality: Public relations is not an alternative to advertising when it comes to kids; it's an absolutely necessary companion.

Myth: *"Kids' clubs are a drain on resources."*

Reality: Over 80 percent of kids' clubs studied report that they contribute to their company's bottom line while growing new customers.

Myth: *"In the milk industry, we have targeted kids for years, but they are still reluctant to make it their favorite snack beverage."*

Reality: A kid can't snack out of a gallon jug.

Myth: *"Children change brands often and show little brand loyalty."*

Reality: Children find security in attaching themselves to an object—a pillow, a blanket, a store, a brand—that enhances their well being. But children's curiosity has not yet been suppressed as ours often has, so they do turn their attention to other objects including other brands.

Myth: *"Kids love products that are just like Mom's and Dad's."*

Reality: Kids love products that are just like Mom's and Dad's, but not as much as they love products that are just for kids.

Myth: *"If your kid's product can only satisfy one need, let it be the need for play."*

Reality: If your product can only satisfy one need, shoot it, and put it out of its misery.

Myth: *"Satisfy the kids and you satisfy the parents."*

Reality: Children loved their free Mystic Magic Magnifier, but parents hated the burned holes in their curtains and tablecloths.

Preface

In 1962, I presented my first research paper on the consumer behavior of children documenting them as a bona fide market. The audience was a chapter of the American Marketing Association consisting of a group of marketers from manufacturing, service, and retail organizations and some academicians such as myself. They practically laughed me out of the place. "Kids as a market? You gotta be kidding." Very few are laughing today, and if they are, it is most likely at themselves for not recognizing the market potential of this emerging group of powerful consumers and its impact on their success.

In 1987, my first book on the subject of children as consumers—that was the title, *Children As Consumers*—was published and received a warm reception. The purpose of the book was mainly to report my various research findings and my thinking on children's consumer behavior in an easy-to-read fashion. The timing was right, I guess. It was widely read in the business community. As a result, I was asked to speak at various conferences, consult with firms that were in or thinking about getting into the market, and work with government units interested in regulating marketing activities directed to children.

I should add that members of some government agencies and consumer welfare groups considered me to be instigating and encouraging marketing efforts to this group. Some of these suggested, in various ways, that I should shut up. But I tried to work around them, go with the flow, and continue my research into the most fascinating area one can imagine. I also began to extend my research efforts abroad, mainly into the Asia-Pacific region.

In 1990, I published a bibliography on the subject of children as consumers as an attempt to serve people who contacted me and asked for more information on the topic. It was titled *A Bibliography of Research and Writ-*

ings on Marketing and Advertising to Children. A lot of people, including a number of academicians, seemed to appreciate the bibliography, bought it, and used it. To me this was a good sign that the topic of children as consumers was no longer a laughing matter, that people were taking it seriously and doing a good deal of research related to it.

In 1992, my third book related to the children's market, *Kids as Customers*, was published. It received a rousing reception from all circles (except of course my own university, which had pretty much concluded by the time my first book arrived in 1987 that this was not a legitimate area of study and that I was mainly skylarking). I was asked to do a great deal of consulting and speaking. I welcomed most of this, since the forthcoming revenue became the principal source of funds for my growing research program, particularly the overseas portion, which is so costly.

That book—*Kids as Customers* instead of consumers—described children as spenders and influencers of parental spending, but went a step further to explain in some detail the forces that were driving the rapid growth of this new market. It also attempted to give more consideration to the marketing efforts to children that had concurrently blossomed. In effect, it viewed children from both sides of the counter rather than just the consumer side as the 1987 book did.

By 1995, virtually every consumer goods industry was somehow involved in marketing to children, either as a primary, influence, or future market, or some combination of these. In addition to all the commercial marketers targeting kids, many nonprofit groups and causes launched programs beamed at this market segment. A growing number of marketers began heading overseas to target children as they sought market growth and opportunity beyond intense domestic competition.

One thing quickly became apparent. A lot of this marketing to kids was mismarketing—that is, it was fraught with mistakes. It seemed that an increasing amount of my work with firms in the children's market involved helping them correct errors and misunderstandings rather than helping them get situated in the market.

From my perspective, these mistakes often appeared to be based on stereotypes—what I call myths—regarding children and their consumer behavior. For example, one widespread myth was the notion that a parent who is also a marketer—what I call a "**marent**" in later chapters—holds special insights into children's behavior. The reality is that many firms have lost millions discovering just how unique its marketers' kids are.

Over the past couple of years I have cataloged these myths, discussed them with business firms and academic colleagues, and finally decided to use them as a format to talk about marketing to children in this book. I do so with some hesitation because such a format can have a "greater-than-thou" ring to it. I sure hope this book doesn't come across this way because I certainly don't have a lock on how to do it when it comes to the kids market. But from years of experience, I often can spot errors and point them out to those who will listen and read.

So within these pages I try to provide a detailed description of children's consumer behavior, this time through a treatment of 26 myths and their realities. Most important among the book's features, I believe, are my efforts to correct these myths, to show what businesses in the children's market may be doing wrong, how they may be doing it wrong, why they may be doing it wrong, and provide practical answers and solutions.

Hopefully some of the two-million-plus marketers, retailers, service suppliers, and social marketers who work in the kids market will heed the advice and suggestions, and consequently satisfy more kids and their families and make more money. That's the key: satisfy more kids, make more money, in that order. The net results should be better products and services for kids and better treatment of kids by recognizing that they are not just 3-footers in a 6-foot world. They are people, too. They are bona fide consumers. They are a market with more market potential than any other demographic group.

So I try to tell it like it is and like it should be, believing that satisfying kids is the most fundamental of all marketing efforts. It will keep a company in business in the fiercest of competition because it will keep kids coming back—for the rest of their lives. But if a firm insists on marketing by myth and doesn't try hard to satisfy kids, it will run out of customers and die!

How This Book Is Structured

The book has three parts: (1) an overview; (2) myths and realities about children as a market (chapters 1-8); and (3) myths and realities about children's responses to marketing behavior (chapters 9-21). The overview is just that, an attempt to put the materials in the book in perspective, and in some cases to summarize some of the significant discussions. It is personalized somewhat due to my 35 years of involvement in the subject matter.

The first eight chapters describe myths and their realities regarding children as a market segment. I demonstrate the enormous market potential children hold today is far beyond the penny-candy potential once attributed to them. I characterize children as not one but three markets—a current market spending their own money on their own wants and needs; an influence market spending mom's and dad's money on their own wants and needs; and a future market for all goods and services. Additionally, I show how kids grow into these three markets from infancy, and describe the parental and marketing forces that shape children's behavior as consumers. I hone in on new family lifestyles that emerged in the late 1980s. I also discuss the types of stores and products that contribute substantially to children's development as consumers.

In the third part of the book—chapters 9 through 21—I detail children's reactions to marketing, specifically, their responses to stores, products, including social products, brands, advertising, promotion, public relations, and packaging. The term "reactions" is intended to connote both positive and negative, avoiding and seeking, liking and disliking, effective and ineffective as they apply to the marketing-consumer relationship. In other words, I try to show what works and what doesn't in terms of correctly marketing to children and their parents.

I follow these discussions with an examination of marketing research efforts among children as consumers, showing how some work better than others. Finally, in the last chapter, I devote some time and space talking about kids as a global market. The first time I went to Taiwan and China to conduct research among Chinese children and their families, I was struck by the number of U.S. marketers who already had a presence there. Today that number is much greater.

Finally, the book contains many color drawings done by children resulting from many of my research efforts. About half are by American children and half by Asian children. I explain briefly in this book, and with more detail in the 1992 book, the reasons why I so often choose this research technique. But I also present them here because I believe they are well worth a "thousand words" when it comes to explaining some concept or fact, and that they can say it more eloquently than I can.

Let me take this opportunity to thank Mindy Ji, Shushan Wu, and Chyon-Hwa Yeh for their research assistance and guidance related to children as consumers in China, Taiwan, and Hong Kong. Their work is apparent throughout the book. At the time of this writing, Mindy Ji is still very much involved in my research program helping me to design and implement studies of children's consumer behavior in China.

OVERVIEW

The Kids Market
Grows Up

In the beginning, the notion of kids as consumers got no respect. Thirty-five years ago, when I first posited the notion that children constitute a viable consumer market, I seemed to be one of a very few who could see the market potential. Now kids are everybody's business.

Today this market segment is coveted by manufacturers of products ranging from autos to zinnia seeds, and by service industries from airlines to zoos. In fact, few consumer industries don't target kids. Just look at how the words children, child, and kid have entered many firms' names:

Advertising and Promotion Agencies: Kid Think, Inc. (Griffin Bacal), Kid Connection (Saatchi & Saatchi), Just Kid, Inc. (North Castle Communications), and Kidcentives (Mello Smello), for instance.

Advertising Media: All major media now sport editions geared for kids: Disney Radio and Children's Broadcasting Corporation (radio), *Sports Illustrated for Kids* and *Crayola Kids* (magazines), Fox Children's Network and Kids WB (television), *My Weekly Reader* and *Class Acts* (newspapers). The Internet also sports hundreds of addresses for kids, such as www.worldkids.com and www.4Kids.com, and the number seems to grow daily.

Marketing Research Firms: Kid2Kid, Kideation (Doyle Research Associates), Kid Facts, Children's Market Research, Inc., and Child Research Services, to name a few.

Retailers: GapKid, Kids R Us, Fit For Kids, and Kid's Foot Locker are some that compete for the children's apparel business.

Many companies have developed branded kids' clubs as a route to maintaining a permanent relationship with children. Some with the word kids in them include Burger King Kids Club, Sega Kids Club, Fox Kids Club, and Westin Kids Club. With the advent of database marketing, kids' clubs have come into their own, not only as a way to communicate with children, but also as a means to distribute to them and study their consumer behavior.

Just think of the thousands of products designed primarily for children. Toys, candy, soft drinks and sweetened cereals have been traditional kids' products for years, and in recent years their sales have expanded. But more important, the list of products for kids that essentially did not exist a decade ago has grown enormously.

• • • • •
The list of products for kids that essentially did not exist a decade ago has grown enormously.

One area that particularly comes to mind is technology: kids' computers, software, and online services. Nickelodeon offers an accessory kit that transforms any PC into a kid's PC. The relatively high costs and rocketing growth of these technology-based products for kids almost overshadow other relatively new product lines such as prepared kids' meals that come frozen, chilled, and shelf-stable, and a whole array of toiletries.

Among the many "adult" brands that now offer kids' line extensions are Dial For Kids (liquid and bar soap), Pert Plus For Kids (shampoo), Kid Fresh (flushable wipes), and Crest For Kids (toothpaste). Usually these kids-also products differ by being scaled down and funned up. For example, Dial For Kids, an antibacterial soap, is formulated with mild, non-irritating cleansers to be gentle to kids' skin. The fun is added by packaging it in bold colors and producing it in such fragrances as screaming strawberry and power purple.

And in virtually all product categories for kids, entertainment-based licensed characters such as the Flintstones and Batman have expanded sales even more—an additional $17 billion in 1996 alone.

Adult services have also been adapted to kids. There is now an array of banking services for kids, investment services including investment camps, and entertainment centers and parks. Some travel agencies have begun specializing in trip planning built around kids. The hospitality industry has awakened to children as real people and now offers services such as check-in, in-room, and entertainment options, many under a kids'-club umbrella such as Camp Hyatt and Best Western Young Travelers Club.

And consider these annual marketing communications expenditures related to kids as a market:

> **Over $1 billion** spent on media advertising to kids, mostly on television. Continued growth is expected as online programming to kids attracts advertisers.

At least $4.5 billion spent on promotion such as premiums, sampling, coupons, contests, and sweepstakes with much growth expected as more nontraditional players such as motels, airlines, banks, and professional sports come into the market with kids' programs and kids' clubs.

Perhaps $2 billion spent on public relations including broadcast and print publicity, event marketing, and school relations, much of this within the realm of kids' clubs. The public relations industry was slow to acknowledge the kid market, but they were pulled into it by integrated marketing firms and other clients who required their services. Now it appears that publicists will increasingly initiate their own programs and thus grow the market even more.

Probably $3 billion spent on packaging especially designed for kids. Kids' packaging is no longer an afterthought, as one major producer of kids' snacks once called it. At least some members of the industry are recognizing that kids' packaging needs often differ from those of adults.

- - - - - -

In the mid-1980s, perhaps one-third of major retail chains made some effort to target kids as a market. Today, that figure is closer to two-thirds and still growing.

These figures are small compared with those found in adult marketing, and are still relatively small when compared to kids' market potential. Nevertheless, they are measures of the seriousness with which business is treating the kids market.

Retailing is another industry that has awakened to the clout of children in the past five or six years and done something about it. My studies show that in the mid-1980s perhaps one-third of major retail chains made some effort to target kids as a market. Today, that figure is closer to two-thirds and still growing. Particularly significant are those who have nothing to sell directly to children, such as auto dealers and insurance brokers, but still target children for their influence and future potential.

And recently we have seen another player become more active in the kids market—**social marketers**. They have always been around in small numbers with even smaller marketing budgets. For example, the Smokey The Bear campaign attempted to teach kids to protect our forests. Today more social marketers are targeting children, often with big budgets that buy into kids advertising and promotion. They assume that if others can sell soap and soup to kids, they can sell social concepts to kids in the same way.

A good example is the Office of National Drug Control Policy in the White House targeting kids aged 8 to 13 with anti-drug messages. For the first time, it is doing so with hard money, almost $200 million, that will vie with toys and snacks for commercial time on television and in other media. Currently, I am working with the World Health Organization and the Centers for Disease Control and Prevention, each of which wants to target children with healthy lifestyle messages. Social marketing to children appears to be growing rapidly and will compete with commercial marketers for a share of children's minds, money, and matter.

Finally, the number of business symposia and workshops that focus on the kids market have multiplied since 1990. The first symposium on this topic in which I participated was the Second Annual Symposium on Children's Research held in 1988 at the Princeton Club in New York City. It was sponsored by Youth Research whose president is Karen Forcade, one of the pioneers in children's consumer research. That first symposium attracted fewer than 30 people including the presenters. Today, at least four organizations regularly sponsor conferences on kids as consumers: Institute of International Research, International Quality & Productivity Center, Strategic Research Institute, and The Marketing to Kids Report. Some hold two or more meetings a year that attract 200 executives from companies that target children.

It's Their Market Potential, Stupid

Why this surge of kid orientation in business? Of new kid-friendly firms? Of kidizement of media, brands, and stores? Why are there now marketing strategies that target kids alongside those that target adults? It's simple arithmetic: People x Dollars = Markets.

I get quite a few calls from the press asking me why so much marketing activity is devoted to kids today compared with a few years ago. Because I am prone to respond with a lengthy dissertation about all the forces that have shaped the market, I keep a sign above my desk that says: "It's the market potential, stupid."

Kids are more than just one market. They are three markets in one and each should receive significant marketing and merchandising effort.

> **First, kids are a primary market.** They spend their own money on their own wants and needs.
>
> **Second, kids are an influence market.** They determine much of the spending of parents.
>
> **Third, they are a future market.** Eventually they will be a potential market for all goods and services.

Put them all together and kids represent more market potential than any other demographic segment. Let me briefly assign some dollar figures to these three dimensions of the market. These three facets of the kids market are discussed in more detail in the chapters that follow.

Primary Spenders

As a primary market, kids spend money they get from allowances and other sources on a wide range of products, not just on penny candy as they did when I first began to write about them. **Figure 0-1** shows how spending by kids aged 4 to 12 has changed during the three decades I have been tracking it.

While these are unadjusted figures, one can see that they were static during the 1960s and 1970s, began to take off in the 1980s, and jumped off the chart by the mid-1990s. Moreover, these figures are understated because they do not account for the same-year spending that resulted from kids taking money from their savings. They represent only our estimates of immediate

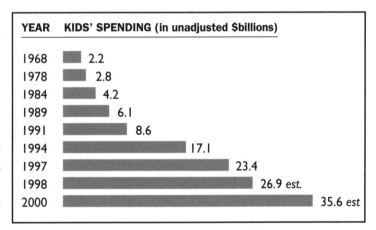

YEAR	KIDS' SPENDING (in unadjusted $billions)
1968	2.2
1978	2.8
1984	4.2
1989	6.1
1991	8.6
1994	17.1
1997	23.4
1998	26.9 est.
2000	35.6 est

FIGURE 0-1

spending from income based on parents telling us how much money their children receive, spend, and save.

No one knows exactly when the critical mass of dollars in the hands of kids first occurred or was first recognized, but myriad marketing activities that focus on kids just as a primary market today took on a life of their own during the recessional years of the late 1980s. For instance, it seems like the candy and gum racks in convenience stores suddenly blossomed with "kidcitement" around 1987 or 1988.

Persuasive Power

The influence market—children directing the spending of their parents' money—has grown with at least as much robustness as the primary market. Of course, kids can't influence parents' spending unless parents let them.

They have always let them, but in the late 1980s parents started ceding unprecedented decision making power to their kids. I have not tracked kidfluence as long as primary spending, but in 1985 it was around $50 billion. It approached $190 billion in 1997, and is anticipated to reach $290 billion in 2000.

Figures of this magnitude spark the interests of marketers. Like primary spending, influence spending has quickly spread among a wide range of products and services. Auto producers, clothiers, and makers of toiletries are industries that started actively targeting kids as an influence market in the late 1980s and early 1990s. Saturday morning television, once the domain of cereal, toys and confections, had to make room for new advertisers such as fast foods and jeans makers.

• • • • •
Growing customers from childhood is a viable long-term marketing strategy for entering a new culture.

When Ted Turner announced his Cartoon Network, primarily for kids, there were questions about a glut of advertising time in kids' television. Hardly. The additional advertising time was easily absorbed by new entries into the kids market, and in fact, the price of 30 seconds of kidvid advertising continued to climb, even more than the precious prime-time slots that mainly target adults.

Tomorrow's Customers

As a future market, kids have the most market potential, for they will eventually buy all goods and services. If a business nurtures kids as future consumers, they are more apt to like that company and prefer its products and services once they get old enough to buy them on their own.

Delta Air Lines started its Fantastic Flyer program in the late 1980s as a way of growing customers for its airline seats. It targets kids aged 7 to 14 with a magazine, birthday greetings, special food on flights, and bargain airfares for their families. Delta knows it has only two sources of new customers—those who switch from its competitors and those the airline grows from childhood. Both are expensive, but the latter are likely to provide more profits in the long run. The more common approach, switching, often leads to profitless competition.

The search for new customers also is why more kid marketers are looking overseas where they can switch customers from less efficient competition. These same international marketers are learning, too, that growing customers from childhood is a viable long-term marketing strategy for entering a new culture. Kids are less culture-bound than adults and more responsive to new ideas, including new products from other nations.

How are kids handling all this newfound attention? Well, they don't know it any other way. They think it comes with the territory, that it is a natural part of becoming a person. They become consumers earlier than they did a decade ago, know more about the consumption function, and seek it out more. They are confident as consumers.

Over the years, I have used drawing studies among children of many nations because it is a good way to get them to communicate. Drawing is an engaging activity for them. Their drawings demonstrate their confidence, knowledge, and positive attitudes as consumers. Take a look at the drawing in **Figure 0-2** (colorplate 0-1). A 9-year-old Korean girl drew this picture in 1995 when asked, "Draw what comes to your mind when you think about going shopping."

FIGURE 0-2

Notice the poise shown by this child, her presence in the store among other shoppers, and her awareness of store-related items that give her the feeling of belonging in the department store. She shows lots of detail: many shoppers, a sales clerk, special prices, a variety of fixtures holding a variety of products including play items and clothing, a TV monitor repeating a sales message, shopping bags with the store's name on them. You can feel the excitement she feels. This same picture repeats itself in various ways in all developed and developing countries, and confirms the newfound stature of children as consumers.

Forces that have Fostered Children's Consumer Clout

Since there have always been kids, and their numbers in the U.S. haven't grown appreciably in the past decade or so, how do we explain their newfound consumer clout? As noted earlier, people x dollars = markets. The number of children aged 4 to 12 declined somewhat in the early 1980s and grew somewhat in the late 1980s. There were roughly 3.8 million births annually in the U.S. through the first seven years of the 1980s, then the number edged up to around 4 million starting in 1988. This pace continued through the first half of the 1990s and then leveled off. In 1998 the U.S. had about 36 million kids aged 4 to 12, up from 34 million in 1980.

This slight increase does not explain the enormous increase in kids' dollar power during the same period, however. What circumstances could have produced this economic phenomenon beginning in the late 1980s? The answer lies in a complex of economic, social, and psychological forces that came together. I will summarize the eight forces here and discuss them in more detail throughout the remaining chapters.

More Earners per Kid

• • • • • • • •

Almost one in every six American children is someone's stepchild.

The choices offered by the birth-control pill, increased educational and labor-force aspirations of women, and double-digit inflation of the 1970s all served to move millions of mothers into the workforce. This in turn gave families more money to spend. In 1970, around half of mothers with children aged 6 to 13 worked full- or part-time. By 1985, 67 percent of mothers with children in that age group worked. Five years later, 73 percent did so. Even with Dad and Mom both working, families didn't hit high-income brackets, but it did allow them to keep up with inflation and maybe get slightly ahead of it. And it also provided money that wouldn't have been there otherwise.

Fewer Kids per Family

The total fertility rate in the early 1960s, during the last years of the baby boom, was 3.5 per woman of childbearing age. By the early 1980s, it had declined to 1.8, or close to half of the baby-boom rate (it has since risen a little to hover around the 2-child mark). Clearly, mothers were electing to have fewer children. The reasons included the soaring inflation rates of the 1970s, the fact that mothers wanted to work or had to work and could not take care of a large number of children, and for some, a new philosophy of one (or two) is enough. Whatever the reasons, there were fewer children per family and more money allotted to each than would otherwise have been the case.

Older (Wealthier) Parents

In the 1960s and 1970s, women viewed age 30 as the now or never age for having children. By the mid-1980s, births to thirty-something women were soaring. Career-first thinking had a lot to do with this. Uncertain economic conditions also encouraged many families to postpone having children. By delaying births and getting careers in place, parents had more money when children were born and tended to shower them with more. Wanting children but delaying having them seems to give children much more importance when they arrive.

Fractured Families

Splintered families mean more gift-giving relatives. Almost one in every six American children is someone's stepchild. While it is often little consolation to the kids, they tend to get more money and things from multiple sets of parents and grandparents. Some additional acquisitions are simply due to being shuttled between households and therefore needing another toothbrush, comb, and bedding. Naturally, some extra toys and snack items go along with the necessities. Some of the money and things parents give to children in these situations are DWI gifts; that is, gifts to help children deal with it.

Single-Parent Households

More single parents mean earlier consumer maturity. Between 1970 and 1990, the number of births to unwed mothers in the U.S. increased two and a half times. During this same period, the number of divorced women almost tripled. The net result was a large number of single-parent households in which kids were expected to participate more in household activities. In these households, children tend to take on the consumer role earlier in life and more regularly, handling money, shopping, buying things for the family and for themselves. For example, our research shows that children in single-parent households often make their first purchases almost a year earlier than those in two-parent households. Distant dads may also be a hidden source of income for children in single-parent households when they provide gifts, money, and vacations for their kids.

Children in single-parent households often make their first purchases almost a year earlier than those in two-parent households.

Grandparents Became More Important

There was a time when grandparents were supposed to see the grandchildren only at Christmas and not meddle in their lives at other times. It was the parents' job to socialize their children—not that of grandparents, with their outdated values. But with both parents working, or with a single parent, grandparents became more welcome. As parents became busier and away from their children more, grandparents started stepping in to help out. It just so happens that this generation of grandparents has money to burn, so to speak. They visit the children more, the grandchildren visit them more, and always they give the children money and gifts. Grandparents tend to spend even more per toy for grandchildren than parents do, and grandparents are one of children's fastest-growing income sources.

The Guilt Factor Grew

Along with all those working, and single, and divorced parents has come a lot of guilt associated with being away from the kids much of the time. A new term, "**quality time**," was invented to justify the lesser time spent with the children. In our material society, quality time often means giving kids more when parents are away and doing more with them when they are together. Long weekends became times to go to Walt Disney World, take long shopping trips, and play family more. In fact, the term family became popular again in the late 1980s and early 1990s, as reflected in the introduction of new magazines such as *Family Fun* and *Family Life*.

Our society also originated another term for children left alone to fend for themselves more: **latch-key kids**. Kids were provided with more entertainment, more to eat, and more money to buy things to fill the time when they were home alone. It was the concept of latch-key kids that stimulated more easy-to-prepare snacks and meals for kids. Many eventually failed, not because they were necessarily bad, but because their preparation often required the children to use the microwave oven, an appliance that was not designed with children in mind.

Parents Worried More about Their Children's Future

The economic uncertainty that arose out of the 1970s' double-digit inflation didn't go away in the 1980s. By the late 1980s, an emerging recession added to this worry, and for the first time produced a great deal of white-collar unemployment in the early 1990s. Losing an executive job after 15 or 20 years with a company became commonplace and consequently a fear.

Confidence in government, religion, education and other traditional institutions waned. The future looked bleak. Parents no longer aspired for their children to do better than they had. They knew they wouldn't. They just worried about their kids having it as good as other kids.

At a time when many families had less, however, they gave more to their children, including more money, more things, more education and training, and more input into family decision-making. For example, parents began to look for after-school classes and activities for their children. Summer became a time for piano lessons, computer lessons, and camps to learn the art of investment.

• • • • • • • •
Quality time often means giving kids more when parents are away and doing more with them when they are together.

Mistakes in Marketing to Kids are Many

Notice the absence of marketing when we are cataloging the various forces that came together to produce children's phenomenal economic clout. The development of new products for kids, increases in advertising, promotion, and publicity, more in-store merchandising directed to kids, stepped-up in-school marketing, and increased marketing research efforts may have contributed directly or indirectly to kids asking their parents for more money and things. But marketers did not create the social changes that resulted in the more powerful children's market. They have merely reacted to them.

Kids are not just mini-adults. They act, talk, and see the world differently.

Given the great potential of the kids market, it is little wonder that so many businesses began to target this group as a primary, influence, or future market. Some have done it well; some have not. Some have done it well in the sense that they demonstrate a good understanding of kids as consumers and provide them with satisfying goods and services while meeting the financial goals of their firms.

Others have made mistakes marketing to children. For some, those mistakes have been fatal. These are mistakes, however, not failures. Some of these mistakes will be mentioned later in the book to illustrate specific points.

During the years I have studied children as consumers, I have had the privilege to work with some outstanding kids marketers as well as with some who were not. There is a big difference, and I can explain it only by saying that some people possess special insights about kids. They realize that kids are not just mini-adults, that they are wired differently, act differently, talk differently, see the world differently. Maybe this special understanding comes from experience, surely some of it does, but it seems to me to be almost an inherent skill.

As I step back and reflect on the marketing mistakes businesses make, I see how often they resulted from misperceptions, misunderstandings, or what I would call myths. Many of the myths about the children's market result from and are perpetuated by marketers who are also parents, or what I sometimes call **marents**. These marents can be recognized by their declarations such as "The one thing I understand is kids. I have three of my own." Or, "Let me take it home and try it out on my kids. If they like it, it'll sell."

In the following chapters, I highlight a number of these myths and spend a good deal of time describing what I believe are the realities. It is the realities that give direction to effective marketing to kids—satisfying their needs and wants, along with business objectives of marketers.

Marketing to Kids is Still Marketing 101

Marketing is a social process. Consumers and marketers come together in a relationship that should produce satisfaction for both parties. If either does not receive adequate satisfaction from the process, it is a marketing mistake and the relationship will not continue. Satisfaction for children as consumers is the fulfillment of needs and wants in a socially responsible manner. Satisfaction for the marketer consists of meeting such economic goals as share of market, revenue, profits, and return on investment.

* * * * * * *
Children are consumers in training. They often need a little more help.

It is marketers' responsibility to satisfy business and consumer needs. This is an awesome responsibility for several reasons. Children are consumers in training. They often need more and different help or service in obtaining satisfaction from the marketplace. Moreover, children think and act like children, but adults put together the marketing mix that is supposed to satisfy them. This creates lots of room for misunderstandings.

Marketing as a social process

EXCHANGE

Consumer Marketer

Satisfaction   Satisfaction

FIGURE 0-3

In addition to satisfying children, marketers usually must satisfy parents, and this can double the difficulty of satisfying both the children and the firm's goals. For example, parents may misunderstand or disapprove of an advertising message designed specifically for children. It may be necessary to concurrently advertise to parents and children with different messages in different media. This, of course, drives up marketing costs and may make meeting the firm's goals more difficult. Potentially even more disastrous is the fact that such advertising is often done through an agency that is already the agency of record for a firm and skilled in advertising to adults (parents), but not to kids. This common decision by the client (an adult) may not be a wise one unless the moon and the stars are aligned just right.

Simply speaking, compared with marketing to adults, there is more chance for error when marketing to children. The failure rate of products ordinarily sold through supermarkets is around 60 to 70 percent. I believe the failure rate for these types of products for children is substantially higher. Hopefully, the discussion of the myths and realities that follows will stimulate some thinking among business executives and help reduce failure rates. If so, more satisfaction will accrue to the children as well as to the businesses that seek to serve them.

WARNING!

Myth/Reality #1

Fooling Kids May Be Easy, But It's Bad Business (and Immoral to Boot)!

In the chapters that follow, we will examine 26 myths. In the process, we'll say a lot about children's consumer behavior and a lot about marketers' behavior regarding children. But there is one myth that I would like to deal with right now. It goes something like this:

Myth: *"Kids are easy to dupe. We can make a million on this."*

Reality: Kids are the easiest of all consumers to dupe. Do it and you'll make millions of enemies.

The point is that kids constitute a market with more potential than any other, and therefore it is bound to attract its share of charlatans. It is as natural as June bugs buzzing around a sun-split watermelon. As I often say in my classroom, make a nice profit and there will be others to share it with you. It's called competition. But among those that come into the market, there will be those who intend to deceive. Given that kids are the most unsophisticated consumers of all, we can expect unsavory types to appear on the scene. This is why some people feel children as consumers deserve extra protection.

Because kids are so easy to fool, it is not possible to list all the ways. We can generalize some major ones, however:

- Market a play product to children that does not hold up under the tough treatment that we can expect them to give it.
- Package a perishable product for kids in such a way that kids can't properly close the package securely on the unused portion.

- Pair a product for kids with a premium and then give most of the communication emphasis to the premium instead of the product.
- Advertise a product for kids to kids and use camera angles to make the product bigger or better than it really is.

There are many other ways to trick a kid, but these are some major ones. Sadly, they are also too common. The Children's Advertising Review Unit (CARU), a part of the Council of Better Business Bureaus, lists many more such practices in the positive form of a code of ethics. Get a copy and read it. It is easy to deceive children as consumers, but it is the worst business sin, and it will create enemies among the children, their parents, consumer protection groups, and all the other marketers who are trying hard to do it right.

One of the more important ways in which I serve as a consultant is to be called in to second-guess a new marketing strategy that will target kids. Sometimes I can see some element of the marketing strategy that has the potential for deceiving kids, and can suggest some changes. If so, it may help the marketer to do a more effective job of satisfying the young customer. Most likely it was not the intent of the marketers to deceive; it was just a typical case of adults developing a marketing mix for the kids market.

My concern here, however, is not with unintended deception, although it causes a lot of problems for business firms; it is with intended deception and its practitioners. The kids market attracts more than its share of them. They won't go away by my mentioning them here. But the marketers who read this book can help. They can appeal such unethical behavior to the CARU or some other self-regulatory group, or to a regulatory group such as the Federal Trade Commission or state's attorney general's office.

PART 1

Kids as Markets

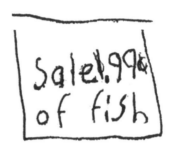

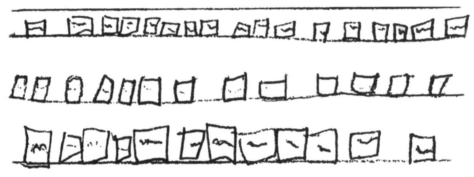

CHAPTER 1

The Market Potential of the Kids Market

MYTH: "Let's face it. Kids don't have the money that teens or adults have."

REALITY: No, kids don't have the money that teens or adults have, but they have more market potential than either of these groups—or any demographic group.

Kids: Three-in-One Market

As observed in the Overview, today's children are not one market but three, and consequently have enormous consumer clout. In fact, in their lifetimes they will make more purchases and influence more purchases than any other age group—more than teens, more than adults.

- They are a primary market for goods and services spending their own money on their own wants and needs. As described in detail in a later chapter, kids aged 4 to 12 have annual income of over $27 billion, spend $23 billion (virtually all discretionary), and save the rest. For example, they spend over $7 billion/year of their own money on snacks, and nearly that much on play items.

- They are an influence market, directing parents' spending toward their own wants and needs through requests, hints, and outright demands. Children as an influence market are currently responsible for around $188 billion of parental spending annually. They directly influence over $110 billion of food and beverage purchases by their parents. (Much more will be said about children as an influence market in chapters 6 and 7.)

- They are a future market for all goods and services that if cultivated now will provide a steady stream of new customers when they reach market age for particular products and services. That is, they have all their purchases ahead of them and eventually will buy all the toys, foods, stocks and bonds, airline tickets and cars—everything—offered by marketers. Thus, marketers can and should begin to get involved with these customers now, while they are children. Chapter 8 talks about this in detail.

Put them all together—primary, influence, and future consumers—and children have more market potential than any other demographic group. This is not airy pondering; this is the thinking that underlies the success of such marketing greats as McDonald's and Coca-Cola! We will look at these economic measures in detail as we treat myths related to them. Here we want to consider the marketing realities and implications of this myth that children have relatively little money.

Kids' enormous buying power didn't just sprout with the sunshiny 1990s. Their income and spending, as well as their influence on parents, have been growing at a rate of 10 to 20 percent a year since the mid-1980s when various social and economic forces came together to affect them. This growth shows no signs of abating. I believe that by the year 2001, children's current $27+ billion will approach $40 billion and their current $187+ billion in direct influence will be well above $300 billion.

• • • • • •
By the year 2001, children's current $187+ billion in direct influence will be well above $300 billion.

Consumer Clout of Kids Apparent to Some Retailers, Not to Others

Virtually all of children's income can be spent on anything they wish to buy—giving them probably more discretionary income than college students. The mere fact that they can withdraw money from savings; the mere fact that they can usually get more money from parents if they need it; and the mere fact that they at least bat .500 when it comes to asking parents to buy them things, gives them consumer clout with a capital C.

Despite this immense buying power of children, retail personnel are often surprisingly rude and offensive toward them. I recall in an observation study some years ago that an 8- or 9-year-old girl was circling the fragrance counter of a major department store with the green of her money showing out of each side of her little hand. It was the Christmas season, and the look on her face and the money in her hands indicated she was definitely in a buying mood—probably for a gift for her mom or grandma. After several circles and no response from either of the exotically dressed ladies behind the counter—a counter that towered above her head—she took an atomizer of fragrance from a display and sprayed it on the inside of her arm, probably as she had seen her mother do. That got the attention of one the clerks, who leaned over and asked, "Where is your mother? Aren't you supposed to be with your mother?" Intimidated, as is often the case for 3-footers in a 6-foot world, the little customer zipped away, perhaps forever.

Regrettably, such naive behavior is still commonly found at the retail level and probably stems in great part from this myth—that kids don't have much money. Just observe for a while the checkout counter personnel at any mass merchandiser, supermarket or convenience store, and you are likely to witness verbal abuse of kids. One clerk at a mass merchandiser, for example, berated a young consumer because he had only two dollars to buy a $1.98 toy. "Don't you know there's tax?" she lectured.

Children have told us in focus groups that they get nervous standing in line at a checkout, and if the checkout person gets on the public address system (as they so often do) and shouts something in that undecipherable code they use, children's anxiety level goes up more. Surely merchants can understand this—what it feels like to a child to stand in a checkout line between two adults waiting to be checked out by an adult—and could do something constructive about it since we are talking about their most important customers.

Notice also the signs displayed in some stores. For example, there is a Cincinnati mall store whose entire offering consists of gifts and play items for children. Yet, as you walk in, one sign on the right reads, "Lovely to look at, lovely to hold, but if you break it, consider it sold." On the left of the entrance is another sign that says, "Parents are responsible for whatever their children break." If children can read these, how unwelcome they must feel. Not to mention the parents who are discouraged from walking in. I've heard this store is in financial difficulties. It certainly should be! And what about those signs you can see on the doors of some convenience stores such as, "Limit of five kids at one time." They make kids sound like a disease! Can you imagine where McDonald's would be today if its clerks normally behaved in such rude and abusive ways or if it displayed such offensive signs? You would be asking, "McWho?"

Not all retailers have their heads in the sand when it comes to the children's market. Far from it. The hospitality industry, for example, has really awakened to this market in the past few years. The Hyatt hotels offer Camp Hyatt programs at many properties that make sure children's stays are fun, comfortable, and rewarding. And how the parents love it! Days Inn, Holiday Inn, and Howard Johnson also acknowledge kids with special gifts and services. Over the past few years, Wal-Mart stores have reorganized their toy section to make sure that more of the merchandise is at kids' eye level, and now Toys R Us is doing the same. Waldenbooks has a special entrance for kids that says, "Kids are welcome," along with a larger selection of children's books. Restaurants such as Bob Evans in the Midwest welcomes children with children's foods, gifts, and entertainment. Even banks are targeting kids with special services. I could mention many more retailers that have re-merchandised their offerings to get children's hands on—not off—products. Why? Because they recognize that kids are people too and constitute a group of powerful purchasers. Now, if only the rest of retailers could discover these truths!

Segmentation Strategies Should Be Different for the Kids Market

It is naturally impossible to place an exact value on the future market potential of all children, but a particular store type such as a supermarket chain can develop an estimate of what one customer is worth if that customer buys most of his/her food goods from that one chain over an average lifetime, or buys half, or buys none at all. The point is that an 8-year-old has practically all of his or her food purchases ahead, and a food store that hopes to have a future must try to develop that child's business, to make decisions now about where its new customers will come from. That's something that Sears, Woolworth, Kmart, Best Products, and 7-Eleven stores, for example, apparently did not do very well, if at all.

The plain fact of the matter is that **businesses have only two major sources of new customers: either they are switched from competitors, or they are developed from childhood.** The standard model is to switch new customers from competitors—from Kmart to Wal-Mart, from AT&T to MCI—which explains Sunday newspaper supplements from supermarkets and mass merchandisers and phone solicitations from long-distance providers. We know this works, but we also know that if customers can switch over, they can just as easily switch back. Over time, this strategy can result in profitless competition—lots of sales, not much profit. It can sometimes even mean the kiss of death if businesses lose their credibility.

Growing customers from childhood is a less common source of new customers, but one based on good business logic. If children are made to feel warm and fuzzy about a store or brand or product, they will bond with it. When they reach market age for that store or brand or product, they will logically migrate toward it. Unfortunately, this can happen even with

● ● ● ● ● ● ●
Growing customers from childhood is a less common source of new customers, but one based on good business logic.

product categories directed at adults, such as tobacco and alcohol. These emerging customers, therefore, tend to be more loyal, to not respond so negatively to higher prices or changes in product features, for instance, and to place trust in the firm. In effect, these nurtured customers are more profitable customers who cost less to keep.

We often see signs in store windows that say, in effect, "Your language spoken here." These signs are welcome beacons to those from different cultures. A customer-growing strategy that focuses on children has the same effect; it makes children feel their language is spoken there, and they respond positively.

A department store, for example, could subscribe to the myth—as many do— and believe that kids have relatively little money to spend, particularly on higher-priced items. But it would be ignoring the fact that if kids want something and they don't have enough money to buy it, as would often be the case, they ask their parents for it and get it at least half the time. It would also be ignoring the fact that kids will spend more of their money at department stores if encouraged by the stores. Those relatively small spending acts, if satisfying, will help bond the kids with the store. When bonding begins, the kids are more likely to keep coming back, and more likely to bring their parents into the relationship.

When a fourth-grade class of 34 students was told by a guest speaker from a local department store that it was thinking of instituting a once-a-month Saturday morning sale just for children, the children's responses were as follows: 41 percent did not believe it or were not interested, 50 percent said they would check it out, and of these, 35 percent said they would tell their parents about the possible sale. If these figures could be generalized to the young population, they offer both good and bad news. The bad news is that even at the early age of 10, 41 percent of the kids doubt the sincerity of the department store. The good news is that half of the kids are interested in the offer, and a number believe their parents also would be interested.

To put it on a bottom-line basis, if a department store effectively targets kids as primary customers—if it can convince them to spend their own money on their own wants and needs at that store— there's a good chance it can convert them into influence customers and future customers, and the store will get a great share of their business during their lifetimes. To not do this surely marks the beginning of the end for such retailers. Witness the trail of dead department stores and drug stores that did not learn how to

> • • • • • •
> *Marketers should target children not as one market but as two or three.*

grow customers, but just assumed them. We could add to this list a bunch of convenience stores, newspapers, and banks.

Thus, it is advantageous for marketers to practice a multidimensional segmentation strategy with children. That is, they should target children not as one market but as two or three. Certainly a department store could not justify marketing efforts such as advertising and promotion that target children only as a primary market, although their expenditures would contribute to paying for these communications efforts. But it could target them as primary, influence, and future consumers, and justify a budget for an integrated marketing program that focuses on youth. Then children would spend some of their money there, which would help pay for the costs of marketing to them. As primary consumers coming to the store to make their own purchases, children provide marketers an opportunity to market to them directly, cut down on communications costs such as media advertising, and bond with them.

Kids can spot insincerity a mile away. They will avoid phonies in childhood and even rebel against them in teen years.

It is also an opportunity to encourage them to influence their parents to shop there. As influence consumers, they come to the store with their parents. This is a rare opportunity to bond with both parents and children, develop links with the household through special offerings such as credit cards and in-store-only specials, and of course, to make major sales such as back-to-school clothing for the children. All the while the store is developing a relationship with this one customer that can be productive for many years. The stores should bear in mind, however, that kids can spot insincerity a mile away. They will avoid phonies in childhood and even rebel against them in teen years.

Delta Air Lines does not target children as primary consumers because children usually don't buy airline tickets. However, it does target them as future and influence consumers. It believes, and rightly so, that if the children have good feelings about Delta, they will, in various ways, recommend it to their parents, and they will choose it when they reach customer age for Delta. Therefore, Delta has an extensive marketing program—the Fantastic Flyer program—that targets children at home, in the air terminal, and in flight. For example, in-flight services include very special meals designed entirely for kids as well as a magazine—Fantastic Flyer—that provides entertainment just for kids. Naturally, the program's activities, such as the magazine, provide information for a database which in turn provides opportunities for one-to-one marketing to these potential customers (flyers). This is refreshingly and effectively competitive.

Has it worked for Delta? Perhaps the answer is best found in some downsizing that Delta had to do, along with many other firms, during the recent recessional years. It cut back on everything, I think, except the Fantastic Flyer program. The fact that United Airlines started offering kids McDonald's Friendly Skies Meals a few years ago, and recently an in-flight kid's audio channel of its own, suggests the Delta program is working. (I've heard that Delta just recently made severe cuts in its Fantastic Flyer program that targets kids. If that is true, I guess its new top management has a secret source of new customers that only it knows about.)

The Term "Little Kids" Shouldn't Imply Little Money

Each year, around 4 million new consumers (excluding immigrants) enter the U.S. marketplace for the first time. These rookie consumers are children freshly socialized into the consumer role by parents, with help from educators and business. They might ordinarily go unnoticed if it were not for their newfound economic prowess. They're just "little kids" to a lot of merchants, but to an increasing number they are important new customers looking for retail outlets in which to buy satisfaction for their needs. They deserve special attention because they are new at what they do, and also because they have all their market potential ahead of them.

Look closely at the child shopper in Figure 1-1 who is standing in the checkout line at a Kroger supermarket. Along with some of her classmates, she was asked to "draw what comes to your mind when you go shopping."

She is one of these new consumers who has all of her purchases ahead of her. But notice her attitude. She is ready to buy; she came to the store to buy. She has knowledge of this store and likes it. See the center positioning of the store name, and in big lettering like a billboard. This tells us she likes Kroger's.

Notice, also, her knowledge of the checkout system, the shopping system in a self-service store. She is aware that you use a shopping cart, load it down, then head to the checkout where there are other shoppers doing the same thing. She knows there's a number for the checkout lane, a checker

• • • • •
Children deserve special attention because they are new at what they do, and also because they have all their market potential ahead of them.

FIGURE 1-1

35

will be there, perhaps with a smile on her face, and the prices of the goods she bought will be registered so that she can see them. She even knows there's a trash can underneath the counter! (Guess how she learned that.) And she goes to a little trouble to tell us the prices are attractive ones by depicting a "sale when red light is flashing" promotion that she generalizes from other self-service stores.

She is fairly confident about it all. Yes, she needs a little help, some extra attention, but she is willing to give a lot in return even though she is just a "little kid." And the Kroger store, or whatever merchant that treats her right, treats her as great market potential, will be richly rewarded. Rest assured, too, that she will return the favor in darling dollars, perhaps for a lifetime.

There is a mall in Canoga Park, California—the Topanga Plaza—that has a Kids' Club. It used to give away balloons to kids that attended club festivities. For hours afterwards, management would watch for those balloons throughout the mall as indicators of the kids and their parents shopping. Observers often couldn't see the little kids because they were over-shadowed by big people, but they could see the balloons that symbolized dollar sales. That's smart marketing; that's smart marketing research.

"Little kids," as they are often called, shouldn't be confused with little money or little spending power. We used to say that little kids should be seen and not heard. Well, sometimes they are difficult to see in the crowd of adults, but more marketers are listening to them. They are listening with a variety of sophisticated marketing research tools—some recently invented—because what kids have to say can make or break a firm. They really do have that kind of clout.

When marketers think of kids, they should think of KIDS—Keepers of Infinite Dollars—with the emphasis on the S. That is, kids are bona fide consumers, they are powerful consumers, and they should be treated with all the dignity of one's best customers—because they are.

CHAPTER 2

When Do Kids Become Consumers?

MYTH: "Kids have little market significance until they are well into
elementary school."

REALITY: Children have consumers clout before they can walk.

Learning to Be Consumers

Children aren't born consumers; neither do they become consumers when they complete a certain level of school. But they are born to be consumers, at least in the United States, and they begin their consumership early in life. According to my research, the consumer embryo begins to develop during the first year of existence, at first slowly, then very rapidly until it becomes a bona fide functioning consumer at around 8 or 9 years of age. At about this point, children begin to absorb an enormous amount of additional consumer competencies as their reasoning powers develop at a higher plane. These consumer cadets, no doubt, learn more than half of their consumer attitudes and skills by the average age of 10.

The development of consumer behavior can be conceptualized by an S-shaped learning curve as shown in **Figure 2-1**. One axis is the degree of consumer competence, and the other is the age of the consumer. The curve shows relatively little consumer competence gained during the early years. Actually, short periods of relatively great gain are followed by a plateau not shown when the curve is smoothed.

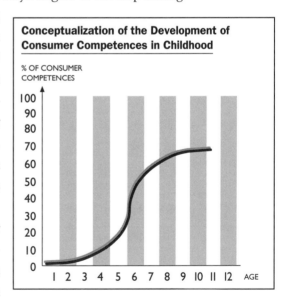

Conceptualization of the Development of Consumer Competences in Childhood

% OF CONSUMER
COMPETENCES

FIGURE 2-1

For example, as will be described below, at around 24 months, children make their first in-store requests to parents who eagerly fulfill them. This marks the beginning of one very important kind of consumer behavior through which children will obtain many satisfying products and services.

The S-curve shows that starting around age 4 or 5, the curve slopes up rapidly, indicating that much consumer competence is accumulating. This is a time when children are learning to make their own purchases. From this point on, the curve takes on verticality until hitting another plateau at around age 9. Note that this new plateau slopes upward, but only moderately, and will continue in this direction for much of the individual's life. Thus, a consumer is born and reaches functionality during approximately the first 100 months of life—a little over 8 years. Many foundations of consumer behavior learned in this early period will manifest themselves throughout a person's life.

If marketers are to successfully target kids as consumers, when do they begin? At what age, what level of consumer competence, what level of financial status? The answer in general is that they should target the children when they begin performing as members of any of the three markets—primary, influence, or future.

Since children are a future potential market for all goods and services—does this mean all marketers should begin targeting them at birth? This sounds ridiculous, but as ridiculous as it may sound, children begin their consumer journey in infancy and certainly deserve consideration as consumers at that time. Being a consumer is a right; being a marketer is a privilege. Therefore, children may be the focus of marketing efforts in infancy, although these efforts primarily are funneled through the parents. In any case, we can identify these starting points—when children first become primary, influence, and future markets. These points should cue marketers who are interested in children as one or more of these markets.

Stages of Consumer Behavior Development

When Maria Sanchez was asked the first type of store to which she took her son, Roberto, she answered, "A supermarket, when he was around 6 weeks old." When asked about the type of store in which her son made his first product request, her answer was, "I think it was the supermarket, also, for some Cheerios. He was around 2." Where did Roberto first request permission to select a product himself? "The supermarket, to get a box of cereal, at around 3, I think."

> • • • • • • • • • •
>
> **The median age of a child's first store visit is 2 months. By 18 months, many children recognize some products on the shelves of food stores that mom provides as rewards at home, usually sweets.**

The scene shifted to a mass merchandiser when Roberto made his first purchase attempt while shopping with his mother at age 5. "At the Kmart for a little toy car," she recalled. And finally, when asked where Roberto made his first purchase completely on his own, she answered, "Down the street at the Circle-K" (convenience store). It is little wonder that Mrs. Sanchez also reported that her son favored the Circle-K convenience store and nearby Kmart. He had had several significant shopping experiences at these two stores, and several years of shopping experience in which to develop special feelings about certain stores.

Let us look more closely at children's development of consumer behavior patterns to understand how Roberto and others come to have certain consumer competence and preferences at certain ages. Through in-depth interviews with 222 mothers from a wide variety of geographic and socioeconomic backgrounds, we investigated what kinds of stores and products were involved in children's first consumer acts, and at what ages these interactions took place. The results are summarized in nine charts by stages of consumer development.

Stage One: First Store Visit

The child's first visit to the store marks the beginning of knowledge about commercial sources of satisfying goods and services ordinarily provided by parents. We asked mothers to recall the first time they introduced their children to the marketplace. The median age of a child's first visit was 2 months. Most had visited one or more stores by the age of 6 months. **Figure 2-2** shows that the first type of store visited in 78 percent of cases was a supermarket (of various sizes), followed by mass merchandisers (9 percent), shopping malls (7 percent), and drug stores (4 percent).

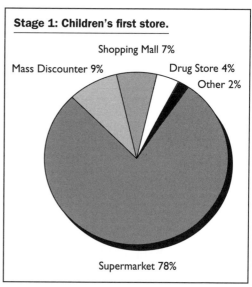

Stage 1: Children's first store.

Shopping Mall 7%
Mass Discounter 9%
Drug Store 4%
Other 2%
Supermarket 78%

FIGURE 2-2

At this tender age, children begin building impressions of the marketplace through sensory experiences—colors, shapes, sounds, aromas, flavors, and textures. At first, they only respond to whatever market stimulus is in their presence, but soon they are able to recall some of these representations in their mind and ask for them. It is important for both parents and marketers to keep in mind that the foundations of children's consumer behavior patterns are constructed before they take their first steps. This finding could be particularly significant to supermarkets, the most frequented type of store by infants, which operate at around 1 percent net profit and are under siege by other retail types such as convenience stores and mass merchandisers.

Stage Two: First In-Store Request

FIGURE 2-3

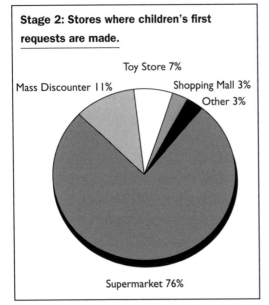

Stage 2: Stores where children's first requests are made.

Toy Store 7%
Mass Discounter 11%
Shopping Mall 3%
Other 3%
Supermarket 76%

When mothers were asked when their children first made a request (through pointing, gesturing, talking) for a product, the median age reported was 24 months, with the earliest being 7 months. Thus, at around 18 months, many children recognize some products on the shelves of food stores that mom provides as rewards at home, usually sweets. At this moment, the child makes the connection and gestures toward the product—usually a brand. To the child it is merely a recognizable set of colors, shapes, and symbols such as the multi-colored rooster on a box of Kellogg's Corn Flakes. Mom interprets this as a request and hands the package to the child who happens to be strategically situated in the observation seat of the shopping cart. Mom's thoughtful response to her baby has just initiated the "gimme" stage.

This stage occurs first only when in the presence of a certain product in a store, or brand of product, or, more precisely, a certain package design. Soon the children will be able to recall the representation of the product in their minds at any time, perhaps when they see the brand advertised on TV or when they simply think of it in the car on the way to the supermarket. This is the beginning of the influence market among children. At this point, the display level, package design, and point-of-purchase presentation that targets children becomes very important.

Not surprisingly, supermarkets are by far the biggest beneficiaries of such first requests—76 percent of the time—since supermarkets are likely to be the first type of store children visit. Following in the distance are mass merchandisers at 11 percent and toy stores at 7 percent. The most requested

product is ready-to-eat-cereal, often by the brand name itself or a brand association ("Tony Tiger," for instance). Children asked for cereal on 47 percent

of first-request occasions, and sweet snack
items 30 percent of the time, often by brand
name as well. Toys finish third at 21 percent.

These first two stages of consumer behavior—perceptually connecting to the marketplace and consciously seeking products from
it—suggest a logical pattern. Parents introduce children to the marketplace (along with
many other environments) as part of the daily
routine of caring for them. By the age of 6
months or so, kids have developed a rudimentary repertoire of some store and product
images. Many of these products are in use at
home, where packages begin to make impressions on children. Cereal, for example, is in-
troduced to children as a good transition food between soft and solid food,
and some sweets are received as rewards.

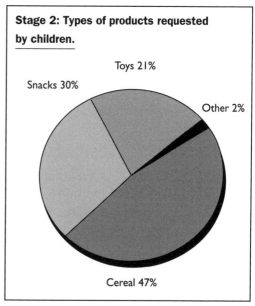

Stage 2: Types of products requested by children.

FIGURE 2-4

Also, parents begin to use TV as a pleasure-giving device, and children
see products there. This connection eventually creates an expectation in the
minds of these toddlers; that is, that a certain store will offer a certain satisfying product. All they have to do is ask for it at shopping time.

Stage Three: First In-Store Selection

It follows that as children learn to walk, to seek independent action, they
arrive at the "I can do it, I want to do it" stage, in which they want to retrieve the requested products themselves. The median age at which this first
physical act toward becoming a consumer begins is 42 months, although it
is often witnessed as early as 24 months. Untethered from the shopping cart
and mother's arms, the child ventures into a maze of fixtures and displays
and, often to mom's amazement, locates and selects satisfying products. "I
couldn't believe it when she came back with this big box of Frosted Flakes,"
is how one mom described it.

The child now believes he or she is performing an adult function, one
that is very fruitful. Very soon the child will test the system by retrieving
products from the shelf without asking. Chances are Mom will go along

with it just for the novelty of it. Another shopper has been born. At this point, if marketers haven't figured out how important a memorable package is, they are racking up losses in the new business column.

This self-selection behavior makes its first appearance in supermarkets 56 percent of the time, followed by mass merchandisers at 23 percent, toy stores at 11 percent, and other mall specialty stores at 7 percent. Clearly, the broad product selection in supermarkets is no longer broad enough for these new consumers. They start to pay much more attention to mass merchandisers such as Target, Wal-Mart, and Kmart.

This shift in store focus can be attributed to kids' insatiable need for play. Of the first products selected in this phase, 28 percent are toys. Cereals continue to be most important selection, at 35 percent; premiums that promise play now occupy an important role in which cereal is selected. Sweet and some salty snacks account for 24 percent of first selections, followed, interestingly, by books at 6 percent and clothing at 5 percent. Thus, the children broaden the scope of their wants and get experience fulfilling them. These experiences are marked in their minds and serve as guides for years.

Selecting a product from a shelf is a hands-on activity and involves a good deal of mental and physical participation on the part of the child. This act, in effect, is taking something desirable, something valued, from another without any repercussions from parents. The experience is likely to leave a number of impressions on his or her mind about the store, its offerings, its physical appearance, and its atmosphere. In turn, these impressions will produce feelings—liking, disliking. The role of self-service and self-selection in facilitating the learning and mastering of purchase behavior

FIGURE 2-5

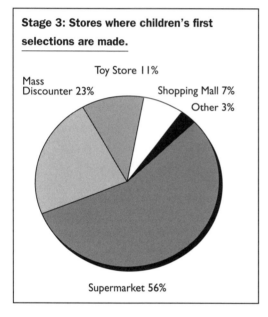

Stage 3: Stores where children's first selections are made.

Toy Store 11%
Mass Discounter 23%
Shopping Mall 7%
Other 3%
Supermarket 56%

FIGURE 2-6

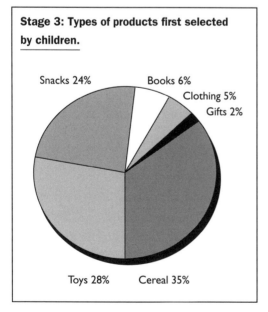

Stage 3: Types of products first selected by children.

Snacks 24%
Books 6%
Clothing 5%
Gifts 2%
Toys 28%
Cereal 35%

should not be overlooked or minimized. For instance, self-service is not yet a common merchandising practice in China. The lack of self-service may at least delay the development of the consumer behavior process, and possibly make it more difficult and more complex.

Looking back on these first three stages in the development of consumer behavior in childhood, we can see that children have a number of positive experiences related to supermarkets. In fact, young children, particularly preschoolers, often talk about one of their favorite stores being a certain supermarket.

Mothers take their children to the supermarket. They permit and encourage them to practice their consumer behavior there. They help to make each visit a favorable experience—buying products requested by children, letting children select desired products, giving children rides in shopping carts, and giving children treats during the visit. They even show the children how to make a successful purchase in the supermarket.

What other type of retail institution has an army of mothers working for it?! And what do supermarkets think about this? It varies somewhat among chains, but what they think seems to be pretty well summarized in what one supermarket manager told me. "I'm not so interested in the kids as I am in the kids' parents." This, of course, is a manager not worried much about his company's future who apparently thinks new customers are hatched out in adult form.

Stage Four: First Assisted Purchase

By a median age of 66 months, hundreds of episodes of consumer behavior culminate in a child's first purchase. Kids have seen their parents and other shoppers do it, and now they want to do it themselves. They have been coming close by making many selections that parents actually buy for them. It's just a matter of taking one more step. They have learned to count and finally have a basic understanding of the concept of money—"this coin will buy this product"—and they recognize that the retailer owns the goods and that "you have to pay the store man."

These cognitions, along with desires that can be satisfied in the marketplace, come together to produce a child's first purchase. Important, also, is the fact that children have ready money at this age.

Somewhere between ages 4 and 6, children request permission to buy something while shopping with their parents and finally get the okay. Parents may have to help, and are usually quite willing to, as the child musters up the

> Somewhere between ages 4 and 6, children request permission to buy something while shopping with their parents and finally get the okay.

courage to consummate the exchange process for the first time. The mathematics of it all are staggering, and can get in the way of what otherwise is a wonderful experience—exchanging money that used to have little value except as a plaything for something coveted such as a toy car.

This big moment is accompanied by a major shift in retail location. A young child's first purchase attempt more often than not takes place at a mass merchandiser (43 percent) rather than a supermarket (19 percent). Almost 20 percent take place at toy stores, 10 percent at convenience stores (where the child is beginning to go more frequently with his time-impoverished parents), and 9 percent at malls.

Toys are the chief object of kids' desires on the first purchase (54 percent of the time), while sweet snacks continue at a reasonably important level of 24 percent. Kids may also ask to purchase gifts for others (8 percent), and they may even buy clothing (5 percent), usually at a mass merchandiser or superstore. Some (6 percent) want to purchase their own cereal or other food items, sometimes fruit for their cereal.

At this juncture in the consumer behavior cycle, satisfying the play need is most important, and while children still have a warm spot in their hearts for supermarkets, these stores don't come to mind very much when they think of purchasing play satisfaction. At this point, also, a child's range of wants has broadened, and only mass merchandisers, maybe superstores, can adequately meet them.

Please note that this most fundamental step in the development of consumer behavior patterns—first purchase—could not take place without money. Fortunately for merchants, an accumulation of money, usually called a piggy bank, has been developing, perhaps since birth.

FIGURE 2-7

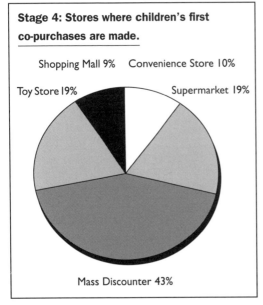

Stage 4: Stores where children's first co-purchases are made.

Shopping Mall 9% Convenience Store 10%

Toy Store 19% Supermarket 19%

Mass Discounter 43%

FIGURE 2-8

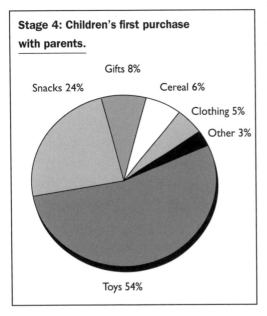

Stage 4: Children's first purchase with parents.

Gifts 8%

Snacks 24% Cereal 6%

Clothing 5%

Other 3%

Toys 54%

It will take quite a few of these episodes of consumer behavior before this consumer cadet will feel comfortable with the exchange process, but we see the emergence of a primary consumer that will reach fruition in the next and last stage. The importance of the checkout personnel in this first-time purchase cannot be overstated.

Stage Five: First Solo Purchase

It is only a matter of time until youngsters want to do the whole thing on their own—to "go to the store and get something." Many children see it as a rite of passage even more than their parents do. The competitiveness of school chums fosters this adventure, and 50 percent of the time it is to a convenience store, just because it is accessible.

The median age for the first independent purchase is 96 months (8 years), according to this study, although about 1 in 4 kids solo before they enter elementary school. In nearly all cases, the retail outlets where kids make their first purchases are convenient ones—close to home, school, and where mothers go. Supermarkets get 14 percent of first independent purchases, malls (usually variety and specialty stores) 12 percent, mass merchandisers 11 percent, and toy stores 8 percent.

Once this independent purchase act has occurred a few times, children begin to feel they have mastered the universe and have grown up several notches. They are likely to make independent purchases frequently for a while to confirm their newfound status as Corporal Consumer. We may even hear them ask, "Mom, do you want me to go to the store for you?"

At this point the child is a primary, influence, and future consumer all at once, a veri-

FIGURE 2-9

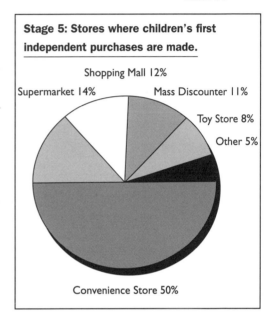

Stage 5: Stores where children's first independent purchases are made.

- Shopping Mall 12%
- Supermarket 14%
- Mass Discounter 11%
- Toy Store 8%
- Other 5%
- Convenience Store 50%

FIGURE 2-10

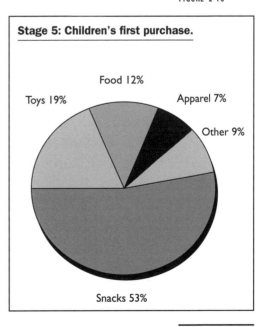

Stage 5: Children's first purchase.

- Food 12%
- Toys 19%
- Apparel 7%
- Other 9%
- Snacks 53%

table mountain of market potential. Figure 2-11 was drawn by a Chinese child who was asked to, "Draw what comes to mind when you think about going shopping." The drawing vividly marks this last stage in consumer de-

velopment. The youngster portrays himself in a major department store stepping up to a toy counter that sells models of airplanes, ships, and cars. The sign above the counter reads, "Ship models on sale," and the sign to the right says, "Welcome. Visit our store." He believes that these signs and similar ones in other stores are talking to him, and has learned how to buy in stores without self-service. He has money waving in his hand, and even though we can't see his face, we can feel

FIGURE 2-11

his confidence and enthusiasm for one of his first major purchases. He is truly a picture of a new consumer who has all of his purchases ahead of him and is anxious to get to them as soon as possible.

It is interesting to ponder how kids feel about the type of store where they make the first purchase. For example, do they subsequently have a soft spot in their heart for this type of store? Or does the experience result in a negative image of the store because of the high anxiety it produces? The results of several studies of children's interactions with stores done several years ago suggest that children aged 5 to 9 hold convenience stores in very warm regard—the stores where they often make their first purchases. They are quick to note that the C-store "has a lot of things for kids like toys and Popsicles," and that they sometimes know the names of people who work there. I have to assume these positive perceptions are due in great part to the fact that they are often the site of children's first independent purchase.

Other Factors that Affect Development of Consumer Competence

I am struck by the remarkable similarity in how children are socialized into the consumer role. Since the mid-1970s, I have often spoke of there being a "standard package" that parents apply in rearing their children as consumers. This study demonstrates this standardization yet again. Two factors, however, do produce some differences in the pace at which children reach particular stages of consumer development; they are single parenthood and gender.

Single Parenthood

As our studies of families' consumer behavior have been repeated over the years, more single parents have entered our samples. The number is now great enough to exert some impact on the findings. When we look at the consumer socialization of children—their learning of consumer behavior patterns—we find that those in one-parent households become indepen-dent consumers earlier than those in two-parent households. This age dif-ference often amounts to a half-year.

Children in these households seem to be viewed as functioning mem-bers at a younger age and get to select and purchase products earlier and more often. It may not be just the one-parent home that makes these differ-ences. Typically, the one-parent family is poor and this may encourage chil-dren to greater responsibility at an earlier age.

Gender

Our findings suggest that boys go through the consumer development pro-cess faster than girls do, at least in the latter three stages—product selec-tion, co-purchase with parents, and independent purchase. It appears that parents expect boys to mature earlier than girls. Also, discussions with par-ents indicate they "hold on" tighter to girls when it comes to making inde-pendent shopping trips to nearby convenience stores. This action probably reflects a perceived increase in criminal activity, including that associated directly with convenience stores, as well as children.

Marketing Implications In Sum

Research shows, then, that young children initially have affection for C-stores and supermarkets. They gradually turn these affections to mass mer-chandisers and specialty stores, the former of which offers wide assortment and the latter, depth of assortment.

Supermarkets might be able to retain more of these young consumers' earliest purchases by offering a wider assortment of goods to children and a bigger welcome mat. Only a few supermarkets are doing this, as far as I know. For example, the Piggly Wiggly supermarkets has its Piggly Wiggly Pals Club. But more than likely, mass merchandisers—Wal-Mart, Kmart, and an increasing number of regional chains—are expanding their offerings to include foods that attract the children at an early age.

In sum, children love to spend money, their parents teach them how to do it, and given the opportunity, they will spend it in one of their favorite stores for one of their favorite brands of one of their favorite products. Eight embryonic years of intense, repetitive buying behavior have produced these preferences and evaluations, which direct children to the stores most likely to best satisfy them. The retail outlet selected for this honor stands to benefit, but only if it takes advantage of this opportunity to serve an important current and potential future market.

CHAPTER 3

Kids Are Better Savers than Their Parents

MYTH: "Children spend all they get."

REALITY: Kids save at a much higher rate than their parents, but spend the savings just as their parents taught them—for high-ticket items.

Kids: Spenders First, Savers Second

Most children don't spend all they get. They are great savers compared with the parents who taught them. It is true that children, particularly preschoolers, are "now" types—"I want it now; Let's get it now." But by the time children have substantial income, they have been introduced to the concept of savings by parents and others and generally agree with it.

This myth of non-saving, like some others described in this book, may have been perpetuated by parents who were also members of the marketing world. I referred to them as "marents" in the overview. There is a tendency for marketers with children to believe they have special insights into the kids market. I have no evidence to support this notion, although it has a logical sound to it, and I do know of some instances in which it appears to have actually misdirected strategic marketing efforts.

This myth probably causes banks and other financial institutions, as well as those that sell high-cost goods such as computers, to ignore children as potential customers. This is a pity because kids do save money for big-ticket items.

Like everyone else, kids are spenders first, savers second. They do love to spend money, they do like to buy things, they do like to accumulate things, and they never run out of ideas for spending more money. But somehow in the midst of all this materialism, they have also been taught the necessity of saving money—that to spend in the future, you have to save today. In fact, they spend around 85 percent of the monies they receive from a variety of sources and save at a net annual rate of around 15 percent.

In various ways children tell us that they save money and that the biggest reason is to spend it on high-cost items—on "things that cost a lot." The drawing in **Figure 3-1** is an example. The 8-year-old Chinese girl who drew this picture told us verbally and visually that she sometimes spends exceptional sums of money on expensive clothing—just as kids this age do in the United States.

When asked to, "Draw what comes to mind when you think about going shopping," she portrayed herself and other shoppers in the Wudaokou

FIGURE 3-1

department store in Beijing—a relatively upscale place to shop. Notice that she has a 100-yuan bill in her hand, a substantial amount of money for her to be carrying, roughly U.S. $12, but not unusual for special shopping occasions such as buying clothing. She makes it pretty clear to the researcher that there are times even for an 8-year-old to get out a large sum of money and go spending. Incidentally, all the urban Chinese children we have studied report having saving accounts at banks, often with more money in them than those of American children.

Children Do Save Their Money; It's the Adult Thing to Do

Children do save their money. They are savings-conscious, they talk about saving money, they study the topic in school, and they understand why they should save. Saving money is conveyed to children as an adult concept. This appeals to their desire to be grown-up.

Take a look at **Figure 3-2**, drawn by a 9-year-old Chinese boy asked to, "Draw what comes to your mind when you think about going shopping." In his drawing we can truly see the results of his teachers talking about saving money. The drawing—in almost engineering style—shows a bank— The People's Bank of China—complete with clock, towers, and the Chinese flag. Underneath the bank building, a caption reads, "If I have money I will put it in The People's Bank of China to help support the construction of our country."

What he is saying in the drawing, as confirmed by a post-drawing interview, is, "When I think about going shopping, I think about the money that

I will need to withdraw that I have put in savings for a very good cause." You can't get much more savings-conscious than thinking of your savings when you think about spending. The reason he gives for saving his money in a bank, "to help support the construction of our country," has been taught to him by his government through school teachers, just as the U.S. government has done from time to time. The net result is that he contributes to his society while learning an important financial habit.

FIGURE 3-2

I have been examining children's consumer behavior for over 35 years, and my records show that they have always saved some of their money, and in fact, their weekly saving rates have grown rather steadily. For example, during the 1970s, children's weekly saving rates were in the 12-to-18 percent range, depending on their ages. During the 1980s and early 1990s, their weekly savings rate grew to 25 to 35 percent, probably due mainly to tough economic conditions and the resulting behavior demonstrated by their parents and teachers.

Also in the 1990s, for the first time, children—almost one-sixth of those aged 11 and 12—had some kind of joint investment plan with their parents, according to the parents. Again, an adult thing to do. Looking into the near future, it appears that children's weekly savings rates will decline to around 20 percent as the "good time" economy of the latter 1990s has produced more spending and less saving. At any point in time, however, the saving rates of children are well above the 5 or 6 percent their parents sock away.

Where Do Kids Keep Their Savings?

Where do children save their money? Roughly half is kept at home in a variety of places—old purses, jars, drawers, and, of course, piggy banks—ready to be spent. The other half is in a commercial depository, usually a savings account at a commercial bank or credit union, or more recently for some older children, in an investment plan.

Some banks offer special savings programs for children as a way to attract new business. These programs take several forms—kids' clubs, bank-and-school partnering, and in a few cases, separate units that serve only children. Parents, teachers, and the kids usually like these kid-specific programs, or at least they like the concept. When kids get a quarterly bank statement in the mail—in an envelope just like mom and dad get—they feel 6 feet tall. This feeling, in turn, reinforces the saving habit and encourages more saving, more adult-like behavior.

Kids' clubs set up by banks to encourage saving have increased in number in the 1990s as banks discover that kids are tomorrow's depositors. The Citizens National Bank in Charles City, Iowa, for instance, has the Thumbuddy Club. It gets kids started with a savings account by putting in the first dollar. It also has special hours for kids on Saturday morning with a specially designated teller window. Members receive a standard bank passbook, membership card, and monthly bank statement. The kids are rewarded with coupons contributed by local merchants. They also receive bonus points when they make deposits. They can redeem the points for premiums such as T-shirts, pens and pencils. The bank benefits by growing future customers as well as attracting their moms and dads to do current business. Parents usually appreciate those who are helpful and kind to their children.

How Much Do Kids Really Save?

The extent and nature of children's saving behavior is illustrated by **Figure 3-3.** It shows income, spending and saving on a weekly and annual basis for 1997.

FIGURE 3-3

National Estimates of Income, Spending, and Saving in 1997 for Children Aged 4-12		
	INDIVIDUAL AVERAGE WEEKLY	**AGGREGATE ANNUAL**
Income	$14.90	$27.9 billion
Spending	10.58	23.4
Saving	4.32	4.5

We typically gather this information by asking parents about their children's weekly income, saving, and spending. We stop the clock, so to speak, and ask, "How much money do your children receive, how much do they save, and how much do they spend?" The figures show they save at a rate of 29 percent on a weekly basis. One of the problems with this methodology is that it focuses only on recent saving behavior and does not tell us how much children later spend of what they have saved. Thus, this research does not reveal the true savings of the children; it does not tell us how much they save over the course of a year or more.

Subsequent research overcomes this difficulty by examining how much of savings was later spent. It turns out that children have an annual saving rate of about 16 percent, or slightly more than half of their weekly rate. In other words, children save at a rate of 29 percent, but they spend some of their savings during the year to give them a net annual saving rate of around 16 percent. Even so, this saving rate is around three times higher than for adults.

Putting these figures into dollar context, American children aged 4 to 12 save an average of $225 per year. They later spend half of it, roughly $112 a year, on top of what they spend as soon as they get it. This means that children put at least $100 a year into a commercial savings account. The typical 10-year-old therefore has $500 to $700 in the bank at any one time, in addition to perhaps $20 to $30 in cash stashed at home—plus about $15 in weekly income.

With this kind of personal financial backing, children have a lot of buying power at their fingertips. This helps explain how they can afford to buy an expensive pair of Adidas, a Polo shirt, or a Liz Claiborne fragrance. Sadly, research sponsored by the Office of National Drug Control Policy has discovered this money also helps explain how 10-year-olds increasingly can afford to buy and experiment with illicit drugs.

We have noticed two particular times of year when children take hefty amounts of money out of their savings. One is summer vacation.

Kids Spend Half of Their Savings

What causes the difference between weekly and annual saving rates? It happens because kids spend some of their savings, just like adults do—usually on high-ticket items. A common scenario goes like this: A child sees a display of athletic shoes in a mall store. The ones that catch his eyes sell for $100. He reports this to his mother, who understandably balks at spending this amount of money for a pair of sneakers. After a week of saying no to the child's requests for the shoes, Mom finally makes a deal: "The most I will pay for a pair of shoes for you," she firmly declares, "is $50. If you want those, you will have to pay the other $50." So he takes $50 out of his savings account and gets the shoes. This sort of behavior contributes to a reduction in children's saving rate over a period of a year.

We have noticed two particular times of year when children take hefty amounts of money out of their savings. One is summer vacation. Parents, and grandparents, too, often take children on trips when school is out. They commonly permit children to take a relatively large sum from their savings to spend while on vacation. This vacation—typically a trip to the beach or an amusement park—has an atmosphere of celebration related to the children's school accomplishments. One of the ways adults celebrate any occasion is to spend, spend, spend, and children gladly copy this behavior. Parents reason that vacation is exactly the type of thing for which money is meant to be saved—after all, it's often the way parents pay for the trip.

The other significant time when kids withdraw money from savings is the "holiday" season, vaguely defined as that period of time between Thanksgiving and Christmas. Our data indicate that when jingle bells start ringing, kids start spending. Unlike their elders, however, they are not spending most of the money on gifts for others, but mainly on themselves. Under the guise of needing extra money for buying Christmas gifts, children often turn to their savings. Interestingly, we have found that much of this additional money is spent on snacks (often at mall food courts) and play items (often at mall toy stores) almost as much as it is spent on gifts for family and friends.

● ● ● ● ● ● ● ●
Children at the early ages of 4 to 6 save at the highest rate, usually near 40 percent.

Who Saves the Most?

Who are the biggest savers? Girls or boys? Older or younger kids? The table in **Figure 3-4** provides some answers by showing children's weekly saving rates by age and gender. A U-shaped curve of sorts appears by age. Children at the early ages of 4 to 6 save at the highest rate, usually near 40 percent. The rate declines during ages 7 to 9, to around 30 percent, then turns up again somewhat for ages 10 to 12.

Preschoolers probably save more because they have not yet mastered the art of spending. They may have no choice in the matter, either, if Mom and Dad guard the piggy bank. When kids enter school, they learn about many things from other children, including more things to want and buy. This is also the first time most kids experience any peer pressure to conform by having the same stuff "all the other kids have." Parental control, teacher influence, and perhaps peer influence, along with an increasing ability to think abstractly—"If I save this much over time, I can buy this later"—all combine to eventually produce greater saving rates as children get a little older.

Girls generally save a slightly larger proportion of their income than boys do. Figure 3-4 shows this to be true of all ages except 11 and 12 when girls and boys save at the same rate. There is no simple explanation for this gender difference, and I know of no clear explanation provided by others. My best guess is that it is probably related to traditional socialization by family members. Boys are permitted more freedom in their activities than girls, and therefore they

FIGURE 3-4

AGE	ALL	BOYS	GIRLS
\multicolumn{4}{l}{**Children's Weekly Savings Rates by Age and Gender**}			

AGE	ALL	BOYS	GIRLS
4	39%	38%	39%
5	40	40	40
6	33	30	34
7	29	29	30
8	25	23	27
9	24	24	25
10	35	33	36
11	27	26	27
12	28	28	28

spend more. Even in Mom-only households, boys seem to be on a longer rope than girls are. This sort of thing is not specific to the U.S. My recent studies in China show essentially the same thing. Saving is encouraged even more in China, and children usually are not permitted to withdraw money from their savings accounts—except for older boys.

In any case, both boys and girls do save money, and they save it at a relatively similar rate, one that exceeds that of their parents. It is a myth to say that they are not savers. They actually follow their parents' advice pretty well. That is, they save some of their money, and they spend some of their savings for relatively expensive items. During the past decade, we have noticed that saving advice increasingly comes from grandparents too, who tend to be strong believers in "saving for a rainy day." What will happen when thrifty Depression-Era grandparents are replaced by baby-boomer grandparents remains unclear.

In 1997, American children aged 4 to 12 saved an estimated $4.5 billion.

Some Marketing Implications

Children who save money are obvious customers for the banking industry. In 1997, American children aged 4 to 12 saved an estimated $4.5 billion. About half stayed at home under the proverbial mattress, and the other half went to commercial depositories. Commercial depositories of some kind consequently receive around $2.3 billion of children's savings during any given year, which suggests that banks hold billions of children's savings at any moment in time.

Financial institutions could have more of the other $2-billion-plus stashed at home if more of them knew how to implement programs that effectively reach out to children. But most banks insist on being adult-like to the exclusion of being simultaneously child-friendly.

Many banks are intimidating to children, who may eagerly bring in coffee cans of change to deposit, only to face less-than-delighted tellers and impatient adult customers. Virtually everything in a bank is on an adult level, including the attitudes of people who work there. Some banks have penalties and service charges that may drain a child's small savings account.

Banks that have seriously targeted children with savings accounts and other services appear to be successful—successful in attracting children's deposits and successful in growing customers for the future. Most banks that target children offer them special savings accounts. There is usually a token deposit to open an account. At one of the Texas Commerce banks, it is 25 cents, while at a NationsBank, it is $25. Banks may offer premiums when kids open accounts. Children are allowed to withdraw the money, although there are often penalties for frequent withdrawals. At least at one Wells Fargo bank, children can make withdrawals through an ATM.

Some investment firms have special programs that attempt to attract children's savings. Stein-Roe established its Young Investor Fund to attract children as investors by offering a portfolio of kid-familiar companies along with a prospectus, newsletter, and coloring book.

A number of products have also appeared on the scene to serve children who are savers—the classic piggy bank and hundreds of other types of banks, computer software to track savings and earned interest, even checkbooks for kids. ParentBanc from KIDCORE, Ltd. offers a package containing checkbooks (decorated with dinosaurs), a mini-calculator, check register, ID card, and wallet. In this case, kids write the checks to their parents so parents can help children manage their money.

It might be smart for retailers such as Wal-Mart and Kroger and malls to implement their own version of "banking for kids." They could offer children savings accounts that would draw interest in the form of discounts on merchandise. These merchants are usually more convenient than banks, usually open more hours and days, and could offer more attractive premiums. Most important, such systems would get children and parents into the stores, where the odds are they will spend more than they save with their earned discounts.

The more broad-ranging implication of children's saving habits for marketers is that children can be motivated to purchase relatively expensive items with their own money. There still appears to be a tendency for many marketers to think children are mini-adults who make mini-purchases. Not so. Children are legitimate consumers who make a wide range of purchases. Sure, they buy lots of candy bars and soft drinks, but they also buy video games, athletic shoes, and small appliances. They often buy these things with money they have painstakingly saved, looking forward to the day when they achieve their goal of buying that Nintendo system with their own money.

CHAPTER 4

What Do Kids Buy?

MYTH: "Children spend all they get on sweets."

REALITY: Less than one-third of kids' spending goes for sweets.
Their fastest-growing expenditure category is apparel.
Children will buy, or ask for, anything they believe will satisfy
their needs.

This myth is a common one among marketers. It seems particularly prevalent, in some form, among managers of small stores. It has its origins in the period prior to the 1960s when it was generally correct, and has been perpetuated by older marketers. The myth was apparent in one of my earliest research projects related to children's consumer behavior, in which I interviewed both parents and children. One mother said something I have always remembered. She noted, "All my kids ever want are sweet things and playthings." This kind of thinking probably started this myth, even though it has been getting less true for at least two decades.

I delivered the paper that resulted from this early 1960s study to a group of professors and business executives. It was titled "Penny-Candy Purchasers" and was intended to establish the premise that children constitute a bona fide market, although a minor one. One of the notable findings presented in the paper was that children aged 5 to 8 bought and consumed two or three pieces of candy per week with an average value of less than five cents each. Today, children buy around four or five pieces of candy per week, with an upper-price threshold bordering on a dollar or more. Yes, kids still buy lots of sweets, but it's not the whole show by a long shot.

The table in **Figure 4-1** destroys the sweets-only myth. In 1997, children spent only around one-third of their own money on food and beverages and two-thirds on a

FIGURE 4-1

How U.S. Children Spend Their Own Money

PRODUCT/SERVICE	EXPENDITURE
Food and Beverages	$7.7 billion
Play Items	6.5
Apparel	3.6
Movies/Sports	2.0
Video Arcades	1.3
Other	2.3
TOTAL (1997)	23.4

wide array of other products. Furthermore, the money spent on food and beverages doesn't all go to sweets. Spending on salty snacks such as potato chips and cheese puffs is increasing. Just take a look at the new Frito-Lay kiosks/displays in supermarkets and mass merchandisers. These four-sided, kids'-eye-level, interactive fixtures offer an array of small-sized, kid-priced (20 cents at my local Wal-Mart) Frito-Lay snacks.

● ● ● ● ● ● ● ●
Kids aged 4 to 12 spend nearly $6 billion a year on sweets.

My best measure indicates that preteens typically spend somewhere around 25 percent of their own money on what is traditionally known as sweets—confections, frozen novelties, and soft drinks. Preschoolers spend more than this. This means that kids aged 4 to 12 spend nearly $6 billion a year on sweets, a hefty amount in the eyes of any confection seller or producer.

Sweets for Kids Make Sense

Children spend as much of their money as they do on sweets, particularly candy, gum, and soft drinks, for at least four reasons. For starters, candies are low-ticket, widely available items. Look at the candy/gum display in any convenience, drug, discount or grocery store to find something for every appetite. Second, sweets are inherently desirable—they taste good. Biologically speaking, sugar of some sort is good "brain food," and who uses their brains more than kids? Third, mothers tend to use sweets as a reward starting in infancy, so we should expect kids to want them in later years if for no other reasons than they taste good and are implicitly Mom-blessed. Sweet flavors may also subconsciously remind children of bonds they formed with mothers in infancy.

Fourth, sweets satisfy kids' play need, probably their most important need. For example, virtually all of the many brands and kinds of bubble gum targeted to kids promise fun and affiliation in addition to good taste. Consider the line of more than a dozen offerings from Amurol Confections. The gums have brand names such as Bug City, Bubble Beeper, Bubble Tape, and regrettably, Big League Chew, all imbued with play through the product, name, and package—ready to bring friends together for fun and games (e.g., who can blow the biggest bubble?).

When one steps back and realizes how many needs a piece of gum or candy, frozen novelty bar, or soft drink may meet for kids, it's little wonder they want them often and buy so many of them. It's little wonder, too, that they want and ask mom for the many kid-targeted sweetened cereals that come with various play dimensions.

Candy's Dandy

I am somewhat surprised that children, in fact, don't spend more of their money on candy, although the total amount they spend on this product line has grown over the past decade. So many varieties of candy are designed for kids that, as noted above, satisfy their most important needs: sentience (taste, flavor, texture), play, affiliation, and achievement. More will be said specifically about kids' important needs in a later chapter.

In some ways the candy industry does a better job of designing and merchandising its products for children than the equally traditional children's toy industry. For example, Impact Confections, Inc. produces a line of combination toys and candy. It labels them Interactive Candy Toys—with light and sound built into them. One example is in the form of a space rocket. This combination of taste and fun has big appeal to kids because it targets their two most important needs.

M&M's® Brand apparently still holds the number-one chocolate-candy position in kids' minds with its M&M's Plain Chocolate Candies, according to some of our research, that of *Confectioner* magazine, and of A.C. Nielsen. It will probably continue to lead as it introduces extensions of the M&M's brand such as the M&M's MINIs Milk Chocolate Candies and M&M's Crispy Chocolate Candies. M&M's products possess a unique combination of attributes highly appealing to children—bright pure colors, sized for little hands, crunchy texture, and popular chocolate flavor.

When we started our research in China, we were surprised to find that in spite of the brand's relative expense, M&M's is the big name in chocolate candy there, too. Chinese children view it as the most desirable imported chocolate brand. Amazingly, M&M's products have not been duplicated by competitors.

A glance in an up-to-date convenience store, such as the many thousands of 7-Eleven stores, shows a fantastic assortment of candy just for kids. Some are so targeted to kids' quirky and intense taste that adults sensibly avoid them. Lock Jaw Sour Gum Bawls from Zeeb Enterprises is one example; The Foreign Candy Company's mouth-blasting WarHeads is another.

There are also those special candies to celebrate Valentine's Day, Easter, Halloween, and Christmas. Some are directed toward adults, but many are definitely kid-oriented. All in all, an incredible assortment of candies in stores and vending machines tempts the taste buds and playfulness of children and tests the limits of their pocket money.

Not usually included in this candy category, but very important to kids,

• • • • •
When we started our research in China, we were surprised to find that in spite of the brand's relative expense, M&M's is the big name in chocolate candy there, too.

is gum. Bubble gum in its many forms is one of the finest examples of mixing sentience and play. Zeeb Enterprises, for instance, offers kids gum in play form such as shapes of CDs and video tapes. The Foreign Candy Company offers bubble gum in several fun forms such as Sidewalk Chalk that "looks like chalk and chews like bubble gum." The Yardstick is a yard-long piece of gum with a package marked off in inches—fun, taste, and education. Altogether, children's purchases represent perhaps 20 percent of the total $1.5 billion gum market in the U.S.

Children also direct parents to buy candy and gum—lots of it. This includes "stocking up" on bagged candies found in supermarkets, as well as those niggling requests for single items at checkout counters. Our estimates show that children influenced an additional $6.6 billion in candy/gum sales in 1997.

The Beverage Mystique

Kids aged 4 to 12 spend more than $1 billion each year of their own money on soft drinks. They tend to "wear them like a badge." There is something almost spiritual about the perceptions children hold about a can or paper cup of Pepsi or Coke. They revere noncarbonated beverages, too, including the many "juice boxes" that have sprung up to become a favorite portable drink for lunchboxes and car rides. With their small serving sizes, minuscule straws, creative flavor mixtures and colorful packages, these are obviously meant for kids.

The kid-oriented fountain drinks offered by most convenience stores and many mass merchandisers hold a particular spot in the hearts of preschoolers. 7-Eleven convenience stores have grown generations of Slurpee lovers by developing a market among the very young. Today, this drink comes in countless flavors and is popular with young and old. Children often buy a big cup of Slurpee after school and cherish it all the way home.

Fruit-flavored and real fruit drinks—chilled and shelf stable—may have also gained popularity with kids as parents have become more nutritionally alert. It appears that fruit drinks and isotonic drinks, together with carbonated beverages and the "kidizing" of vending machines, have expanded the beverage market among preteens. There's a Wal-mart store in a small town located near an elementary school. In the afternoon, children gather outside around the soft-drink machines drinking, socializing, and

There is something almost spiritual about the perceptions children hold about a can or paper cup of Pepsi or Coke.

loving life. What a wonderful way to satisfy kids while getting them a step closer to shopping inside the store.

But Life Is More Than Sweets

By the same token, we can expect children to want products other than sweets for a combination of reasons. They have been taken to stores since they were about 2 months old and have visited all types of stores many times by the time they learn the exchange process and actually participate in it. During this pre-purchase training period, they have asked for and received many types of satisfying products. They have experienced thousands of exposures to a vast array of products in stores and through advertising, many just for kids. It is no wonder they have many more wants than those related to sweets.

Also, as children grow older, many parents ironically encourage children to cut back on the sweets they initially taught them to like. Maybe they do this because they become more concerned about fat and tooth decay than they were when the children were very young. They may also feel they have less direct control over what children consume once they're in school, so they feel compelled to advise them more strongly. Admonitions from parents and others may cause some children to consume fewer sweets and more alternative products such as fruits and yogurt. In this and other ways, children's spending is diverging from its "penny candy" origins.

• • • • • • • •
Children spend more than $6 billion a year on toys—more than one-fourth of the $22 billion toy business.

Toys Are Second Biggest Expenditure

Kids spend a great deal of money on sweets, but three-fourths of their spending goes to other things. Children spend more than $6 billion a year on toys—more than one-fourth of the $22 billion toy business. It is their second-largest expenditure after food and drinks.

Children love to browse through the self-service mass merchandise stores that have all enlarged their toy offerings in recent years, feel the merchandise, and buy a $1-to-$5 toy—a Beanie Baby, Barbie item, kite, or action figure. They also make more expensive purchases such as video games, but usually ask parents to buy these.

Children's spending money usually comes to them in small amounts, so play items in the $5-or-less range have a lot of appeal. Low pricing undoubtedly helped make Beanie Babies one of the most successful toys in history and helped the industry to post its first real significant increase in annual sales in many years. Pricing within children's financial reach also surely explains the many successes in action figures.

One thing noticeable in the toy sections of mass merchandisers is that most items are at children's eye-level. Children may find the merchandise in a Toys-R-Us store more exciting, but even the store's giraffe mascot can't reach some of it. When an item for kids is displayed out of reach, they feel the same way they do when parents place snacks or other off-limit items on the top shelf of the pantry or on top of the refrigerator—offended. If they can't even see an item, they can't even ask an adult to get it for them.

● ● ● ● ● ● ● ● ● ●

Kids expect (not just prefer) soft-drink cups to possess a national beverage brand name such as Coke or Pepsi rather than the name of the retailer. In the same way, clothing and shoes say something about kids, and they want to be sure it's the right thing.

Clothing Is Hot

Children's spending on most categories of goods has been growing, but probably none faster than apparel. In 1984, their clothing expenditures of $40 million were not significant enough to warrant a separate line item in our estimates of children's spending. By 1987, however, we separated apparel as a purchase category and estimated it at $690 million. This figure grew to a whopping $2.5 billion by 1994 and $3.6 billion in 1997.

Apparel is hot for a variety of reasons. One thing that makes it important is its conspicuousness. Anything children consume that: (1) can be seen, and (2) has a stand-out quality—the two elements of conspicuousness—is of great concern to kids (and often to their parents). For example, in a proprietary study of children's views about kids' meals, a number of children showed concern for soft-drink cups printed with store names. Given that these cups were so conspicuous—they traveled with the kids and revealed what the kids drank—the kids expected (not just preferred) them to possess a national beverage brand name such as Coke or Pepsi rather than the name of the retailer. In the same way, clothing and shoes say something about kids, and they want to be sure it's the right thing. This concern even extends to underwear—apparel that isn't normally visible, although it has become so.

Many parents can tell you about all the clothing they have bought that kids would not wear. That's expensive, of course, and parents permanently scarred by the last recession now seem more receptive to kids buying or selecting their own clothes. Yet parents are also aware of the conspicuous nature of kids' clothing and sometimes want their own say in it. Parents, particularly those with an only child, seem to say, "Look at my child and see who this family is." Brands such as Polo, Guess, OshKosh B'Gosh, and Reebok speak a language of their own, often on an international level.

Power struggles can ensue when parents want one look while children want another. But children usually win in the end. One of the ways they win is to buy clothes with their own money.

There's a good chance that the $3.6 billion shown in Table 4-1 would be even higher if children's apparel were easier for children to buy. Specialty stores, such as shoe stores and clothing stores, have done little to encourage children to breeze in, browse, and buy. Ditto for department stores who act more like drug stores—very adult—but are still on children's minds as places to buy apparel.

Many department stores and specialty stores give lip service to the kids market, but pretty well ignore them as customers.

The mass merchandisers, such as Wal-mart, Kmart, and Target, are the ones making it easiest for kids to buy clothing. As these types of stores stock more of the fashionable children's items typically found in department and specialty stores, and they make children feel they are bona fide consumers who are welcome, we will see this category of children's products grow even more.

Children's apparel manufacturers that have traditionally relied on department stores and specialty stores eventually will seek out mass merchandisers just as fragrance vendors have. Even more significant, children will direct parents to these stores for more of their clothing, unless, of course, department stores and specialty apparel stores begin to genuinely recognize children as a market. The operative word here is "genuinely," because many department stores and specialty stores give lip service to the kids market, but pretty well ignore them as customers. Observations made from an unobtrusive location in a major mall monitored salespeople's reactions to kids in a well-known athletic-shoe store. The observer's notes record that: "The salesperson is often on the phone and rarely hangs it up if kids come in to shop. He just watches the kids, sometimes with a frown." That's not genuine.

Movies and Many Other Things

Children spend almost $2 billion annually on admissions to movies and spectator sports, mostly movies. This does not include what they spend on snacks and beverages while there. Children's spending on movies is flat and likely to stay that way as home-entertainment options increase, and as movies cater to young adults and baby boomers.

Somehow the movie industry seems to have lost sight of the fact that probably three-quarters of movie successes have been those targeting kids—G-rated Disney movies, for example. These G films are also the basis of the enormous success of movie-driven tie-ins, such as *The Lion King* with

Burger King. The fact that a movie outing for a family of four can cost up-wards of $50 (including monster-sized portions of popcorn and soda) won't boost children's movie attendance, either. This surely suggests that in some way movie makers and their partners should get children to movies at re-duced prices to build demand for tie-ins—the old give-them-the-razor-and-sell-them-the-blades marketing approach.

The amount of spending by children on spectator sports is unlikely to grow much in spite of rapidly growing marketing dollars targeted to kids by professional sports. I don't think I have ever seen so much marketing effort be foiled by the product itself. The professional sports industry fails in prac-tically every area of attracting kids to its events. It surrounds itself with adult-based controversy related to payoffs, drugs, sex, and vulgarities, adult-based products such as beer and tobacco, and boastfully wraps itself in adult pricing. Then it shouts to the kids to "come on out." In spite of the move toward families doing things together in outdoor settings, profes-sional sports are not likely to benefit.

Children spend slightly more than $1 billion a year in video-game par-lors. This figure probably will not grow much, either, partly due to more home-centered entertainment. These retailers also target teens more than preteens. A void is developing in the video arcade business as it moves away from preteens that a national brand such as Sega or Nintendo, or even con-venience stores, could fill. Children see their visits to video parlors as social outings, even a precursor to dating. But their parents are becoming negative about these establishments as they increasingly see them as teen "hang-outs." These businesses have an opportunity to practice market segmenta-tion by focusing either on under-12s or over-12s. They could also do both, as long as they physically separate the two groups. They could modify the game mix, add age-appropriate snacks and other entertainment, and prob-ably grow the business again, maybe big time.

Finally, kids spend over $2 billion on a whole host of other items. This miscellaneous category includes gifts for parents such as cut flowers and potted plants—children have helped make supermarkets successful florists. It also includes a host of gifts for themselves—accessories for their rooms such as bedspreads, rugs, and lamps, and accessories for themselves, such as jewelry and fragrances. These items tend to cost more than the average chocolate bar or Beanie Baby. Their sales to kids probably would amount to even more if retailers made them easier for kids to purchase, for example, through a layaway plan for kids. Kids find some of these purchases complex and intimidating, too, and they could benefit from some sales assistance.

This miscellaneous category of kids' spending also includes gifts to charities and causes. Social marketers are increasingly targeting children as sources of money and assistance to clean the environment, help the church, and expand museums and zoos. Children generally respond to these appeals because it gives them a chance to do a grown-up thing. This spending should increase as social marketers improve their general marketing skills.

They'd Buy More If...

We are likely to see children's choices broaden into more expensive items as their incomes continue to increase, but only if retailers give them the chance. It is at the store "where the rubber meets the road," where customer and product come together. All the products designed with the kid-purchaser in mind are here. But many stores make it difficult for kids to buy.

FIGURE 4-2

For example, children's strong preference for M&M's is illustrated well in **Figure 4-2**. When asked to draw what comes to her mind when she thinks about going shopping, this young girl took the opportunity to complain about stores. She drew herself shopping in a supermarket, but also demonstrated that stores display her favorite M&M's items and other desirable products in hard-to-reach locations.

A drawing study in South Korea yielded a similar consumer complaint. In **Figure 4-3**, a Korean child illustrates her ability to shop for food goods in the marketplace, in this case an open marketplace. But she also depicts store personnel who ignore young consumers and watch television instead.

FIGURE 4-3

Producers of kids' products, who obviously have a vested interest in kids' buying habits, are working with retailers to make it easier for kids to shop. Many confection makers work daily with convenience stores and supermarkets to make stores more kid-friendly. They know that, theoretically, kids would buy everything from convenience stores if they could. They are accessible, small enough for kids to feel comfortable, kids often know the store clerks, and low ceilings force practically everything to kids' eye-level. Convenience store managers and owners don't necessarily see it this way. "There is no way you can make a living on kids," says one C-store manager. That's true. Kids aren't the chief buyers of C-store staples such as gasoline, beer, or cigarettes—but they will be eventually.

So kids look to other store types for many of the products and services they buy. They are doing precisely what their parents have taught them— try out a variety of stores until they find the right comfort zone in which to spend their money. In some ways, children are like flowers sowing themselves. All merchants have to do is nurture the seeds that drift their way, and they will have a steadily blooming crop of new customers.

CHAPTER 5

Children's Income: Filling the Piggy-Bank

MYTH: *"Children don't work for their money."*

REALITY: The fastest-growing source of income for children is earnings—second only to their allowances. Children earn around one-third of their income.

Children Are Working More

Children's income has been growing over the past decade at a rate of 10 to 20 percent a year, far faster than that of their parents. By 1997, children aged 4 to 12 had an average weekly income of about $15, spent $10.58 of it and saved the rest. Chapter four shows children spending more of their growing income on more expensive items, particularly apparel. This chapter will deal with the question of where children get an average of $15 per week, totaling almost $28 billion a year. Contrary to myth, they are increasingly working for it.

It seems logical to many adults to think of children as unproductive since they possess few or no work skills at such an early age. But they do work. They perform a variety of tasks that they and their parents perceive as work, and that their parents ask them to do. As a rule, we are not talking about part-time jobs for preteens, although some older children within the 4-to-12 group do work outside the home. We are mainly referring to household tasks. Just as women who aren't in the paid labor force nonetheless "work," so do children who help around the house.

Children see themselves as working a lot. School is work. Even some recreation is "work," such as after-school soccer practice or piano lessons. And when they come home at the end of a hard day at the office, so to speak, Mom wants them to work more, as she so often does.

When the government of China declared a 2-day weekend—a comparatively long weekend in a country where children were used to attending school 6 days a week—we asked children to, "Draw what comes to your mind when you think about the long weekend." In effect, we were asking what they would like to do after school, or expect to do after school, given this "extra" time. A large number of the children were clearly interested in playing and shopping, but a significant number "told" us they would do more work. Some, such as the little girl in **Figure 5-1**, revealed they would do more housework. She can be seen cleaning the windows beside her study desk. The caption says, "Me cleaning windows." Her desk suggests she will also do some school work.

FIGURE 5-1

Figure 5-2 offers another perspective on spare weekend time. This young man shows himself at an art class, obtaining skills and knowledge in addition to those learned at regular school. The caption above the art teacher's head reads, "Art class, 6 to 8." The clock above registers 7:00, and the dark object to the right is a finished artwork, rolled up and ready to take home to show his parents.

FIGURE 5-2

The combination of work in the home and work outside the home now accounts for almost one-third of American children's income. Moreover, we believe the growth in work-for-money will continue as changes in values related to childrearing continue to extract more responsibility from children of younger ages. In a focus group interview conducted by a bank, one child put it this way: Child: "In the afternoon, I usually help fix supper. Then after supper I help clean up. On Saturday I help clean house and do the yard." Moderator: "That's a lot of work. Why do you do all that?" Child: "My folks make me do it. And I make more money so I can buy more things I want."

To the marketer interested in children as spenders, such reports and other research suggest children are learning the relationship between working, earning money, and spending money early on. They also suggest today's kid is a more significant member of his or her household, in the sense of being more responsible, more involved, even to the extent of being involved with the purchase of household goods and services. That's important to marketers, too. Now let's look in some detail at how kids get money.

Kids' Income Sources

Children, like adults, may have several income sources. The types and amount of income children receive tend to be a function of both parenting style and children's persuasive skills. Some parents, for example, are more permissive toward their children than others; some are more authoritarian, and some more neglectful. Children seem to sense various parenting styles and develop requesting skills that most effectively match them.

Our research over many years has documented children's income, changes in it, changes in parents' and kids' attitudes about it, and its sources. **Figure 5-3** shows the five major sources of income for children aged 4 to 12, and how they are currently distributed. They are allowances, household work, gifts from parents, gifts from others, and work outside the home. Other minor sources of income for some children that are not examined here include income from absent parents, court-ordered child support, contest winning, as well as interest and dividends. Children's income sources are not merely interesting in themselves; they are related to how children spend their money.

FIGURE 5-3

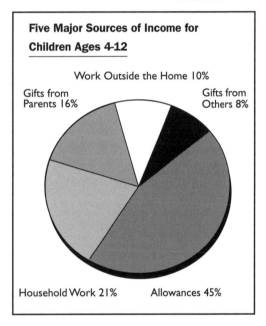

Five Major Sources of Income for Children Ages 4-12

Work Outside the Home 10%

Gifts from Parents 16%

Gifts from Others 8%

Household Work 21%

Allowances 45%

Allowances

An allowance, the largest single source of income for approximately 60 percent of American children, is a no-strings-attached periodic distribution of income to children from parents. "I get $5 a week every Saturday," is how one child described it. If children have to perform defined tasks to earn their allowance, it is not considered an allowance but placed under the heading of Household Work.

Allowances currently account for around 45 percent of the average American child's income. This category has been the most important source of children's income since the 1960s when we started tracking it, but it used to be more important. In the mid-1980s, it stood at 53 percent, then began declining steadily about one point a year. It seems to have leveled out at around 45 percent in 1992, where it remains today.

There is a good deal of discussion in family and parenting magazines about the extent and purposes of allowances for children. Parents who provide allowances usually do so to teach money management to children. Through allowances, parents believe children can learn several money concepts: (1) saving in order to buy a more expensive item or an unanticipated item; (2) budgeting so they can buy what they want when they want it; (3) spending behavior as a result of regular income, including making errors.

Some would argue that when children are paid to perform tasks in their households they are treated as employees rather than as bona fide members of the household. Therefore, parents should not pay their children to do things that they should do just because it is their home. Some parents report they prefer not to give their children allowances, but that children pressure them because all their friends get allowances. Parents never seem to know what is the appropriate amount for an allowance, but often follow the rule of one dollar per week for each year of age. Parents who give allowances also prefer not to give children additional money such as the price of a movie ticket. But, again, they often report being pressured to do so and giving in.

Why have allowances lost share? At the same time allowances were declining, children's income from doing household tasks was increasing almost a point a year—from around 15 percent in 1985 to 21 percent today. We believe this shift reflects the recessional years of lost incomes, lost jobs, and lost confidence in the economy, and increasing concern for the future welfare of children.

From 1985 to 1992, U.S. median household incomes stayed about the same or declined slightly. Yet children's income increased dramatically, suggesting a redistribution of wealth within households from parents to children. It appears that parents, badly bruised by the recession, turned to their children and said, "We worry about you, we'll watch out for you, but no more free lunch; you've got to work for it." Gradually, parents gave a greater share of their income to children, particularly if the kids agreed to assume more responsibility in the household. The new work-for-money duties of children may have freed up parents to work longer hours or take on more part-time work, so perhaps parents felt somewhat more generous toward children.

Furthermore, with tough times and increased pessimism about the prospect of better times, parents may have felt obliged to teach children to be more responsible so they might take better care of themselves. In both

• • • • • •
At the same time allowances were declining, children's income from doing household tasks was increasing almost a point a year.

cases, securing the future of children was paramount. The net result was a boost in children's income of at least 20 percent a year (unadjusted) with a new system for earning it.

It should be noted that the declining impact of allowances on children's total income may produce some errors in reporting kids' income and spending. For example, one large market research firm regularly asks children if they get an allowance and, if so, to state how much money they receive and how often. This amount is then reported as their income. Since allowances average only 45 percent of children's total income, such reporting substantially understates children's buying power.

Household Work

As noted, children's income from working in the home has grown from 15 percent in the mid-1980s to approximately 21 percent today. Virtually all children now do some household tasks. In fact, they now perform 11 percent of total household work in the U.S., according to a study reported a few years ago in *Parents Magazine* by Karen Levine (mothers do 70 percent and fathers do 16 percent).

There is plenty of dialog among child psychologists and others about the pros and cons of children being paid to work in their homes and little agreement about what is right. There was a time when moms' role was strictly homemaker and children's role was mainly "going to school" and "going outside to play." With more working and single parents, families need more help and cooperation from children. Many parents see this as a blessing in disguise. It is a chance to teach children to be responsible for their earning power, to work together with others, and to manage money. So, increasing numbers of children sort laundry, dust furniture, carry out garbage, sit with younger siblings, do yard work, and make salads for supper.

A handful of children whose numbers are growing are using their parents' home-office equipment to earn money, sometimes in a questionable fashion. We discovered, for example, in a research project during the Christmas selling season of 1994 that some children of the "cyber generation" are earning money with fax machines. They do homework for other students, fax it to them, and collect money the next day at school. Some also fax drawings to grandparents with the hope of receiving monetary gifts later. (Maybe they think grandparents can fax a check back.) A few parents also reported that older children do some word processing for them, perhaps a more legitimate type of household earnings.

• • • • •
Increasing numbers of children sort laundry, dust furniture, carry out garbage, sit with younger siblings, do yard work, and make salads for supper.

"Everybody works" as a family concept appears to be here to stay whether or not kids like it. It is possible that this change could be construed by some as taking childhood away from the child. But we are not describing an "all work and no play" situation. Play is still the central focus of kids' lives in the United States. Perhaps, though, the pressure to learn to earn is making some children more resourceful. They are simply adding work responsibilities that help them earn money to buy more things for play.

Work Outside the Home

Work Outside the Home accounts for around 10 percent of kids' income. Together with Household Tasks, this provides children with 31 percent of their total income from some kind of work. Work Outside the Home, as used here, means efforts such as babysitting, picking up aluminum cans, selling door-to-door, yard keeping, and sometimes formal part-time jobs. Income from outside work has remained steady at around 10 to 13 percent of income for children under 12, with tweens, those aged 9 to 12, earning most of it.

We expected this figure to rise along with that of Household Tasks, but an unexpected intervening factor prevented it. Fearing for the safety of their children in this new meaner world, parents are more reluctant to let their children have a newspaper route or go through the neighborhood looking for yard work. For preteens, income from work outside the home is not likely to increase, and may even decrease. However, as noted, resourceful children are discovering how to utilize technology to earn money outside the home while remaining at home, just as their parents increasingly do.

Another force may help children earn money outside the home—the financial-services industry. Some older children, 11- and 12-year-olds, earn money on investments and savings. Summer camps and after-school classes teach children about investing as a way to earn money. Some parents also invite their kids to join them in various investment efforts. It is possible that we may not be far from the time when children earn much of their money with their minds instead of their muscles, the way most people do when they graduate from college. We may one day hear our children saying things such as, "I bought it with the money I earned in the market."

Gifts from Parents

The 16 percent of income in the form of Gifts from Parents also has remained steady during the past few years for almost all children. These are handouts, so to speak—"Here's $5 to go to the movies;" "Here's $5 for a

Fearing for the safety of their children in this new meaner world, parents are more reluctant to let their children have a newspaper route or go through the neighborhood looking for yard work.

good report card." The recession probably took its toll on this source of income, also. Again, many parents would prefer to see children earning their own money, although some still tell us, "I give my kids money whenever they need it." The latter group may put their children in a position of having to ask for money, which tends to foster the nag factor (see the next chapter for more on this persuasive tactic). It also may foster more dependence and less responsible behavior.

In general, however, a majority of parents prefer not to dole out money to their kids without some degree of accounting for it. In effect, they see it as contrary to good money management. Further, they often are troubled by children regularly receiving money from other people such as grandparents, absent parents, and others that goes beyond some logical level they have in mind.

A significant share of parents use money gifts as rewards for various accomplishments such as learning a long list of Bible verses.

Our research does suggest that a significant share of parents use money gifts as rewards rather than handouts. The rewards are for various accomplishments such as learning a long list of Bible verses, participating in school plays, and of course, good grades. Also, as noted, more parents are sending their children to "school after school"—that is, to after-school educational undertakings such as piano, dance, and computer classes. These are additional opportunities for parents to reward children with money, as well as treats such as pizza and ice cream.

Gifts from Others

Finally, the 8 percent of total income kids receive as gifts from others has been growing rapidly and is a category to watch. This line item mainly consists of gifts from grandparents who in the 1970s and 1980s were the forgotten family members, but in the 1990s are increasingly important in their grandchildren's lives. American grandparents—60 million and growing—have money and time, and their input to their grandchildren's household is more welcome than it used to be. Grandparents are again seen as possessing fundamental wisdom, whose help with the children is increasingly appreciated by working, single, or otherwise busy parents. This 8 percent, still a small percentage of total income, has increased from 5 percent before 1990.

Other Sources of Income

Other currently minimal sources of income for children are not included here and may not have been accounted for when we conducted our research. Therefore, income figures used throughout this book are probably understated. A growing number of children have several parents due to divorce and remarriage. These children may also have additional step-relatives—grandparents, aunts and uncles—because of this situation. It is difficult for field researchers to obtain accurate information about money children receive from all of these sources, but they should be acknowledged since they are increasing.

Kids Working—Not a Bad Idea

● ● ● ● ●
Success in investing in securities during the 1990s appears to be filtering down to children from their parents and school teachers.

While it is unlikely we will soon witness detergents and household cleaners targeting children in ads that promise to reduce the drudgery of their day-to-day chores, it is nevertheless true that kids are doing more work around the house. This work provides them with additional income at an increasing rate, and, in turn, this growing income gives children more spending power. We think the amount children earn from household work will continue to increase as pressures grow from dual-working parents who need help in the house while they are gone, single-parents who need a partner to share household duties, and grandparents who believe work is inherently good. Parents also want children to fill up their non-school time, and work is one productive way to do this, as are after-school classes. Parents are increasingly encouraging both, and are willing to invest in both.

Also, children seem to be more interested in working, in earning money, and in innovative ways to earn money. The nation's significant success in investing in securities during the 1990s appears to be filtering down to children from their parents and school teachers and creating some interest among children as a possible source of income. Some children's publications talk to children about working and earning money. For example, the magazine, *U,* published for children by USAA , a large insurance/financial organization, has regular features on "Earning money" and "Investing money."

The idea of kids working is hardly a new concept. According to child sociologists, one of the prime values of having children is their potential to be productive members of the household, as well as people to nurture and love. Although child labor laws properly prohibit the exploitation of children in the workplace, there are opportunities for retailers and others to institute internship programs in partnership with schools and parents, whereby children work a few hours a week in well-supervised situations for pay—to earn while they learn. The kids could learn a lot of economics, social skills, science and math, as well as work habits that surely would enhance their earning power later in life.

CHAPTER 6

Little Naggers with Growing Responsibilities

MYTH: "Children are constantly nagging their parents to buy them things."

REALITY: Children do ask for many things because that is what they have been taught since infancy. Much of their requesting is viewed by today's busy parents as responsible behavior—not nagging.

In this chapter we will examine how and why children become naggers, as parents so often call them, and how parents increasingly view nagging behavior as essentially responsible behavior. In the next chapter, we will demonstrate the results of requesting on family spending and marketers' profits.

The Gimmes

Parents call them the "gimmes," referring to kids' requests that often start with the command: "Gimme!" The term presupposes that children have access to a great deal of product information from advertising or point of sale, and that they bombard their parents with requests for these products without regard for the family's financial limits. Marketers often speak of this phenomenon as the "nag factor" and "pester power." These somewhat negative characterizations obscure two facts: (1) children are taught by their parents to ask for things even before they can walk, and (2) the "new family" that came about in the late 1980s assumes children are active participants in family decision-making. In fact, today's child may have so much decision-making power in the new family, we can aptly describe the household as a "filiarchy" in contrast with the traditional matriarchy of American families and patriarchy of Asian and European families.

Do Parents Unknowingly Teach the Gimmes?

Parents try from early childhood to instill two principles related to children requesting things and children taking things without requesting them: the concept of **ownership** and the concept of **parental provision**.

Concept of Ownership

• • • • • • •
Today's child may have so much decision-making power in the new family, we can aptly describe the household as a "filiarchy" in contrast with the traditional matriarchy of American families and patriarchy of Asian and European families.

Early on, at least in contemporary western culture, parents teach children that everything belongs to someone—"This is yours;" "This is mine;" "This belongs to the store." This soon comes up in children's interactions with others. For example, if parent A and child A are visiting parent B and child B, and if child A sees a toy in the possession of child B, child A may take it. Child A has not yet learned the concept of ownership and will probably embarrass parent A in front of parent B. Parent B may say, "B is so selfish; let A play with it." But parent A will apologetically state, "A must learn not to take things that are not his," then turn to A and say something like, "Give that back; it is not yours. You must never take things that are not yours."

Similar situations usually end up happening in stores, too. At some point after a child begins to walk, she may take a toy or snack item from a store shelf. Mother says to her, "Put that back where you got it." The child replies in a logical tone, "No, I want it." At that point in time, the mother may take advantage of the teachable moment and instruct the child with such statements as, "You cannot take things that are not yours;" "That belongs to the store;" "You have to pay for it." (This is also the beginning of parental teaching of the exchange process.)

These kinds of statements are all intended to teach the same thing—the concept of ownership or property. This basic value is equally applied to interpersonal and marketplace relationships. It follows, in both cases, that the child has to ask for whatever it is she or he desires. This brings up the concept taught concurrently with ownership—parental provision.

Parental Provision

In this corollary to the concept of ownership, parents teach their children that it is parents' obligation to provide for them—i.e., "If you want anything, ask me for it." Often the two concepts are put together in statements such as, "That's not yours. If you want it, ask for it." Again, parents are teaching a very basic value, but one of many that must be instilled as part of the children's value system, developing along with muscles, appetite, and a desire to walk next to instead of riding in the shopping cart.

In both situations—ownership and parental provision—children are taught a set of values. When successfully absorbed, the child will have learned to make requests such as, "Can I play with it?" and "Mommy, will you buy this for me?" The nature of these requests, when they first occur, will bring a smile to mom's face. "It's working," she may think to herself.

Yet, only a few years later, that smile will be replaced by frustration with a child who falls down right in front of the frozen novelty section of the supermarket, kicking and screaming, because her request for a Dove ice cream bar was not honored. Mom may even declare, "I don't understand you, Rosemary, all you ever do is want, want, want!"

What has happened is that Rosemary and all the other kids have learned too well what Mom and Dad have taught. They have even perfected the art of asking with a lexicon of its own, including: "Puleeze!" "I'll never ask for anything again!" And here's a classic: "You never want me to have anything I like!" Almost as if in collusion with each other, children have developed a set of appeals and a style of asking that are difficult to refuse. Appeals such as, "Don't you want me to be healthy?" pleading, "I'm begging you!" and threatening, "I'll quit school!" have been learned through a combination of creative trial-and-error and tips from friends.

The important point is that the children are strongly motivated to learn the art of asking; this is how they get virtually everything they need or want. Both mothers and marketers know this, but Mom usually takes the credit and the marketers get the blame—credit for having taught the children how to properly ask for things, blame for children asking so often and for so many things.

As a side note, mothers can legitimately blame some marketers for teaching children at least one bad habit regarding ownership. Advertisements sometimes use the basic theme of it's-so-good-it's-worth-stealing (breakfast cereals, for example). Young children who think literally may agree with this message, particularly if it supports their logic.

The Role of Children's Requests in the Family of the 1990s

What we see when we glance into today's families and examine parents' responses to children's requests is a substantial change from the 1980s to the 1990s that generally can be summarized this way:

> • • • • • • •
> *Children are strongly motivated to learn the art of asking. Mom usually takes the credit and the marketers get the blame—credit for having taught the children how to properly ask for things, blame for children asking so often and for so many things.*

NO (1980) "Don't nag me. I know what's best for you."

MAYBE (1990) "All right, I hear you. I'll consider it."

YES (1995) " I understand you prefer that. I'll get it when I go shopping if I can find it on sale."

Today's family lifestyle assumes parents expect purchase requests from kids and that most will be accepted and fulfilled. The changes in family character that took place in the 1980s are described in the overview of this book, but let me summarize them here in order to put this myth in perspective. They also will come up again when we discuss the next myth about children's purchase influence. The changes, briefly, are as follows:

Smaller Families

Parents are having fewer children and therefore tend to give each child more things and more say-so in obtaining things. Parents may say to their child, "I think you ought to learn to play a musical instrument, don't you? I want you to give some thought to what kind, and from whom you might learn." To which we might hear, "I want to learn to play the electric guitar, and I know a video we can buy to teach me."

Single Parent Households

There is an increasing number of one-parent households in which the child is expected to participate more in household decision-making, including deciding what he or she can have, as well as what is good for the family. "I need to buy another car," the single parent may say, "Would you like to help me select one?" Which is a perfect cue for, "Yeah, let's get a minivan so Tommy and Joan can ride to school with us."

Parents with Discretionary Dollars

Many parents, particularly those with a college education, postpone having children until they have launched careers and reached a certain level of financial security. By the time children arrive, they are the object of substantial monetary attention. Such parents may solicit children's desires regarding big-ticket items. For example, "When school is out, we will take a vacation. Where do you think we ought to go?" And like any superstar who has just accomplished the great feat of completing second grade, the child answers, "To Disney World!"

Mom and Dad are Working Late Again

Both parents are working in more two-parent families, and many work longer hours, requiring more household participation (read responsibility) on the part of children. Mom may call home in the afternoon and ask her child what he wants to eat tonight. When the child suggests ordering a pizza for supper, it simultaneously simplifies things for parents and satisfies one of children's elemental desires, not to mention parents' secret longing for a slice with extra cheese.

More Money, Less Time

The "guilt factor" has grown among some working parents. Their focus is on "quality time," a term that can translate into giving kids a lot of what they want in an effort to make up for time not spent with them.

Yours, Mine, and Ours

A greater number of children live in stepfamilies now. They may receive more because they have more parental figures in their lives. Sometimes children receive things from parents striving to make up for, or distract children's attention from, family difficulties.

Keeping up Appearances

Parents worry their children will not have it as good as other children. Therefore, they may give children things so they can stay ahead of, or at least keep up with, other children. This new thinking fits in well with the appeal, "You want me to learn, don't you?" when a child requests a computer that's loaded with video games.

The overall result of all these lifestyle changes is that today's family has fewer children with more power. Children have been ceded more decision making power by career-oriented parents who desire more togetherness when they can manage it, and who want their children to have a productive, well-adjusted life when they are apart.

Is it True that Children Constantly Nag their Parents to Buy Them Things?

How often do children ask for things? When are they most likely to ask for things? To the extent that answers to these questions can be cast into averages, various research among children and their parents finds the following. Children aged 4 to 12 make around 15 requests in a typical visit to a shopping setting with parents, around 5 requests a day at home, and on a vacation, approximately 10 requests a day—in all, around 3,000 product/service requests a year.

Roughly speaking, parents honor these requests 50 percent of the time. This figure is probably higher if you consider parents' delayed responses to requests in ongoing purchases for kids. Further, if parents and children agree ahead of time to buy a type of product, for example, a pair of athletic shoes, and once at the store, children request a specific item within that product line, say a certain brand or style, this kind of request is honored around 90 percent of the time.

Fulfillment rates vary slightly by age and gender. Parents tend to meet most of the requests of the youngest kids, then starting around age 6 or 7, they cut back as kids' requests reach beyond the financial means of the family. However, there is a tendency for parents to increase fulfillment rates for older children around age 11 or 12. From age 7 on, parents usually fulfill more of boys' than girls' requests, although parents are not likely to admit this. Parenting style may also enter into these percentages. An authoritarian parent will make a greater share of purchase decisions for her children than a permissive parent who permits or even encourages children to make many more of the purchase decisions.

FIGURE 6-1

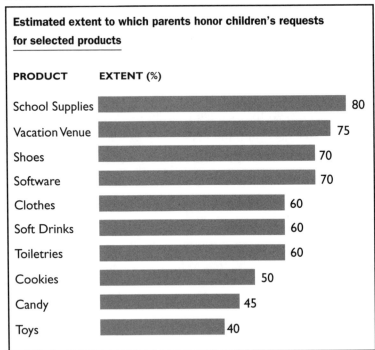

Estimated extent to which parents honor children's requests for selected products

PRODUCT	EXTENT (%)
School Supplies	80
Vacation Venue	75
Shoes	70
Software	70
Clothes	60
Soft Drinks	60
Toiletries	60
Cookies	50
Candy	45
Toys	40

In one of our studies of parents of tweens, we asked parents to what extent they honor requests made by their children for certain products. We averaged their responses and smoothed them to round numbers. The chart in **Figure 6-1** shows the results. Fulfillment rates range from 40 percent for toys to 80 percent for clothes and school supplies.

We might expect parents to fulfill more requests for toys than clothes since clothes are relatively more expensive. But the number of requests for toys is much, much greater, which drives down the extent to which parents honor them. Responses to requests for snack items tend to be similar, as are responses for clothing and shoes. Software requests—not video games but "edutainment" software—are honored at a high rate due to the lower frequency of requests. Also, parents see computer software for kids as an aid to learning, which gives it a high priority.

We might ponder why parents tend to meet only half of their children's requests if in fact the requests are viewed as responsible behavior. There are various reasons:

- Parents are aware that some of their children's requests are not serious, but act as practice for more important requests.

- Some requests are for products deemed inappropriate by parents due to their excessive cost, poor quality, lack of nutrition, or inherent dangers.

- Some children push requests to the outer limits of parents' budget barriers. In spite of children's newfound decision-making power, parents often moderate children's purchase requests and still try to apply sensibilities when needed.

Let's examine in a bit more detail the 15 or more requests during a typical visit to a supermarket to determine to what extent they constitute "constant nagging." After all, the number sounds large even to a marketer. What kinds of requests might we expect from a typical 8-year-old who goes supermarket shopping with her working mom on a Saturday?

We can expect the requests to begin at the mention of going to the supermarket and continue during the drive to the supermarket. An 8-year-old has good knowledge of supermarkets having already visited them several hundred times. Some moms have a few rules about the gimmes; some don't. These rules are intended to deal with various situations before they occur and may sound like: "You can select the cereal you want and the beverage you want for your school lunch. And you can spend one dollar on whatever you want. But don't ask me for anything else. Otherwise, you will have to sit

· · · · · · · ·
Children aged 4 to 12 make around 15 requests in a typical visit to a shopping setting with parents, around 5 requests a day at home, and on a vacation, approximately 10 requests a day—in all, around 3,000 product/service requests a year.

in the car while I shop." So we won't count the requests that occur before the family reaches the store.

Upon reaching the store, Mom has in mind a scheme of moving throughout the store that will maximize her efforts. It probably is not the one the child has in mind. So as Mom heads for the fresh fruits and vegetables first, a request (1) for cereal occurs. "Just wait," Mom suggests. In order to look like a team player, a suggestion (2) for apples is quickly made. Mom agrees. The child feels good about the acknowledgment of her suggestion and makes another (3). "Let's get strawberries, too." Their first disagreement occurs, with Mom saying they are not in season and therefore cost too much. Of course mom fails to count on her daughter's childlike logic: "If they are not in season, why are they here?" followed by another request (4), "Then, let's get some strawberry ice cream." "Maybe," Mom answers.

As the two move to the fresh bread display, the little girl rushes ahead shouting another request (5), "Let's get some doughnuts like you got before." Notice the strategy. If Mom has bought them before, she surely would buy them again. Mom bargains. "If you want sweets, we'll get some SnackWell cookies." To which daughter suggests (6), "I'll go get some." But she is told to wait.

Then, in the area of the fresh and chilled meats, Mom asks, "What kind of lunch meat do you want for your sandwiches next week?" "I don't want lunchmeat; I want Lunchables." That's number seven (7), and our shoppers are far from done. Before leaving the chilled meats, there will be a request for cheese (8), and maybe for a "What's this? Let's get one (9)." There will be several requests at the cereal display (10, 11, 12), another at cookies (13), ice cream (14), and frozen novelties (15). Several of these requests probably result from top-of-the-mind information derived from this morning's TV viewing.

In dry foods, we hear three or four (16,17, 18) "Get somes," for certain brands of macaroni and cheese, sandwich spread, and salty snacks (chips, etc.). The long display of soft drinks will elicit one or more requests (19). Pet foods will draw a few suggestions since kids have been given more say-so about them in the past few years (20, 21). A freestanding display of *Pocahontas* videos will get a special request (22) with, "You can get $5 back!" Finally, the checkout display provokes requests for gum and batteries (23, 24).

Total Score: two dozen requests. Actually this is a relatively small

> • • • • • • •
> *Actually, two dozen requests is a relatively small number— one per thousand items— for a store that stocks more than 20,000 items.*

number—one per thousand items—for a store that stocks more than 20,000 items. Mom may even be unaware that there were 24 requests if the shopping trip went smoothly. And on closer examination, she might admit that most of the child's requests were generally helpful, and that she did not buy any "shut-ups," as retailers call items purchased to keep children quiet.

Our assumption in this scenario is that one child is shopping with Mom. When two or more are along for the trip, the requests multiply, not only due to the larger number of children, but due to the competitive factor. **Figure 6-2** shows a drawing of a mother and two children shopping in a supermarket that was part of a study of children's perceptions of the marketplace. In a post-task interview the child, Katherine, told us her drawing showed her mom, her sister Elizabeth sitting in the seat of the shopping cart, and herself standing beside the cart. She said she could remember when she used to sit in the observation seat now occupied by Elizabeth and

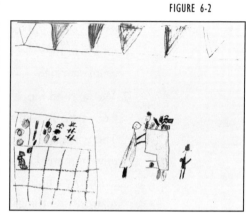

FIGURE 6-2

her mom would buy her things. She went on to say that now she helps her mother by "Running and getting the things that Elizabeth wants," in addition to the things that she, Katherine, wants. So, Mom has one pointing and one running, and you can see by the smile on her face how happy she is about it.

An important point here is that children's purchase requests are always relatively large in number when in the presence of the products. We can call these impulse purchases (a questionable term for young children) or some other term that suggests quick response to merchandising methods. Whatever term is used, it doesn't change the fact that strategically displayed products that appeal to consumers' needs will prompt requests and purchases, not only among kids but adults too. That is the way merchandising works. This means that if Mom doesn't want to hear 24 requests, she should not take the kids shopping with her. The fact that she does hear them, however, suggests that she feels she should permit many of the requests, and that she even values many of them. Bear in mind, also, that many mothers see these shopping situations as a set of teachable moments in which children can be molded into effective consumers.

Children's Requests May Lend Efficiency to Parents' Purchases

Yes, mothers may even value children's requests and expect them because they recognize their suggestions can lend efficiencies to the family's purchase mix. There are several ways these efficiencies may occur.

1. When mothers buy things their children ask for, those things are more likely to be consumed by the children than those moms choose independently. Many parents know this lesson well, particularly when it comes to expensive purchases such as clothing. Those who refused to buy torn and worn jeans a few years ago probably wasted money on those they did buy because the kids would not wear them or wore them sparingly.

2. We learned more than 20 years ago that children obtain information from school, media, and friends to which parents do not have access. This is no less true today when it comes to nutritional matters, environmental concerns, and particularly high-tech products. Let's face it, many parents have a poor education and simply do not understand many of the things their fourth-graders talk about. It really is true "Parents don't know everything," as some kids say. Just look at the hundreds of computer software titles for kids, the fastest-growing segment of that industry. Kids know about these; many parents do not. Good information produces more effective purchases.

3. Purchase requests by children can simplify life in a family where all parents work. Families make many purchase decisions, always under time pressure. If the children suggest something from KFC for dinner, that's fine with Dad; he can pick it up on the way home from work and feel confident everyone will enjoy it.

4. By allowing kids to decide on those things consumed mainly by themselves, parents can minimize shopping time and shopping errors. Through a lack of information, or because parents don't always understand their children as well as they think they do, parents often make mistakes when they buy kids' things without kids' close supervision.

5. Finally, fulfilling the requests of kids in such a way that the kids are happy and healthy brings parents and children closer together in a more loving relationship. All parents want these loving relationships with their kids, and the kids want them, too. If deferring to kids helps

produce it, so much the better. This may sound like "buying" love, but this isn't necessarily the case; it may simply be acting out of mutual respect for the needs of one another. A house full of love is a wonder-working household that also reduces its costs.

What the Critics Say About This

Social critics often zoom in on the asking-buying situation discussed here to prove marketers cause children to ask for things they don't need and to ask for more than many parents can financially provide. While I would argue that parents teach their children to ask for things, as well as limitations on requests, these critics would argue that marketers, particularly through advertising and eye-level displays, offer too many things for children to want. They would say that marketers capitalize on parents' teachings by dangling things in front of the children and suggesting that children ask for these things.

They would carry their argument even further by suggesting that marketers cause children to want so many things parents cannot afford that the children may steal the items, even kill for them. We will discuss this critical matter more when we talk specifically about advertising to children in the last part of the book. But for now, if we focus on the typical rather than extreme situation, it appears marketers are merely responding to markets that result from parents teaching their children to ask for things.

In Sum

Children have always asked parents for things, but a new family structure facilitates and encourages these requests by ceding more decision-making responsibility to kids. Parents and children in these families share a greater exchange of respect and responsibility. The net result is more requests and a wider range of requests from children. In turn, more marketers have become aware of this new family dynamic and are responding to children as an influence market with more communications.

CHAPTER 7

Kids' Influence on Parents' Spending

MYTH: *"Children influence over $187 billion of parents' purchases annually ."*

REALITY: Children *directly* influence over $187 billion of parents' purchases annually, and *indirectly* influence at least $300 billion more.

Pounds of Power: Direct and Indirect

How often have you heard this scenario?

(Baby crying loudly.)

Mom: "Whatsa matter, baby?" (Baby continues to cry.)

Mom: "Do you want your bottle?" (Baby continues to cry.)

Mom: "Do you want your ducky?" (Baby continues to cry.)

Mom: "Do you want mommy to hold you?" (Mommy holds baby and baby calms and coos.)

From such conditioning as this, children eventually learn to articulate what they want, learn to ask for it, and learn that moms and others will provide it most of the time. This can be termed direct influence. Likewise, as a result of children's repeated requests, parents learn to anticipate what pleases their children and provide it without them asking for it. This is what we call indirect influence. In total, children's direct (active) and indirect (passive) influence give much direction to their parents' purchase choices. In fact, it appears that children in U. S. families may in various ways influence household spending of $450-500 billion annually.

Compared with a decade ago, today's "little kids," as they are often called, have a lot of sway over household purchases. Pound for pound, inch for inch, they exert more influence on family purchases than their fathers do. The patriarchal family of the early 20th century that gave way to a matriarchy in mid-century now looks more like a "filiarchy" in which kids are increasingly in charge. No longer do children make decisions for the things they primarily consume, they also have much to say about the purchase of things the entire family consumes.

Look closely at **Figure 7-1**. It shows a shopping setting in Beijing, China. It was drawn by a fifth-grader who was asked to, "Draw what comes to mind when you think about going shopping." It shows our subject in the middle of the drawing with her mother. They are leaving the Yansha Friendship Shopping Center, which consists primarily of a major department store. Their arms are full of bags with the store's name on them. This is the subject's way of saying they bought many expensive items and that she helped choose them.

FIGURE 7-1

Notice, also, three other mother-daughter shopping teams, which is the illustrator's way of saying parents and children regularly shop together as equals. This is normal in China where children's influence rate on household purchases is around 67 percent. It is also normal in the United States. As we are indicating in this discussion, and as this child shows in her drawing, children's influence is normal, is direct at the point of purchase, and is indirect in the sense that most parental purchase behavior gives much consideration to it.

Spending Under the Influence

When Mom goes to the marketplace, chances are that one-third of what she spends will go for her kids. If the kids accompany her, it usually will be more than one-third. But count on it, whatever mom spends—and if she is a middle-income American, she probably will spend around $13,600 a year on her one school-aged child—the kids will influence most of it, directly or indirectly. Most moms, most of the time, are spending under the influence.

We know that households with school-aged children outspend households without children by at least one-third. Households with children spend around 40 percent more on apparel, 35 percent more on entertainment, and 20 percent more on personal-care products.

The influence kids have on parental spending is both direct and indirect, based on the degree to which children actually participate in the decision-making process. Determining how much of each type of influence comes to bear on many purchases is difficult, since it's often a combination of both.

Direct Influence

In the case of direct influence, children take an active role in their household's purchases; they hint for things, ask for things, recommend things, and outright demand things, with various words and/or gestures. For example, a 2-year-old may point and shout from the observation post of a shopping cart, "Get Sugar Bear," after spying a box of Post Sugar Crisps on the supermarket shelf, while a 6-year-old may retrieve a box of frozen treats, carry it to the cart, and ask, "Can we get these?"

The hospitality industry knows that kids sitting in the back seat of a car on a family road trip are making about one-third of the decisions about where the family will spend the night.

Most of the literature regarding children's consumer behavior talks about direct influence, probably because it is easier to discern and measure. For example, in a series of observations in a Limited Too store, which specializes in children's wear for tween girls, one mom brought her two daughters to the door of the store with instructions to look around and that she would be back soon. Within 15 minutes she was back, and approached her daughters with, "Did you see anything you like?" This question resulted in requests for four or five items. Observation studies like this produce measures of frequency of requests in different store settings. The requests from the two girls in the Limited Too store are much easier to measure as influence than the consideration Mom may have given to the two girls' preferences while she was shopping in other stores. Yet retailers must be sensitive to both types of influence, know when both are operative, and try to satisfy both parents and children.

Direct influence does not take place just at the point of sale, although this is where parents are likely to feel the most pressure. The hospitality industry, for instance, knows that kids sitting in the back seat of a car on a family road trip are making about one-third of the decisions about where the family will spend the night—perhaps just moments before they approach the exit that leads to the motel advertised just a few miles back on a strategically placed billboard. This is why Days Inn has Fred Flintstone as a spokesperson and plush Freds available to children at check-in. It is why Best Western has a Young Travelers Club and play-laden Adventure Pack at each motel. And it is why both companies target an increasing amount of their outdoor advertising to families—over $15 billion of the $70 billion hotel/motel business, and growing. Neither Days Inn nor Best Western targeted children a decade ago, but both have recognized children have a wide range of influence on parental purchases—not just on sweet things and play things.

However, not all requests are made at the point of purchase. Many purchase requests to parents are made at home, prompted by activities such as studying, playing, snacking, and watching TV. Sometimes, in-home requests are simply a result of running out of something—"Be sure and get more Coke when you go to the store, Mom." Parents have told us many times it is rare to announce a shopping trip, particularly to the supermarket, without hearing a chorus of "getmes" from the children.

Direct influence, as described here, refers to several dimensions of family purchase behavior:

- Number of requests by children;
- Range of products requested;
- Amount of decision-making power ceded children by parents; and
- Combinations of types of direct influence.

As a rule, when the term direct influence is used here, by researchers and marketers, it refers to measurement of the degree to which children influence the parental purchase of a single product.

The degree of direct influence children have on specific purchases by parents varies for several reasons. Let me mention what I believe are the most important ones.

Nature of the Product

Generally speaking, children have most influence on the purchase of products consumed primarily by them. Their influence usually will be less for products for the family, and even less for products specifically for adult members of the family. So kids are probably the principal decision makers for their toys, clothing, snacks, items for their rooms, and their entertainment. They have a lesser degree of influence on the family television set, camcorder, furniture, meal elements, and toiletries (although items such as these have increasingly entered children's decision domain). Children's influence normally is minimal for such items as parents' clothing, jewelry, cosmetics, and alcoholic beverages. Their indirect influence, to be described later, may be substantial in the latter two categories, however.

Children's Ages

The influence kids have on their parents' purchases tends to vary by the ages of the children, although not in a clear linear direction. The chart in **Figure 7-2** conceptualizes this age-related influence according to the extent to which requests are honored. The chart suggests that requests by infants and toddlers—they may be verbalized or gestured—are almost always fulfilled. At these ages, children's needs and wants are almost totally the responsibility of parents, and whatever requests children make—for food, play, or entertainment—parents usually comply.

FIGURE 7-2

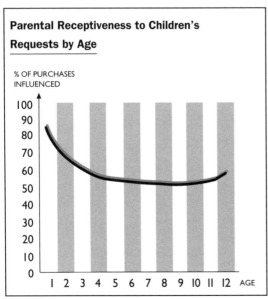

Beginning around age 2 or 3, children's requests increase rapidly along with their variety—the "spoiled brat" begins to appear as a result of virtually 100 percent satisfaction—and it becomes more difficult for parents to meet them, logically and financially. The positive responses of parents taper off until they reach roughly the 50 percent level, then hover there for the remaining childhood years. Parents begin to honor requests a little more often, particularly expensive requests, as children reach the "tween" years of 10 to 12, apparently because they view the request as more mature and less frivolous.

Stage of Decision Making

When parents make purchase decisions, they go through essentially three stages or steps: (1) need recognition; (2) search; (3) choice. Children's influence may vary for these stages, yet researchers usually generalize their influence as influence on the purchase. These three stages are more distinctive for expensive durable goods such as autos, camcorders, furniture, and television sets. For routine smaller-ticket purchases, the stages are blurred and children's influence, to the extent it occurs, can legitimately be termed influence on the choice, the last stage, in which a product is selected and bought.

For more expensive durable goods, children are often a major influence in need recognition. The idea for a new household item may come from them. It may be a simple suggestion such as: "We need a new television set that gets all the channels." If parents agree, they initiate the search stage and eventually the choice and purchase stage. In such a case, we would say that children have substantial influence on the purchase of a new TV.

Children may also participate in the search stage for items in which they have some expertise. Recently parents have been relying more on their children to help shop (search) for home computers and software because children often know a lot about features and may even be the computer's principal users.

Children directly influence about 12 percent of the annual $8.2 billion in sales of pet foods.

Finally, children may participate in the choice and/or actual purchase for some products once chiefly the domain of parents. Children are increasingly instrumental in all stages of the decision process for expensive apparel—athletic shoes, designer brands of dresses, and coats, for example—once primarily chosen and purchased by parents. Now, the last bastion of parental authority is even falling as kids are increasingly permitted to help select the colors, models, and body styles of the family auto. It was kids who practically invented the minivan and required parents to buy one. And it was kids who asked them to trade it in for a sport-utility vehicle.

Parenting Style

It seems that during the past decade, parents' styles of rearing children—their patterns of thinking and behavior regarding children's development—have become homogenized. My ongoing research in children's consumer behavior suggests a "standard package," of sorts, that most parents adopt for raising their children. Most of them do it about the same way.

However, some parents remain more strict or conservative than others. To the extent we can assign figures to it, it appears that perhaps one in four parents could still be classified as strict when it comes to letting children participate in decisions about family purchases. Stricter parents tend to make major purchase choices with very little input from children, at least until the children are in their tween years.

Estimates of Kids' Influence on Selected Product Purchases

The table in **Figure 7-3** estimates children's direct influence on sales of 75 items. The second column gives a measure of industry sales, the third shows an estimate of children's degree of influence on industry sales (not on family purchases), and the fourth shows the aggregate dollar value of children's influence. Be aware that many of the figures are educated guesses based on a variety of sources of information—industry publications, assessments by industry members, published measurements by marketing research firms, research results from our studies of children's influence based on what children and parents say, and combinations of some of these measures.

The list does not include some products and services kids certainly influence—for example, vacations, airline travel, eyeglasses, prepared foods sold in delis, and swimming pools. We are unable to obtain enough information to make estimates. Therefore, the total estimate is probably understated.

The table suggests, for instance, that children directly influence about 12 percent of the annual $8.2 billion in sales of pet foods, or $984 million. The table also reveals that children's influence on all foods and beverages totals well over $100 billion in sales. The estimated grand total of children's dollar influence on all 75 categories is $187.7 billion.

Children's direct influence on family purchases has been growing at a rate of around 15 percent a year during the 1990s. We believe that growth rate will continue, perhaps even increase slightly. Thus, children's influence on household purchases will reach almost $290 billion in 2000.

> • • • • • •
> *Parents are usually well aware of the brands their kids like most and buy them even without the children requesting them.*

Assessing Children's Indirect Influence on Family Purchases

For all the items listed in **Figure 7-3** and many others, children also have indirect influence. In the case of indirect influence, a decision maker, most likely Mom, takes her children's wants and needs into account when she buys things. Children's preferences are acknowledged and satisfied, but in this instance the children are passive participants in the decision-making process.

For example, in a recent study of children's consumer behavior in China, we asked parents how often their children make the purchase decision for each item on a list of products. They gladly provided us with estimates—the average was around 67 percent—but many mothers volunteered additional comments on the questionnaires, saying that even though children might not ask for a certain product, their likes were taken into consideration. This is indirect influence.

We posit in a later myth/reality discussion of branding that children possess an evoked set in their minds that contains the couple of preferred brands of each product they consume. These are the brands they ask their parents to buy, over and over. Thus, parents are usually well aware of the brands their kids like most and buy them even without the children requesting them. Parents possess a record of their children's most desired brands in what we call the "evokked set," the second k designating kids, to distinguish it from parents' personal evoked sets.

SELECTED PRODUCTS	INDUSTRY SALES ($ BILLIONS)	INFLUENCE (PERCENT)	INFLUENCE ($ BILLIONS)
Amusement Parks	5.0	45	2.3
Athletic Shoes	5.6	20	1.1
Autos	221.7	8	17.7
Bakery Goods	26.1	10	2.6
Baking Mixes/Dough	2.8	15	0.4
Bar Soaps	1.5	20	0.3
Batteries	3.5	25	0.9
Beauty Aids (Kids')	1.2	70	0.8
Bicycles	2.9	40	1.2
Blank Audio Cassettes	0.4	15	0.1
Bottled Water	2.0	9	0.2
Bread	13.0	20	2.6
Cameras(still) and Film	4.6	12	0.5
Candy & Gum	19.0	35	6.7
Canned Pasta	0.6	60	0.3
Casual Dining	21.0	30	6.3
Cereal, hot	0.7	27	0.2
Cereal, cold	8.0	50	4.0
Clothing (Kids')	18.4	70	12.9
Condiments	5.0	10	0.5
Consumer Electronics	36.0	12	4.3
Cookies	5.4	40	2.2
Costume Jewelry	4.0	12	0.5
Dairy Goods	40.2	12	4.8
Deli Goods	11.1	9	1.0
Eyeware	13.5	10	1.4
Fast Foods	89.8	35	31.4
Fragrances (Kids')	0.3	70	0.2
Frozen Breakfasts	0.6	15	0.1
Frozen Dinners	4.0	15	0.6
Frozen Novelties	1.5	75	1.1
Frozen Sandwiches	0.3	30	0.1
Fruit Snacks	0.4	80	0.3
Fruits & Vegetables, canned	3.0	20	0.6
Fruits & Vegetables, fresh	52.1	8	4.2
Furniture, Furnishings (Kids)	5.0	35	1.8
Greeting Cards	6.2	15	0.9
Hair Care	3.8	10	0.4

Estimates of Kids' Influence on Selected Products Purchases, 1997

FIGURE 7-3

continues . . .

FIGURE 7-3
CONTINUED

Estimates of Kids' Influence on Selected Products Purchases, 1997

SELECTED PRODUCTS	INDUSTRY SALES ($ BILLIONS)	INFLUENCE (PERCENT)	INFLUENCE ($ BILLIONS)
Hobby Items	1.0	40	0.4
Home Computers	4.5	18	0.8
Hotels, mid-price	5.5	12	0.7
Ice Cream	8.7	25	2.2
Isotonic Drinks	1.0	15	0.2
Jellies & Jams	2.6	23	0.6
Juices & Juice Drinks	11.8	33	3.9
Meats, fresh	43.1	12	5.2
Meats, packaged	17.1	18	3.1
Microwave Foods	2.3	30	0.7
Movies	1.6	30	0.5
OTC Drugs	11.0	12	1.3
Peanut Butter	1.4	40	0.6
Pet Foods	8.2	12	1.0
Pet Supplies	3.7	12	0.4
Pizza, frozen	0.9	40	0.4
Pudding & Gelatin	0.9	25	0.2
Recorded Music	3.4	22	0.7
Refrigerated Puddings	0.2	20	0.0
Salad Dressing	3.0	10	0.3
Salty Snacks	13.6	25	3.4
School Supplies	2.3	35	0.8
Seafood	8.0	15	1.2
Shoes (Kids')	2.0	50	1.0
Soda	58.0	30	17.4
Software, learning	1.3	50	0.7
Soup	3.0	20	0.6
Sporting Goods	30.0	15	4.5
Spreadable Cheese	0.3	20	0.1
Sun Glasses	2.0	10	0.2
Toaster Products	0.3	45	0.1
Toothpaste	1.5	20	0.3
Toys	14.0	70	9.8
Video Games	6.0	60	3.6
Video Rentals	11.0	25	2.8
Wrist Watches	5.9	12	0.7
Yogurt	1.6	12	0.2
TOTAL	**$932.7**		**$187.7**

Parents and researchers have informed us about this indirect influence for more than three decades, but we have not been able to quantify much of it and therefore have tended not to treat it separately. More than 30 years ago, for example, William Wells, a professor of psychology and marketing at the University of Chicago, spoke of children's indirect influence as "passive dictation" in Joseph Newman's anthology, *On Knowing the Consumer*. He explained it this way:

> "If you ask a woman who chooses the brand of dog food used in her household, she replies that she usually does. If you ask her how she goes about it, however, you find that she usually tries a number of brands and then continues to buy the one the dog likes best. The same kind of thing happens in respect to children. The mother buys a lot of different brands and then continues to buy the one the children will consume. It is this aspect of the children's consumption that has been seriously underestimated in replies of mothers to direct questions."

Wells implicitly acknowledges the difficulty in measuring this passive dictation of children and notes, in effect, that it has received little consideration in the marketing equation. In spite of its great importance, this is generally still true today.

In some proprietary studies, we have attempted to measure children's indirect influence or what Wells calls passive dictation. For example, in one study, we asked parents: "To what extent does your purchase decision for school supplies favor your children's preferences?" and "How often when you purchase back-to-school clothing do you purchase the brands your children prefer?" From these and a number of similar other probes, we have found children's indirect influence rate for certain products is at least as great as their direct influence. As a specific example, in one investigation of urban households with children, children's total influence on bakery cookies purchased was around 85 percent—approximately twice that of their measured direct influence rate. This is significant given that households with children buy substantially more bakery cookies than those without children. This appears to be true of many products purchased by households with children.

Measuring children's indirect influence is fraught with difficulties, but business firms should nevertheless make the attempt to get some idea of whom to target. For example, when we ask Mom how often she purchases brands her children prefer, we don't know how much other members of the household also prefer those brands. In such cases, assigning all indirect influ-

• • • • • • • • •
An investigation of urban households with children revealed children's total influence on bakery cookies purchased was around 85 percent—approximately twice that of their measured direct influence rate.

ence to children may be incorrect. Also, when a researcher asks a mother how much consideration she gives to her children's preferences in the purchase of products, there's a good chance of getting a socially desirable response such as: "Of course I give my children's preferences consideration when I buy." In spite of these problems and others, marketers sometimes makes estimates of children's indirect influence. Perhaps some of the errors are canceled out by combining these estimates with those of direct influence.

> ● ● ● ● ● ● ●
> *The average U.S. household spent $13,664 per child in 1996, or $683.2 billion for the approximately 50 million kids aged 2 to 14.*

Since indirect influence of children is not visible or audible, it is difficult to estimate its impact on total household purchases; yet, it is typically greater than direct influence. Take utilities. The cost of heating a home, or cooling a home in Houston, can be a major outlay. Likewise, the cost of a good water supply is no small matter. Children have major impact on all kinds of utility costs. In Houston, for example, school children often adjust the thermostat for the central cooling system when they get home in the afternoon to cool down. This increased use of electricity is a subtle but major influence on a major family purchase. Ditto for the large amounts of water used by kids in their play, frolicking in the yard sprinkler and "swimming" in the tub. The net result is a large expenditure by parents determined in part by children.

In addition to the items listed in Figure 7-3, children indirectly influence other major purchases, such as cable TV, telephone, electricity, camcorders, computers, day care, remodeling, landscaping, school meals, jewelry and watches, to name some. Once we account for all the passive influence of children on the obvious (soft drinks) and the less obvious (utilities), we believe the bill is at least $300 billion in addition to the $187 billion of direct influence.

We derive this figure by using and adjusting various estimates of what families spend on their children. Of course this figure is only a crude estimate that varies by income group, education, size of family, parenting style, and other factors. Using data from a couple of government agencies, we estimate a household average expenditure of $13,664 per child in 1996, or $683.2 billion for the approximately 50 million kids aged 2 to 14. Children directly influence around $187 billion of this amount, leaving $496 billion. Of this latter figure, our research on children's influence suggests children indirectly influence somewhere around 60 percent, or $298 billion. Thus, children are potentially responsible for influencing around $485 billion of parental spending.

Again, we must caution the reader that this is at best a "guesstimate."

It, for example, surely overestimates expenditures per child where there are more than one in a family, while probably underestimating the indirect influence factor of 60 percent. But it does give a ballpark figure of the amount of household spending for which children are responsible, and does help explain the great amount of marketing activity targeted to the youth market.

Marketing's Response

There is a tendency—it started in the early days of television—for the business community to focus much attention on kids' direct influence on items consumed primarily by children—ready-to-eat cereal, toys, sweet snacks, for instance. Such sway, of course, represents billions in potential revenues. But with the advent of the "filiarchial" family of the 1990s, kids' influence, direct and indirect, now goes well beyond products traditionally aimed at them and probably approaches 50 to 75 percent of all household purchases, depending on factors such as the nature of the product and parenting style.

We might logically list alcoholic beverages and tobacco products as items whose purchases children do not influence. But this is no longer true. Some children tell us they nag their parents to stop drinking and smoking, or at least to change to different products. It gets more difficult all the time to classify any specific product category as entirely free from children's influence.

Indeed, children influence one large group of expenditures in a largely unacknowledged fashion—i.e., contributions to charities and social causes. Children are commonly enlisted to contribute money and time to these and influence their parents' giving as well. Children bring home recycling ideas to their parents, for example, as well as other social causes they learn about from school, friends, and TV programming and ads. Social marketers are increasingly aware of children as an influence and apt to use them as a channel of communication to parents and other relatives. Business firms can also take this route to introduce their products—products that could help parents reduce smoking, drug use, overeating, and sedentary lifestyle, for instance.

In spite of these household dynamics, few businesses that traditionally target adults have reassessed their segmentation strategies and elected to give more consideration to children's needs and their consequential influence on family purchases. Electric utilities would be well-advised to do so; so would those who make and sell appliances, particularly microwave ovens. How

Social marketers are increasingly aware of children as an influence and apt to use them as a channel of communication to parents and other relatives.

many microwave-oven manufacturers are stepping forward with products geared to the entire family? The point is that children's influence on families' purchases has been rapidly growing for a decade, but attempts by marketers to satisfy this demand still seem woefully inadequate.

CHAPTER 8

Tomorrow's Customers Today

MYTH: "We don't target kids. All of our customers are adults."

REALITY: The firm must have a secret source of new customers only
it knows about.

When Do Customers Become Customers?

This myth, that "...all of our customers are adults," seems to be normal
strategic thinking for many industries that offer products only for adults—
major appliances, autos, tools, and lawn maintenance products, to name a
few. Neither is it uncommon in industries that produce clothing and computers for a wide range of age groups. The myth implies that all the people
who buy things from these companies are adults; that is, that its current
customers are adults, and therefore it follows that all market development
efforts should concentrate on adults.

But what about a firm's future customers? Are they adults, too? Must
they be adults before they can be targeted? This is the narrowness and
naïveté of this myth. As a business firm that thinks this way tries to builds a
larger customer base, it looks to adults who are customers of competitors
and ponders the tactics that will attract them. For example, Sears is attempting to climb out of a decade of doldrums by intensely targeting
women for its clothing line. This means it must attract customers from
other clothing retailers such as The Limited, as well as traditional department stores such as JC Penney. But Sears' future clothing customers include
those who have not yet reached adulthood—youngsters.

Business firms that subscribe to this myth apparently also subscribe to
the notion that they have only one source of new customers—competitors.
They regularly attempt to attract customers from others—MCI from AT&T,
Best Buy from Circuit City, and so on. Some do it with seemingly great

success. For example, Wal-Mart does a great job of switching customers from Kmart and other mass merchandisers. But along comes Target chain and takes customers from both Wal-Mart and Kmart. Then Wal-Mart awakens to the fact that customers who have switched to a competitor can be switched back, and then Kmart . . . , and then Target. . . . Gradually they all discover they are eating up precious resources with switching strategies, such as one-upmanship advertising. In effect, they are doing more business and making less money.

They are perplexed, and may blame suppliers of tactical efforts such as advertising agencies. But they will probably stay at it because they believe in this. These marketing gymnastics are called competition, even intense competition. Maybe so, but not necessarily clever competition.

A business may reason it can go global to expand its customer base with new customers in foreign lands while avoiding tough competition here. Many do. But they discover they must take customers from competitors or grow them from childhood, just as they do domestically. In fact, a company that moves marketing efforts to overseas cultures will have to give even more emphasis to growing customers from childhood, because children are more receptive than adults to goods and services from other countries. We will say a lot more about this later in the book.

Customer or Product Focus?

Companies not only ignore future customers, they may not concentrate on customers at all, or at least very much, but instead on products, concepts, or technology, and expect customers to come to them.

Customers' needs are not for products; products are for customers' needs. There is nothing more pathetic than a product (or store) looking for a customer after, rather than before, its development. But it happens all the time. Companies come up with concepts as a result of some special technology or ability or people, then they go looking for buyers within the domain of competitors to satisfy their ROI goals. A customer becomes a customer when he or she makes a purchase—rather than being nurtured to become a customer.

At any moment in time we can look back over the trail of "dead bodies"—failed marketing efforts— and wonder what went wrong, the cart or the horse. We probably should not blame either as much as the destination chosen for them or the path on which they were positioned. The cart—the product—probably came about because of some special abilities of the firm

> ● ● ● ● ● ● ● ● ● ●
> *There is nothing more pathetic than a product (or store) looking for a customer after, rather than before, its development. But it happens all the time.*

rather than unmet consumer needs, and because some executive championed it. Next, the horse—the marketing group—was chosen to fit the cart. Perhaps some VP of sales or marketing with experience in the particular concept was brought into the company just to "make it go." Then the product was launched with great fanfare down a path leading right to competitors' doors.

Two Sources of New Customers

Customers don't become customers at the point when they switch over to a new product or retail concept. They become customers a long time before that, in the sense they are more prone to buy from one firm than another. As noted in the Overview, there are two sources of new customers, not one.

Certainly companies can obtain customers from competition, and they should if their offering is superior, but they also can develop them from childhood. The product/marketing path does not have to lead to competitors; it can lead to customers before they make their first purchase. It is not only possible but logical for a business to nurture children as future customers so that at some point they see that particular business store, brand, or product in a favorable light, they feel an association with that business, and eventually they view that business as a source of much satisfaction. At any point along this cognitive development path, children can be considered future customers. When they reach market age, they can be easily converted into loyal customers—loyal in the sense that they want to do business with the nurturer.

Building Relationships with Future Consumers during Childhood

I am gratified by the growing emphasis on relationship marketing in many industries today. But when I look closer, I am somewhat surprised that the relationship building is usually only with current customers. With the aid of a database that lists and describes perhaps millions of current customers, businesses merge and purge, slice and dice, until they delineate customers with greatest potential, who supposedly will spend the most with them, then give those customers most or all of their marketing emphasis.

But the thinking behind this strategy can mislead the very firms that practice it. The customers who will spend the most in a store or on a product or brand are those with all their purchases ahead of them—consumers-in-training, kids. These customers with the most potential are not

• • • • • • •
Children are more receptive than adults to goods and services from other countries.

in databases of companies that focus on products and services mainly for adults. But these companies should be thinking about assembling databases of future customers. They could consist of individuals or organizations of them such as schools, athletic teams, and clubs. Since the products a firm offers are temporary—who knows what they will be 15 to 20 years from now—it is more logical to focus on corporate names, images and brands than on specific products as a platform for marketing to future consumers.

Children and their parents make it relatively easy to build relationships with children. It does not require invention from "scratch;" the pieces are already in place. Children's consumer socialization comes in a standard package, so to speak. Most parents tend to teach their children consumer behavior in the same manner at about the same ages discussed in Chapter 2. The kinds of products to which they are introduced in early childhood; the concepts of brand, advertising, and promotion; the various kinds of stores; the reasons for purchasing or not purchasing—all are typically standard elements in children's consumer education as a result of socialization by parents. Consequently, it is relatively easy for producers and retailers to begin a relationship with children as future consumers. For example, in three-quarters of cases, supermarkets are the first type of store children visit. Therefore, parents have done the hard work of bringing the child and the supermarket together that might ordinarily be the task of marketing. It is up to supermarket management to give permanency to that pattern by reinforcing it with an appropriate relationship program.

Since the products a firm offers are temporary, it is more logical to focus on corporate names, images and brands than on specific products as a platform for marketing to future consumers.

Building Brand Awareness

One of the basic behaviors parents teach their children is to go into the marketplace and satisfy their needs through certain products and brands. In effect, children learn to find need-satisfying objects and stick with them, not keep taking risks of seeking new objects—products, brands, stores.

For example, in a 1993 study by Yankelovich Partners, 71 percent of consumers agreed with the statement, "Once I find a brand I like, it is very difficult to get me to change brands." In that same study 77 percent of consumers agreed with the statement, "I prefer to buy products made by well established companies." Parents implicitly and explicitly teach children to think this way.

Notice the drawing in **Figure 8-1** of a shopping setting in Beijing, done by a third-grader who, along with his classmates, was asked to, "Draw what comes to your mind when you think about going shopping." We see four stores and a street vendor. What this child is saying in the drawing is, "When I think of going shopping I think of several retail outlets, and one in particular." The three stores on the right side of the tallest building are labeled "food store," "clothing store," and "toy store." But the tallest one, the one on the left with a traffic director beside it, says, "Landao department store," not just "department store." The Landao department store has become part of this child's brand repertoire. This is how a store should want its future customers to respond.

FIGURE 8-1

An increasing number of companies have established **frequency programs**, such as those initiated by airlines, as a means to attract and keep customers. Now we can find them in supermarkets, shoe stores, and offered by producers of food goods, greeting cards, and securities. The idea, of course, is to keep the customer buying exclusively or mostly from that one company. Customers buy into these programs to build up points and discounts. These programs appear successful in maintaining a level of loyalty among a large body of consumers, although some may say by economic force.

Consumers' affiliation with frequency programs usually begins when they buy something from a company for the first time. Fly American Airlines for the first time, and chances are several different airline personnel at several different times will ask you to join its frequent-flyer program. You may or may not join depending on the attractiveness of the offer. But if you're a first-time adult purchaser who has been a friend of the airline since childhood, there would probably be no need to ask you to join. You would want to. In fact, the smart airline would have asked you to join even before you bought your first ticket.

What Does a Grow-from-Childhood Program Look Like?

It is not difficult to look into an industry and identify firms that primarily practice one or both market growth strategies. A supermarket that inserts elaborate flyers in the local newspaper every week and offers "unlimited triple coupons" is most likely deep into the strategy of switching customers. Likewise for the auto dealer who shouts, "Find your best deal, bring it to us, and we'll beat it." Converting customers from competitors is hard work, you have to shout, and you constantly have to watch your current flock of customers to see that none has been stolen away during the night.

On the other hand, if you fly Delta Air Lines you will see copies of *Fantastic Flyer* magazine on board and you will see children receiving special meals. If you have a child with you, he or she will probably be asked to join Delta's Fantastic Flyer program (club) for children. This company is growing customers from childhood. Over at United, you will find McDonald's meals on board many flights, but they are not for you. Maybe eventually. But for now, they are strictly for kids. While United's program is not as elaborate or as mature as that of Delta, it is another marketing effort intended to grow customers from young flyers.

Speaking of McDonald's, consider the fast-food industry. It is rather apparent that McDonald's grows customers from childhood; it also seeks to lure customers from competitors. Its playgrounds and kids meals are undeniable telltale signs of its commitment to kids as a current and future market. The Burger King Kids Club makes it generally apparent that the number-two fast-food chain does the same thing, but historically with somewhat less emphasis on children. Wendy's and Hardee's are more focused on competitors as a source of new customers, although from time to time both target kids. Even when they seek out kids, however, it tends to be as an influence market. At the other end of the continuum, Jack In The Box (what a wonderful name for a kids' marketer) is almost always focused on products and/or price to switch adult customers from competitors. Can these different strategies explain why different companies rank differently on the fast-food chain of success? Can they explain why McDonald's is number one and has been for a long time, both here and overseas? What other explanations are there? It does hamburgers better than anyone else?

Stores and manufacturers often start growing customers around the time children enter school. Many companies target their brands to kids in school, by donating computer equipment, or providing teaching aids with the company's name printed on them. Local retailers furnish athletic uniforms, scoreboards, and transportation, always with their name visible. If a child learns word processing on an Apple computer in second grade, he or she may well consider this brand when it comes time to buy one for high school or college work.

I watched the decline of Sears over a period of many years in spite of its lock on the tool business with its Craftsman brand. I used to wonder why it didn't join with Fisher-Price, which makes a lot of scaled-down, funned-up adult products for kids. Both names—Craftsman and Fisher-Price—have a fine reputation for durability. Fisher-Price could produce and market a complete line of Craftsman tools for kids, and I'm sure sell lots of them, while growing customers for Sears. This could be an effective customer-nurturing program with good payoff for both companies. But I think Sears has focused on products more than customers, and on switching customers from competitors more than from developing them from childhood. And it almost lost.

Growing Customers vs. Switching Customers

The table in **Figure 8-2** goes out on a limb and compares the two strategies—growing customers from childhood versus getting customers from competition—on several dimensions, even though a firm would most likely practice both. For example, the table suggests nurtured customers require more time before they make their first purchase, but that once they start buying, they stay with the firm longer than switched customers. This suggests a greater investment in nurturing customers, but also the potential for greater lifetime return-on-investment. The switched customer may not stay long and not return the invest-ment, which can place a company in a robust but near-profitless position.

FIGURE 8-2

A Comparison of New Customers Nurtured from Childhood with New Customers Switched from Competitors

DIMENSION	TYPE OF CUSTOMER	
	NURTURED	SWITCHED
Length of time to first purchase	long	short
Length of stay with marketer	long	short
Degree of satisfaction expected	high	moderate
Likelihood of complaining	low	moderate
Response to higher prices	mild	strong
Response to new offering	eager	reserved
Response to competitors	mild	strong
Long-term payoff	high	low
Recommend firm to others	always	maybe

Figure 8-2 also suggests nurtured customers will be more satisfied than switched customers. This seems logical since a nurtured customer has had time to become familiar and comfortable with the business and how it satis-fies needs. This further suggests nurtured customers will be less likely to complain, but if they do, they will probably make a lot of noise, given their higher expectations. They may also be more responsive to new offerings and less responsive to competitors. Finally, we can expect nurtured customers satisfied by the relationship to recommend the firm to others.

A typical business should practice both customer-building strategies, especially since there are often too many intervening variables to say which clearly works better than the other in a particular industry or firm. Yet focusing on childhood as a source of new customers has an enormous advantage from a long-term perspective; it appears to keep a company in business for the long haul. In sum, the nurtured customer is more likely than the switched customer to be described as a "good customer" or "preferred customer." Chances are at some point, someone in a business will break out the 80-20 principle and assign the 20 to nurtured customers— that is, the 20 percent of customers who account for 80 percent of business.

So why don't more firms grow customers from childhood? Probably the most basic reason is because they do not think long-term. Decision makers on their way up or out may not think seriously of building a secure future for a company. Instead, they try to do something immediate and noticeable—like increase sales—to secure their position. Also, because it does not offer an immediate payback, growing customers from childhood is hard to justify when a firm is operating on a narrow margin.

Finally, measuring the success of customer-nurturing efforts is very difficult—virtually impossible in terms of future sales. While we can track changes in attitudes among young consumers toward a company and its products, measuring how and when those favorable attitudes convert to buying behavior is difficult at best. A degree of faith is required, and faith is a luxury rarely allowed in business. However, as more database marketing experience accumulates, firms are increasingly learning the actual lifetime value of a loyal customer. This measure is prodding more companies to practice strategies that will obtain new customers early and keep them as long as possible. Gradually but increasingly, these businesses are reaching down to the beginnings of consumer behavior, or in effect, moving backward into a market growth strategy that targets children.

PART 2

Children's Reactions to Marketing

CHAPTER 9

Barriers to Understanding the Kids Market

MYTH: "The one thing I understand is kids. I have three of my own."

REALITY: The company experiences millions in losses demonstrating just how unique those three kids are.

The Good, the Bad, and the "Marent"

In the Overview, we introduced a person termed a "**marent,**" a contrivance connoting a marketer who is also a parent with kids. The term suggests that not only is she or he a parent and marketer, but one who believes he or she possesses special understanding of marketing to children as a result of occupying these two roles. He or she can be heard saying: "The one thing I understand is kids; I have three of my own."

A marent is not to be confused with a "wiwak," also common in firms that market to children. Wiwaks express confidence in understanding children as consumers by virtue of having once been children themselves. Wiwaks can be recognized by the way they start a strategy or tactic statement with: "When I was a kid...." For example, "When I was a kid, we played in cardboard boxes. I bet we could sell a million today if we decorated them with pictures of athletic stars." Wiwaks rely on their own experiences as kids, while marents rely on the experiences of their own kids. Both marents and wiwaks are valuable for ideas they bring to the table, although the marents' more forceful suggestions may appear more in tune with the times.

Even though marents are probably in tune with the times, their voice-of-authority demeanor can be dangerously misleading, particularly if they hold lofty positions in the organizational chart. From such a vantage point they may cause a business to incorrectly allocate funds and energies, resulting in less effective marketing efforts to children and even enormous losses.

marent \mär-rent\ n 1: a contrivance connoting a marketer who is also a parent with kids. The term suggests that not only is she or he a parent and marketer, but one who believes he or she possesses special understanding of marketing to children as a result of occupying these two roles.

Effective decision makers act on the basis of research results as much as possible, while less effective decision makers act without research. Marents may make decisions without a research base, relying on their proclaimed knowledge of kids, or they may regularly give consideration to research results but bias them with their personal "intuition." Too often the results are less than bell-ringers.

I'm not suggesting that being both a marketer and parent is inherently bad, any more than it is bad to be both a CEO and a golfer. The danger is in believing such people possess special insights because of this duality. When I visit firms who target children and families, I often hear statements such as:

- "When we are working on an idea for a new kid's product, I run it by my kids first to see how they feel about it."

- "When I'm in China sourcing new premiums and I see one I like, I immediately ask myself what would my kid think of this."

- "I sometimes wish my kids could attend some of our (ad) agency's presentations to see what they think."

- "Every member of the (product team) has kids, so we should be able to get it right."

- "I think every buyer should take his kids to the toy show with him. He'd probably do a better job."

On the surface we might agree with some of these statements, and may have even made similar statements ourselves. But the underlying danger is the possibility of making major business decisions on the basis of responses, or perceived responses, of one or a few children, far from a representative sample.

Implicit in this myth is another one that says that "My kids are like most other kids," or "Most other kids are like mine." Therefore, "If my kid likes it (or dislikes it), others will too." Again, this thinking has some logic to it since kids seem to have so much in common. Push this thinking to the point of making a $10 million decision on it, however, and it begins to look very dicey.

It seems important, in light of this implicit myth, to point out that kids have a lot in common with their own parents, perhaps even more than with kids in general. Parents knowingly and unknowingly impose their values on their children. I often explain children's thinking and behavior with the following generalization: $C = f (P, E)$; that is, Children =

---

wiwak \we-wak\ n 1: common in firms that market to children. Individuals who express confidence in understanding children as consumers by virtue of having once been children themselves. A wiwak can be recognized by the way he or she starts a marketing strategy or tactic statement with: "When I was a kid...."

function of (Parents, Environment). In long form, what children are, how they think and act, are a function of parental and environmental forces constantly at work, even before they are born. This is actually a takeoff on the formula of German psychologist, Kurt Lewin, who explained human behavior with the formulation of B = f (P, E)—i.e., behavior is a function of the person and his environment.

Children, particularly those under age 9, are still developing their own persona, and for much of their lives they typically mirror one or both parents. This is obviously true for physical characteristics. We often hear people say about a child: "He looks just like his father," or "She acts like her mother." An older study found such statements were also often made about adopted children. This suggests that children resemble parents, not necessarily physically, but in the sense they reflect their parents' thinking and behavior—even gestures and voice inflections. When we apply these findings to marents, we realize that one of the reasons they put so much faith in their children's thinking is because it confirms their own.

The graphics of kids ready-to-eat cereal packages are notoriously deceptive. Most exaggerate the size of the cereal, for example. Information about premiums is often deceptive, too.

Deception and Ignorance

Accurate records aren't maintained on marketing mistakes made in the kids' market, but they seem to occur more often than in the general consumer market. Failure rates of new products targeted to children appear to exceed the 65 to 80 percent experienced among all new consumer products, according to various record keepers, including Barry Feign who writes for *Food and Beverage Marketing* magazine.

We see much erroneous and ineffective marketing to kids across all product lines, suggesting no one has a lock on doing it right or wrong. Interesting, too, the errors seem to be as prominent among products traditionally aimed at children, such as toys and snacks, as they are among "kid" versions of adult products such as cosmetics, software, and frozen dinners.

The term marketing mistake, as used here, refers to failures resulting from blunders such as targeting all kids aged 2 to 12 with one ad message on one TV program, packaging salty snacks for kids in packages that don't cater to their limited dexterity, concept testing a product only among parents, offering premiums whose use requires adult supervision, and displaying products for kids in stores well above their eye level. We have all seen these rather obvious errors; amazingly they are repeated over and over and over.

Another set of marketing mistakes result when marketers knowingly or unknowingly ignore children's limited abilities to fully understand communications. For example, the graphics of kids ready-to-eat cereal packages are notoriously deceptive. Most exaggerate the size of the cereal, for example. Information about premiums is often deceptive, too. Use of the word "free" is a good example. An item may be free—with a big purchase, such as $19.95 for a year's subscription to *Racing for Kids* featured on a Kellogg's Frosted Flakes box. The average child might think the free *Jonny Quest* comic book promoted on a box of Honey Nut Cheerios is a regular comic book like you buy at the newsstand. But that was not true of the three I ordered; they contained just 12 pages of comics.

I predict that one of these days a real competitor in the ready-to-eat cereal business is going to initiate a premium program for children that is completely honest and forthright, one that copies the success of the novelty candy industry in combining play with food. For example, a cereal that targets children aged 3 to 8 might make a deal with a miniature-car maker to include one in each cereal package. Over time, this would create a relationship built on trust and continued expectations. While the car might be plastic and of less value than the store-bought versions, the cobranding of a well-known toy and cereal is likely to have a lot of selling power and command a premium price—without deception.

Some packaging deceptions rank alongside the disclaimers in very small print presented at lightning speed within TV ads targeted to children and adults, too. Ultimately, kids and parents grow weary of this kind of marketing, distrust the brand, and quit buying it. In spite of longtime existing guidelines for advertising and marketing to children developed by a number of trade associations, many deceptions are still practiced.

Aside from deliberate deception, many marketing mistakes in the children's market are due to the sheer inexperience of producers, retailers, and service suppliers. Manufacturers tend to develop products for the kids market through simple brand extensions, e.g., Kleenex Tissues For Kids, Ozarka Fluoridated Water for Kids, Duncan Hines Kids Cups cupcake mix. Some may have never marketed to kids and have no sense of the inherent difficulties. Advertising agencies, for example, often get into the kid business by default; their clients are producers who extend their brands to kids. Surely this is tantamount to the blind leading the blind.

Many marketing mistakes result in outright failure, while some drive children away from a firm's offering, perhaps forever, and others offend parents. If repeated often enough, most will attract the attention of regulators.

> ● ● ● ● ● ● ●
> *If parents in general did have a special understanding of children, shelves wouldn't be sagging under the weight of books and magazines written to help parents cope with and understand kids.*

All will limit children's satisfaction and therefore the financial success of the business. Such marketing mistakes would not be so prevalent if marents actually understood kids as well as they claim.

If Not Marents, Who Best Knows How to Market to Children?

Remember the movie *Big*? It starred Tom Hanks as Josh, a 12-year-old mystically transformed into a man. The man-boy got a job as a computer clerk at a toy company. Since he was really just a kid in man's clothing, Josh naturally could tell the company what was a great toy and what was not. Sales flourished, and so did Josh, with a bigger office, title, pay, and of course, jealous coworkers.

Every firm that chooses to target kids as a market needs a Josh on the payroll—at any pay he wants. Preferably an army of Joshes. Because the record is clear; no Josh, no consistent success. Most of the time it will be feast or famine, with marketing errors usually starring in a leading role at annual board meetings.

Children are difficult to understand, no matter who you are and what experience you have. But it is the ultimate in marketing folly to select children as a market target and not have the best understanding possible. After all, marketing is charged with the satisfaction of consumers, a more challenging task when it comes to children, who are unable to make the adjustments to marketing efforts adults routinely make. It's harder for children to discount puffery in advertising, reseal products sold in difficult packages, or return unsatisfactory products for refund or exchange. Marketers who intend to be in the marketing-to-kids business need to try harder, and they need to hire experienced help.

Since businesses don't tend to have access to real-life Joshes, who can they count on to help them understand kids? Wouldn't parents who are marketers have a better appreciation of children's consumer behavior than a person who has not been a father or mother? The answer is a resounding NO. First of all, if parents in general did have a special understanding of children, shelves wouldn't be sagging under the weight of books and magazines written to help parents cope with and understand kids. Moreover, the number of child psychologists, psychiatrists, and pediatricians who write those books and magazine articles would be significantly smaller.

At most, it seems that a keen understanding of children's consumer behavior is distributed randomly among a very small number of adults. If I had to go looking for them, I might start with elementary-school teachers.

Teachers can offer a more objective viewpoint, because the kids they deal with aren't their own. Furthermore, they know lots of children, all types.

The Few, the Insightful, the Best Kids' Marketers

A few people in the business world possess a "sixth sense" about kids. These are people I have met, worked with, and seen in action during my associations with business. I use the term sixth sense to imply there is no simple explanation for their insightful interpretations of children's thinking and behavior related to such marketing objects as products, stores, and communications. But they are repeatedly successful in their endeavors.

I'd like to coin another term such as "kids smarketers" to describe them, but this seems almost insulting to special people who possess special kid smarts. Some are parents; some aren't. Some have a lot of experience in marketing to children; some have only a moderate amount. Some have formal education in fields related to children; some don't.

I don't know how many of these marketing practitioners are out there. What I do know is that their number is relatively small, that of the hundreds of people I know in children's marketing, I could identify perhaps a dozen or so I would classify as manifesting this sixth sense. I will mention four examples. I cannot say why and to what extent these four people possess it, but I'm confident they do based on my repeated observations of their work. In alphabetical order they are:

- George Carey who is CEO of Just Kid, Inc., a relatively new integrated marketing firm at Stamford, CT. He participated in developing and marketing a number of successful products for children while he was at Saatchi and Saatchi, and more recently in his role as head of Just Kid Inc.

- Colleen Fahey who is Senior Vice President and Group Creative Director of Frankel & Company, a marketing service agency at Chicago. Colleen has excelled in developing and marketing promotions to children for many clients.

- Donna Sabino who is head of research and strategic planning at Sports Illustrated for Kids magazine. Donna has been with this most successful magazine for kids since its inception, and surely can be credited with most of its success. She seems to intuitively understand what children want in a magazine, and with her insights and much research, consistently gets it right.

- Cheri Sterman who is Director of Child Development at Binney & Smith in Easton, PA. Binney & Smith produces Crayola brand products.

> Probably no firm has been more successful for so long in manufacturing and marketing products to children than Binney & Smith, and surely Cheri Sterman and her sixth sense about children has been a major contributor to that success.

I would be hard-pressed to identify any characteristics common to these four executives that explain their success in marketing to children. I don't want to imply they haven't made their share of mistakes, and I don't want to suggest they don't rely on research for their decisions, of course they do.

Three in four did impressively kid-incisive work as non-parents, all are relatively young to be holding the positions they do, and only two had formal training in a discipline related to understanding children. But all four have a track record of success in understanding children and directing marketing efforts to them. None of the four could be readily classified as a marent in the sense they had kids when they got into the business and claimed special insights as parents. In fact, others proclaim their special insights for them. Maybe they are real-life Joshes.

One other relatively large group of businesspeople demonstrate a strong understanding of the kids market. They never undertake a marketing effort that targets kids without first researching it thoroughly. They are cognizant of the large number of potential errors in marketing to children. They do not entirely trust their own judgement, as a marent might, and they seek current research information every step along the way.

Some of these now-savvy marketers may have been marents and wiwaks in the past, ones who have learned from their own mistakes. In any case, their number is growing, which is good news for both companies and children. The CEO of one promotion firm, a marent surrounded by other marents, rarely involved market research when designing premiums for kids. Because of on-again, off-again success, the business finally but reluctantly introduced research. Today, it is quite successful, known for its research-based and creative kids' premiums, and has an impressive list of clients who market to children.

Basic Things to Know about Kids

Perhaps the biggest reason why adults have difficulty marketing to kids is because kids are different. **Figure 9-1** summarizes some special characteristics of children that cause potential marketing mistakes. For example, children love the term, "Free," but when they see it, they believe it. To add, "with two proofs of purchase" in small print is simply misleading to a kid.

Children love the term, "Free," but when they see it, they believe it. To add "with two proofs of purchase" in small print is simply misleading to a kid.

Special Characteristics of Children that Cause Marketing Mistakes

CHARACTERISTIC	EXAMPLE OF POTENTIAL MARKETING MISTAKE
Children are literal	Making imprecise statements such as, "Free (with two proofs of purchase)"
Children are gullible	Exaggerations, such as "lowest prices in town"
Children are relatively short	Displaying products for kids at adults' eye level
Children are shy	Expecting children to ask for a refund when a product is not as advertised
Children have limited dexterity	Expecting children to properly open and close a typical chip bag
Children have limited ability to think abstractly	Expecting children to keep the receipt in case a refund is necessary
Children's most important motive or need is play	Expecting children to ask parents to buy software for its educational value
Children's second most important need is sentience—to express their developing sensory system	Expecting children to want bland dinner entrees

FIGURE 9-1

Either it's free or it isn't. Likewise, kids are gullible, and believe much of the puffery communicated to them.

Even though we call them "little kids," marketers often ignore the inevitable fact of children's small stature and limited strength and dexterity. Children will never be more than an influence market for milk packaged in 8-pound gallon jugs.

Children have difficulty thinking abstractly about distance and time. Solving problems in their head is pretty difficult until they are around age 11. Yet purchase rules such as "keep the receipt" are the same for kids and adults. Children's seemingly innate shyness—probably around half could be classified as shy—interferes with their ability to maneuver through public transactions.

For most kids in the United States and elsewhere, play is the most important need (beyond essentials such as food and shelter). Play fills time, educates, develops social skills. To kids, there is no time that isn't play time. Play is kids' work. Expecting kids to eat without playing, or eat instead of playing, does not consider their most basic need. Play should not be viewed as the opposite of work or learning, but as a facilitator. This is what "edutainment" software is all about.

Finally, kids love to explore with the sensory system they are constantly discovering. They like to experiment with extremes—very sweet, very sour, very bitter-tasting foods. Just look at some of the candies they love, so sour adults can barely tolerate them, but kids adore them (or at least bravely claim to). When I was a kid—I can't believe I said that—we sugar-coated dill pickles and thought they were winning recipes for what tastes good. Yet food producers are somehow convinced that kids' notorious "picky" eating habits indicate they prefer bland foods. Many kids may not want their corn and peas mixed on the plate, but they sure like hot Creole spices sprinkled on them.

> • • • • • • • •
> *Food producers are somehow convinced that kids' notorious "picky" eating habits indicate they prefer bland foods.*

What I Am Saying Is This

I once had a statistics professor who would completely fill the boards of two classrooms during one lecture with formulae and problem solutions, what we students unkindly called "beta sigma." Then, a few minutes before the end of class, he would fold his huge notebook, shake the chalk dust from his hands, and ask: "So what am I saying?" Fortunately for me, he would answer his own question with: "What I am saying is this."

So what I'm saying is this: I have wandered around quite a bit in the discussion of this myth, gave people some names, called people some names, and praised the names of others. Through it all, I am saying that a lot of people out there in the business of marketing to kids claim to know a lot about it simply because they are parents. But the plain fact of the matter is that many are "marents" making a lot of mistakes in marketing to kids. On the other hand, a few business executives out there seem to have a knack for doing it right. These "kid smarketers" are successful in satisfying kids and making money, and we can learn from them. I wish all of my students interested in marketing to children could intern under one of these experts. In fact, I wish I could, too.

Take a look at the drawing in **Figure 9-2**. It may look a little strange to you if you haven't been to China. An 8-year-old girl produced this

FIGURE 9-2

when we asked her to: "Draw what comes to your mind when you think about going shopping." The picture has two children selecting a common candy in China, a sort of cross between rock candy and candied apples—little crabapple-like fruits dipped in sugar water, threaded on a stick and sold on street corner for around 15 cents. Notice the excitement in the illustration—the sunshine, butterfly, bird, grass and flowers. These *tong hu lu* are a favorite snack item for Chinese children when they go shopping with parents, like a box of popcorn at the movies.

If one saw them for the first time on display on their "trees," one might doubt they would sell so well to kids. First of all the fruit is sour, the hardened sugar coating is solid sweet, and being openly displayed in the streets of Beijing, they are coated with dirt and soot. But a kid smarketer would recognize all these features as attractive to children—the contrast in sweet and sour, the healthy fruit with the not-so-healthy sugar coating, the stickiness, and of course, the incidental but nonetheless appealing dirt—all in one wonderful, inexpensive product just for kids.

CHAPTER 10

Children's Favorite Stores

MYTH: "If a kid has money, he'll spend it before it burns a hole in his pocket."

REALITY: If kids have money, they'll spend a lot of it before it burns holes in their pockets, but they will try to spend it in a favorite store.

The implication of this myth is that children have something in their bloodstream compelling them to spend any money they get as soon as possible. It's just not so. We find no more spending compulsion among most children than we do among most adults. Moreover, as we indicated earlier, children usually save around one-third of the weekly monies they receive, at least until they've accumulated enough for a major purchase. But the major error in this myth is the implication that children will spend their money in any retail outlet convenient when the burning starts. The truth is they will spend it in a deliberate fashion at their favorite stores.

Several years ago, we were curious about the favorite stores of children who live in small towns with few shopping choices. Would they all favor the same supermarket, convenience store, or dollar store by default? Or might they simply not have a favorite? We went to a town of 2,500 population for answers. In one part of a study among third-graders, we asked them in an appropriate research setting to: "Draw your favorite store." We assumed they would draw some kind of retail setting, and if it was really their favorite, it would show.

Well, they did what they were asked, and the results were intriguing. Two-thirds of the children drew a mass merchandiser store in a nearby city; they didn't have one in their town. About two-thirds of those drawings represented a Wal-Mart and the rest a Kmart. What a way to get a measure of out-shopping. These children, we learned, saved much of their money and looked forward to spending it in their favorite store outside of their hometown during weekend forays to major shopping areas.

Figure 10-1 shows one of the drawings done by a late-blooming 8-year-old. While he had trouble picturing himself—he had not yet formed his own self-concept—he had no trouble portraying his favorite store. Just notice the smile on his face, the abundant shopping cart in the center of the page—it looks almost like a Trojan horse—and most of all the Kmart store (brand) name, center front, surrounded by rainbow-decorated clouds. He couldn't say it much clearer than this in an interview: Going to Kmart is like finding the pot of gold at the end of the rainbow.

FIGURE 10-1

Kids' Favorite Stores

Children gave us a hint they have favorite stores when first, third, and fifth graders told us in which store they would spend $100 they had hypothetically won. As shown in **Figure 10-2**, roughly half of all ages mentioned mass merchandisers by name, one in four said "the mall" or a specific mall, and the other fourth mentioned a wide range of specialty stores, department stores, and supermarkets, all by name. None said he or she would spend the money in any store or in any store that carried a certain product. They may generalize the products they would buy with terms like "things" and "stuff," but they are specific about the stores.

Why did three-fourths designate a particular store? The kids gave such answers as, "It's a great place to buy things," "They have the best kind of shoes for kids," "I like to buy things there," "It's a lot of fun," and, "I like the stuff they have there and they're friendly." In other words, they chose a particular store to spend their money in because they have emotional involvement with it, they have feelings about it. In sum, if kids have money, they want to spend it, but they want to choose where they spend it. They often tell their parents, "It's my money; I ought to be able to spend it the way I want to." And they usually do.

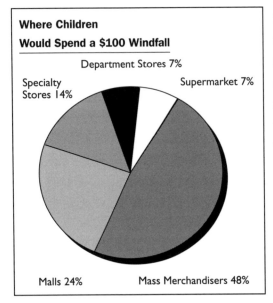

Where Children Would Spend a $100 Windfall

Department Stores 7%
Specialty Stores 14%
Supermarket 7%
Malls 24%
Mass Merchandisers 48%

FIGURE 10-2

Children tend to generalize across stores with the same name. That is, they usually perceive all Wal-Marts, Krogers, 7-Eleven stores, and so on as alike. This certainly works in favor of the store chain trying to develop kids' business. However, children also do some generalizing within store types in that they may see different convenience stores as much alike if the stores' physical features look alike, even if the stores' names differ. This works against the store chain trying to develop kids as a market and should encourage them to seek a distinctive and attractive representational design such as the McDonald's Golden Arches.

When children first make independent purchases, their favorite stores are mainly convenience stores.

Both children's preferences for specific stores and their generalizations among similar names and store types appear to reflect what they have learned from their parents as well as their own experiences with stores. Consequently, astute store managers should make a special effort to target mother-and-child shoppers with special offerings that leave good impressions on both.

More detailed analysis reveals that children's three favorite types of stores vary somewhat by age, as shown in **Figure 10-3**. For example, children tend to prefer supermarkets less and mass merchandisers more as they grow older. Most children grew up, so to speak, in supermarkets, and they harbor many good memories of shopping there with Mom. But as children's need for play begins to dominate, they find many more satisfying products at a Kmart or Target store. Such stores offer many snack items also found in supermarkets, but they have a relatively enormous offering of play items not found in supermarkets.

Notice, too, from Figure 10-3 that when children first make independent purchases, their favorite stores are mainly convenience stores. But notice further how quickly this liking disappears. Our research suggests that children like the accessibility of these stores—within walking or bicycling distance—the relatively wide range of "things for kids," and the relatively small size of the stores, which makes them manageable for the kids. But it appears this is virtually a one-way love affair, with most C-store chains alienating kids rather than grasping the opportunity offered "on a silver platter" to build a relationship with them.

FIGURE 10-3

Kids' Favorite Stores		
YOUNG	**MIDDLE**	**TWEEN**
Convenience	Mass Discounter	Mass Discounter
Supermarket	Supermarket	Specialty Store
Mass Discounter	Specialty Store	Supermarket

Thus, kids' attitudes toward stores suggest that they have favorite stores just like they have favorite brands, favorite relatives, and favorite teachers, and they very naturally try to form an affiliation with the stores they like. (The affiliation need becomes a very important need of children at around age 8 or 9.) While this statement is not profound, it could mean a competitive advantage for a store or store chain that nurtures relationships with these newly fledged consumers. It could mean a competitive advantage for a store's brands, too, since children are generally brand-conscious.

The concept of favorite store, according to my research, seems to be a common notion among youth throughout the world. In China, for example, children make many purchases at street vendors who set up shop in every neighborhood of large cities. They are licensed by the state to sell goods, and each stall or stand has a large license number on the front of it. They do not have names such as Wang's Foods or Chang's Clothing, although you often will see Western brand names displayed. Chinese children identify the merchants by these license numbers and tend to have favorites such as number 27. The favorites are based on experience, family preferences, and word-of-mouth among peers, much as they are in the U.S. and in other countries.

FIGURE 10-4

Figure 10-4 exemplifies this pattern. In this drawing, an 8-year-old illus-

trates two sellers, one of a mobile nature and one of a permanent nature. The mobile seller is saying, "I'm selling snacks," and the youngster has probably bought snacks many times from this merchant. But the child's favorite is demonstrated by the prominent and very decorative #38 where the seller is emphasizing "red and big apples." The original color drawing shows the stall in bright blue and yellow, although in reality almost

none are painted, and it is laden with red apples at an attractive price. Smiles on the seller's face and those of customers leaving with both hands full attest to the retailer's status as a favorite.

How Kids Develop Relationships with Stores

Children have almost as many experiences per time period with retail outlets as their parents do, and they consequently have many occasions to form favorable and unfavorable opinions about them. My research over the years suggests stores also perform a significant role in children's imaginations, fantasies, and play. Children often "play store" in which they pretend to shop and buy. These physical and cognitive experiences with retail outlets start very early in life.

Let us look closer at children's developing consumer behavior patterns to understand how they come to have preferences for certain types of stores. Through a survey of 222 mothers with varying geographic and socioeconomic backgrounds, we investigated what kinds of stores were involved in children's first adventures into retail consumption, and at what ages these interactions took place. We will summarize the results as they apply to explaining how children form relations with stores in childhood. A more complete presentation of the findings was presented in Chapter 2.

Stage One: The Observation Stage

Kids' first experiences with stores begins in infancy at an average age of 2 months during what we call the observation stage. At this point a child's visit to stores is primarily a sensory affair. They see lights and colors, hear many different sounds, and smell many aromas. In 78 percent of cases, this first visit is to a supermarket. From this point on, children become acquainted with the marketplace on a regular basis, probably visiting one or more stores an average of once a week.

Stage Two: In-Store Requests

By the time they are around 18 months, they discover the marketplace is a source of desirable things that mother ordinarily provides. In stage two, in-store requests, children first ask for products they see on display. These first requests occurs at a median age of 24 months. Again, this usually happens in a supermarket. Supermarkets, therefore, are typically the recipients of children's first consumer acts. These early experiences tend to give children warm feelings toward supermarkets in general, and we can expect them to have one or more favorite supermarkets when we ask them about stores.

Stage Three: In-Store Selection

In this stage, children make their first in-store selections. That is, they actually retrieve a product from a retailer's shelf for the first time at around 42 months. This emotional experience reinforces the notion that the store has good things to buy, although at this point they do not fully conceptualize the purchase process. In 56 percent of cases, this consumer behavior takes place in a supermarket, and in 23 percent of the cases it happens at a mass merchandiser. This latter figure indicates that children are getting familiar

Children first ask for products they see on display at a median age of 24 months.

with other types of stores besides supermarkets. Obviously, the opportunity to become acquainted with various store types is a function of parents, who also provide commentary on store quality.

Stage Four: First Assisted Purchase

Stage four in children's consumer behavior development happens at an average age of 66 months (5-1/2 years)—their first assisted purchase. This very significant event nearly always occurs in one of three retail outlets—mass merchandisers (43 percent), supermarkets (19 percent), or toy stores (19 percent). From the standpoint of gender, this particular research effort suggests supermarkets are more important to girls than boys as a venue of first purchase attempt. Thus, children's experience with different kinds of stores continues to expand as they make their first purchase with parental assistance.

At this point the children have a rudimentary understanding of the exchange process—of money for goods—and realize that they can obtain the products ordinarily provided by parents through the purchase process. Particular stores now become even more important because of the products they offer and the atmosphere in which they offer them. Thus, children become more evaluative in their choices of stores in which to buy. In other words, they form likes and dislikes.

Stage Five: First Independent Purchase

The last stage of consumer behavior development that qualifies the child as a bona fide consumer is the one in which he or she makes a first independent purchase, at a median age of about 8 years. Half of the time it will take place in a convenience store, 14 percent of the time in a supermarket—somewhat more frequently for girls—and 12 percent of the time in a shopping mall, according to this research. This critical first purchase is likely to occur in a convenience store primarily because of its proximity to home or school. In discussions with corporate management of convenience store chains, they don't seem to assign any significance to the fact that children often make their first independent purchase in these outlets. But for children, it is a very emotional experience and contributes to the child bonding to a particular C-store.

Stepping back and looking at these five stages of consumer behavior development, with each stage continuing and new ones overlaying the ones before, we can see that by the time children make that first independent

> • • • • • • • • • •
> *Children tend to make their first independent purchase at a median age of about 8 years. Half of the time it will take place in a convenience store, 14 percent of the time in a supermarket—somewhat more frequently for girls—and 12 percent of the time in a shopping mall.*

purchase at age 8, they have had a great deal of experience with a relatively wide range of store types. At the end of their eighth year, they have made at least 750 store visits, with and without parents, perhaps 7,000 to 10,000 purchase requests to parents, 3,000 to 5,000 of their own selections, and probably a couple hundred assisted and unassisted purchases with their own money for their own wants and needs.

What Makes a Favorite Store for a Kid?

By reexamining data from several studies conducted since 1990, we uncover some consistent findings that suggest the elements of a favorite store for children. These factors, or attributes, in order of importance to kids, are as follows:

1. **Kid-Friendly Atmosphere.** If we had to list the single most important attribute of a kid's favorite store, it would be that it is kid-friendly. It is difficult to measure this component except in that children repeatedly mention it more than any other, although not in so many words. They use phrases such as, "They like kids," "They don't like kids," "They treat you bad," "I feel good there," "I hate to go there," and "I like to go there."

    While kid-friendliness is hard to measure, it certainly is possible for a store to go to children through focus groups and perception scales, for instance, and ask them to evaluate a particular store on this dimension and others. Features such as pint-sized shopping carts in a supermarket, bicycle rack at a C-store, kids' products at eye level in a clothing store, and video broadcasts for kids in certain areas of a department store are vivid indicators of kid-friendliness. By all means, thoughtful gestures by store personnel toward kids will place the store in the kid-friendly category. Interestingly, children learn rather early in life to avoid store personnel apparently because parents often disparage these people and because of their own general aloofness with kids.

2. **Kids' Products.** Children are unlikely to vote a store as a favorite unless it has products they want to buy. A mass merchandiser with a wide selection of kids' clothing, toys, and snack items, or a toy store with its depth of offering will be important to kids, but probably not a home improvement store or a jewelry store.

    It is not enough to have kids' products. They must be ones children perceive as popular brands/styles, and they must also be within

> • • • • • • •
> *By the end of their eighth year, most children have made at least 750 store visits, with and without parents, perhaps 7,000 to 10,000 purchase requests to parents, 3,000 to 5,000 of their own selections, and probably a couple hundred assisted and unassisted purchases with their own money for their own wants and needs.*

acceptable price ranges. Brands are tools children use to identify goods and services, and if the clothing offering, for example, at a department store does not include certain popular national brands, the clothing is not really for them. Also, during the past decade, children have become more price-conscious and expect products to be offered in ranges with which they are familiar, as well as those their parents find acceptable. Children do respond to sales prices, although older children seem to become quickly jaded by continued sales prices such as the "25% off" signs that are permanent fixtures in most department stores and specialty clothing stores.

3. **Eye-level Accessible Displays.** Kids are all too familiar with out-of-reach products. After all, they are 3-footers in a 6-foot world. Even in a kids-centered store such as Toys R Us, many play items are not accessible to children (unless they use the ladders scattered throughout the stores, not a good idea). Moreover, items of interest to children are still sold under glass and behind counters in some stores.

Children first experience out-of-reach items at home when parents want to keep things away from them. When the children experience this in a store, they know the store is not for them. Children want a hands-on display of products for themselves. When they see a product of interest to them, they want to be able to touch it, taste it, handle it, operate it, try it on. This means, in general, that kids prefer a self-service or self-selection environment. Salespeople are always adults, and by this definition are a bit intimidating. Self-service is generally more desirable than personal service.

4. **Communicates with Kids.** Children perceive a store as a good place to shop if its mix of communications specifically includes them. This means in-store communications such as signage and video displays, as well as advertising, promotion, and publicity that reach kids through schools, television and radio programming, magazines, newspapers, and particularly mail. A store with a relationship program with children that involves sending occasional mail pieces, such as the Burger King Kids Club, is sure to gain favor with them.

Also, kids' relationship programs often have a spokesperson, such as a cartoon personality, that automatically communicates their child orientation. For years, McDonald's has used Ronald McDonald to symbolize their kid orientation, but recently it has chosen to extend his reach to the adult world. One might question the wisdom of this.

• • • • • • • • •
Kids are all too familiar with out-of-reach products. After all, they are 3-footers in a 6-foot world.

5. Others Like It. Finally, kids favor stores favored by their parents and/or friends. Younger children, those aged 4 to 8 like to say their favorite store is also a favorite of their parents. Older children aged 9 to 12 often tell us their friends patronize the same store they do. In both cases, the desire to conform leads children to like the same stores favored by those they admire.

These five attributes are not unusual or overly demanding, but what any store management would do to attract and keep a market. A good example of one chain targeting children that makes use of all five is the Limited Too. Capitalizing on the good reputation of The Limited stores among women (moms), Limited Too stores initially targeted girls from infancy through teenhood. After lackluster success, management began to realize most of its business was coming from tween girls and their parents—the age group frequently in malls where stores were located. The 300-plus stores were repositioned to focus only on this age group, essentially 8-13 years. It recognized this young consumer was fashion-aware and needed a place to shop for clothing and adornments that understood her needs as a becoming-woman. It also had to please mom in terms of styles and price lines. It transformed its more traditional adult-oriented stores into an friendly and exciting shopping experience for tween girls. At the time of this writing the stores are still being revamped, and management reports rapidly growing sales and profits.

• • • • • • • •
In study after study, children report McDonald's is their favorite fast-food restaurant. Yet in other studies, children report their favorite fast food is pizza.

Marketing Implications

If children have a favorite store, a favorite fast-food restaurant, for example, that restaurant will receive much of children's restaurant patronage, perhaps for many years. Most others will be eliminated from children's choices. Therefore, it behooves stores wishing to attract children as part of their market to institute features such as those described above. Not all of them perhaps, but it at least has to offer satisfying products in an atmosphere perceived as kid-friendly.

The kid-friendly feature could be a "cookie credit card" at a supermarket, a kids' corner in a music store, free video games at an auto dealership, or a kids' waiting lounge at an air terminal. Consider McDonald's again. In study after study, children report it is their favorite fast-food restaurant. Yet in other studies, children report their favorite fast food is pizza. McDonald's enjoys a lot of patronage from children, more than any other restaurant, even though it does not sell the most desirable foods in the eyes of children.

What McDonald's does well is to satisfy the important needs of children, mainly play, with its kids' meals and playgrounds.

It's never too soon to start courting children's favor. Children's adoption of stores as their favorites begins very early in childhood. Stores that acknowledge children at an early age with kid-friendly beacons will surely have an advantage in the future over those that don't.

What about Non-store Retailers?

We have been discussing favorite stores as children's preferred places to buy things. We have shown children also form dislikes for certain stores, understandably so in view of the ill-treatment they receive. But what about other outlets for buying things? What about vending machines, catalogs, direct mail, and web sites?

All told, children's non-store purchases probably amount to less than 5 percent of their total purchases. But kids didn't invent stores, and they don't need stores, certainly not any particular store. They simply require need-satisfaction, just like any other consumer. As our research shows, kids don't have to have a favorite store in their home town; they can have one in a nearby city.

Types of retailers come and go. The traditional door-to-door retailer has nearly vanished. Malls, at the time of this writing, have lost some popularity. A decade ago, the vending machine looked as if it was on its way out, but it may save itself with coin slots now commonly in kids' reach and products favored by children. Can you remember when vending machines had the coin slot at the top and brand names no one had heard of?

On the up side, catalogs are experiencing a boom under the direction of a new breed of specialty vendor, yet at the same time, the century-old Sears-Roebuck catalog finally became too much of a millstone around its company's neck. Web sites are following in the footsteps of mail-order catalogs and abound with specialty offerings. The combination of these two, print and electronic, appear to have a bright future.

While it is still difficult for kids to buy from these latter two sources, they are beginning to do it jointly with parents just as they did when they first started shopping at stores. So far, kids seem to like catalog and Internet shopping, although it lacks the affiliation they experience when shopping at the mall with friends. But if vendors using these two retail "outlets" can figure it out without "gooing up a good deal," they can grow a new generation of non-store shoppers from an early age.

Notice the poise shown by this child, notice her presence in the store among other shoppers, and notice her awareness of store related items that give her the feeling of belonging in the store—in this case a department store. She shows it as it is, with many shoppers, a sales clerk, special prices, a variety of fixtures holding a variety of products including play items and clothing, a TV monitor repeating a sales message, shopping bags with the store's name on them. You can feel the excitement she feels. This same picture repeats itself in various ways in all developed and developing countries, and confirms the newfound stature of children as consumers.

COLORPLATE I, FIGURE 0-I

**Budding
consumers
asked to:
"Draw what
comes to
mind when
you think
about going
shopping."**

COLORPLATE 2,
FIGURE 1-1

Look closely at the child shopper in Figure 1-1 who is standing in the checkout line at a Kroger supermarket. The center positioning of the store name in big lettering tells us she likes Kroger's. She is aware that you use a shopping cart, load it down, then head to the checkout where there are other shoppers doing the same thing. She even knows there's a trash can underneath the counter!

COLORPLATE 3,
FIGURE 2-11

Figure 2-11 was drawn by a Chinese child. The youngster portrays himself stepping up to a toy counter in a major department store. The sign above the counter reads, "Ship models on sale," and the sign to the right says, "Welcome. Visit our store." He believes that these signs and similar ones in other stores are talking to him, and has learned how to buy in stores without self-service. He has money waving in his hand, and we can feel his confidence and enthusiasm for one of his first major purchases.

The 8-year-old Chinese girl who drew this picture told us verbally and visually that she sometimes spends exceptional sums of money on expensive clothing—just as kids this age do in the United States. She portrayed herself and other shoppers in the Wudaokou department store in Beijing—a relatively upscale place to shop. Notice that she has a 100-yuan bill in her hand, a substantial amount of money for her to be carrying, roughly U.S. $12, but not unusual for special shopping occasions such as buying clothing.

COLORPLATE 4,
FIGURE 3-1

This 9-year-old Chinese boy's drawing—in almost engineering style—shows The People's Bank of China—complete with clock, towers, and the Chinese flag. Underneath the bank building, a caption reads, "If I have money I will put it in The People's Bank of China to help support the construction of our country." What he is saying in the drawing, as confirmed by a post-drawing interview, is that "When I think about going shopping, I think about the money that I will need to withdraw that I have put in savings for a very good cause."

COLORPLATE 5,
FIGURE 3-2

· ·

*When asked to draw what comes to her
mind when she thinks about going
shopping, this young girl took the opportunity to complain about stores.*

COLORPLATE 6,
FIGURE 4-2

Children's strong preference for M&M's is illustrated well in Figure 4-2. When asked
to draw what comes to her mind when she thinks about going shopping, this young
girl took the opportunity to complain about stores. She drew herself shopping in a
supermarket, but also demonstrated that stores display her favorite M&M's items and
other desirable products in hard-to-reach locations.

A Korean child illustrates her ability to shop for food goods in the marketplace, in this case an open marketplace. But she also depicts store personnel who ignore young consumers and watch television instead.

COLORPLATE 7,
FIGURE 4-3

COLORPLATE 7,
FIGURE 5-1

Children see themselves as working a lot. School is work. Even some recreation is "work," such as after-school soccer practice or piano lessons. This little girl can be seen cleaning the windows beside her study desk. The caption says, "Me cleaning windows." Her desk suggests she will also do some school work.

COLORPLATE 8,
FIGURE 5-2

Figure 5-2 offers another perspective on spare weekend time. In this case, the illustrator shows himself at an art class, obtaining skills and knowledge in addition to those learned at regular school. The caption above the art teacher's head reads, "Art class, 6 to 8." The clock above registers 7:00, and the dark object to the right is a finished artwork, rolled up and ready to take home to show to parents.

When asked to, "draw what comes to your mind when you think of going shopping," these young illustrators give importance to the role they assume when shopping with their parents.

In a post-task interview, young artist, Katherine, told us she could remember when she used to sit in the observation seat now occupied by her sister Elizabeth. She went on to say that now she helps her mother by "running and getting the things that Elizabeth wants." Mom has one pointing and one running, and you can see by the smile on her face how happy she is about it.

COLORPLATE 9,
FIGURE 6-1

Look closely at a shopping setting in Beijing, China drawn by a fifth-grader. It shows our subject with her mother. Their arms are full of bags with the department store's name on them. This is the subject's way of saying they bought many expensive items. Also notice three other mother-daughter shopping teams, which is the illustrator's way of saying parents and children regularly shop together as equals.

COLORPLATE 10,
FIGURE 7-1

The three stores on the right side of the tallest building are labeled "food store," "clothing store," and "toy store." But the tallest one, the one on the left with a traffic director beside it, says, "Landao department store," not just "department store." The Landao department store has become part of this child's brand repertoire.

This drawing may look strange to you if you haven't been to China. These tong hu lu, displayed on "trees," are a favorite snack item for Chinese children when they go shopping. They like the contrast in sweet and sour, the healthy fruit with the not-so-healthy sugar coating, the stickiness, and of course, the incidental but nonetheless appealing dirt—all in one wonderful, inexpensive product just for kids.

Figure 10-1 shows one of the drawings done by a late-blooming 8-year-old. While he had trouble picturing himself—he had not yet formed his own self-concept—he had no trouble portraying his favorite store. Just notice the smile on his face, the abundant shopping cart in the center of the page—it looks almost like a Trojan horse—and most of all the Kmart store (brand) name, center front, surrounded by rainbow-decorated clouds. He couldn't say it much clearer than this in an interview: Going to Kmart is like finding the pot of gold at the end of the rainbow.

COLORPLATE 13,
FIGURE 10-1

The concept of a favorite store seems to be a common notion among youth throughout the world.

COLORPLATE 14, FIGURE 10-4

In China, children make many purchases at street vendors who set up shop in every neighborhood of large cities. They are licensed by the state to sell goods, and each stall or stand has a large license number on the front of it. They do not have names such as Wang's Foods or Chang's Clothing, although you often will see Western brand names displayed. Chinese children identify the merchants by these license numbers and tend to have favorites such as number 27. The favorites are based on experience, family preferences, and word-of-mouth among peers—much as they are in the U.S. and in other countries.

In this drawing, an 8-year-old illustrates two sellers, one of a mobile nature and one of a permanent nature. The mobile seller is saying, "I'm selling snacks," and the youngster has probably bought snacks many times from this merchant. But the child's favorite is demonstrated by the prominent and very decorative #38 where the seller is emphasizing "red and big apples." The original color drawing shows the stall in bright blue and yellow, although in reality almost none are painted, and it is laden with red apples at an attractive price. Smiles on the seller's face and those of customers leaving with both hands full attest to the retailer's status as a favorite.

Take a look at the drawing in Figure 11-1 rendered by a 9-year-old asked to: "Draw what comes to your mind when you think about going shopping." The young man tells it like it is—a jungle of sorts, with just about everything bigger than he is. There is little distinction among store elements except for a sale sign: "99¢ fish" in aisle 10. Out of all the hundreds of fixtures and thousands of products, their brands, and promotions, price stands out.

COLORPLATE 15,
FIGURE 11-1

COLORPLATE 16,
FIGURE 12-3

COLORPLATE 17,
FIGURE 12-4

Figures 12-3 and 12-4 reveal the importance of floors to children. The first is by an American 3rd-grader, the second by a Chinese 3rd-grader. Although an ocean apart, they still assign great significance to store floors. And for good reason. They have fond memories of many fun hours on the floor. It's their playground at home, and probably at day care too. And since they are still close to the floor, they give it a lot of attention. Thus, placing ad messages in floors—tiles, carpet, whatever—is a logical way to target children at the point of purchase. In fact, if done properly, it could assist children in finding merchandise in large, complex and changing shopping environments, such as large mass merchandisers.

Figure 13-1 was rendered by a third-grader asked to draw a cereal box. This young artist displays two promotions, both in the center of the drawing and both connected to the brand name. The position of these two promotional statements indicates how important they are to the child. The one just below the brand name states that "Theres a pussle on the back," probably referring to a game printed on the back panel. This is part of the cereal's play offering to children. The second promotion in even bigger print says, "Free toy inside." Again, a promotional offer related to play. Thus, the cue word cereal elicited a rendering of a brand name cereal, Lucky Charms, and also a dual offer of two play items— all from the mind of a child who expects something, in fact, multiple somethings.

COLORPLATE 18, FIGURE 13-1

. . . . . .

McDonald's has been a huge success in China, as in the U.S., particularly with kids.

This drawing is from a 3rd-grade Beijing child who, along with his classmates, was asked to draw what comes to mind when you think of the new "long" two-day weekend. The child perceives the long weekend as a time to play, and a time to put on your favorite jogging suit and run with your friends to a McDonald's breakfast. Note the accuracy of the Golden Arches sign.

COLORPLATE 19, FIGURE 14-2

Half of the children asked to, "draw a cereal box," provided a side panel showing in great detail the required nutritional information of the cereal.

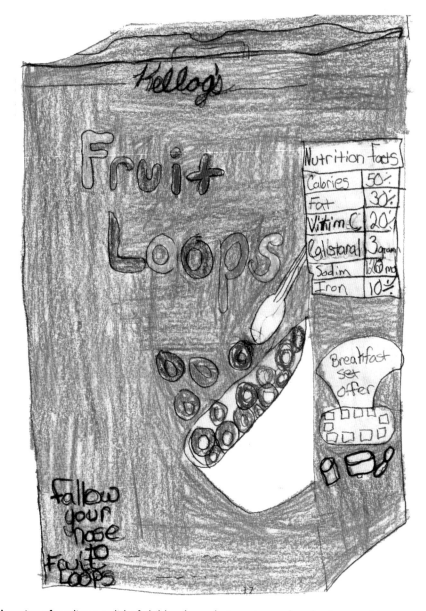

COLORPLATE 20,
FIGURE 16-1

A series of studies we did of children's ready-to-eat cereal packaging provides strong evidence of the importance of packaging communications. We twice replicated a study done in the 1970s to understand the perceptions children have of packaging. In the mid-1980s, we asked first- and third-grade children to "Draw a cereal package." The first graders did a pretty good job. About half supplied a brand name and some brand-specific graphics on the front panel. Virtually all of the third graders provided front panels with brand names, usually exactly the way the packages illustrated them, including many graphic features such as colors and slogans. The children showed us very vividly that a package is not just a package; it's a Cheerios package, for example, with very specific graphics, a detailed picture they carry in their heads.

In 1996 we repeated the study and found one major difference. Half of the children provided a side panel showing in great detail the required nutritional information of the cereal. In this particular case, the child acknowledges "Nutrition Facts," and lists them such as "calories," "fat," "vitim (vitamin) C," and "sodim (sodium)."

When asked to, "draw what comes to mind when you think about going shopping," a brand name may get more attention than the generic name of the product.

Notice the prominence of a brand name, Esprit, in this young girl's drawing. Not once, not twice, but three times she displays this rather complicated word (for a 9-year-old) on store offerings. She even wraps it around her own shirt. Moreover, she illustrates it exactly as the brand owner does! And then, bless her heart, she misspells "shirts" and "skirts" and writes "shrits" and "skrits."

COLORPLATE 21,
FIGURE 17-2

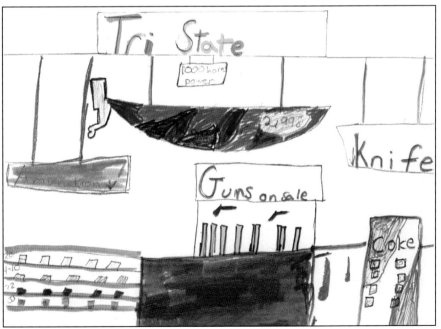

This youngster is keenly aware of the adult products he can buy or ask his parents to buy.

This fourth-grader's drawing says: "I like to go shopping at the local sporting-goods store, get a Coke from the machine, and look at hunting and fishing equipment. I can either buy things with my own money, such as a knife, or ask my dad to buy something for me such as a rod-and-reel combination." He knows too, from reading his own magazines, for example, that many of these products are just for him.

COLORPLATE 22,
FIGURE 18-1

A completion test that was part of a study among Chinese children to determine their likes and interests regarding TV viewing.

COLORPLATE 23,
FIGURE 19-1

The characters are children drawn by children. Their faces are not visible, and the picture on the TV set is vague to reduce directive bias. In this scenario, a girl is asking a boy what program he wants to watch next. Male respondents are asked to write in the empty balloon over the boy's head what they believe he will answer. Girls responded to a reverse scenario.

Chinese children seem very aware of their multi-tiered role as primary, influence, and future consumers.

COLORPLATE 24,
FIGURE 20-2

This 9-year-old, after being instructed to draw what comes to his mind when he thinks about going shopping, shows himself among other young shoppers in a department store. The sign above the appliance area states that appliances are on sale, while the sign above the clothing counter says, "Welcome, hello, customers."

CHAPTER 11

What Kids Know About Pricing

MYTH: *"Children don't care at all about price."*

REALITY: A majority of kids are price-sensitive, will state a
preference for a low price, and recognize that similar stores
may differ in price.

Textbooks usually define price from a marketing perspective as the amount of money charged for a product or service, and from a consumer perspective as the amount of money paid for a product or service. But in some focus group research we conducted for a software producer, young respondents offered a different perspective. We were discussing their knowledge of a particular product—a video game system. We asked: "How much do you think it costs?" One 10-year-old boy answered, "Too much!" quickly followed by chants of "Yeah, too much" from other participants. His, "Too much" may have meant too much for his income, his parents' income, or too much for the satisfaction he would receive from it. In any case, kids are aware of and sensitive to price.

Kids aged 4 to 12 have an average weekly income of almost $15, spend around $10.50, and save slightly over $4.

Earlier discussions pointed out kids have money of their own to spend, as well as access to a substantial amount of their parents' money. Kids aged 4 to 12 have an average weekly income of almost $15, spend around $10.50, and save slightly over $4. Also, at any point in time, a typical 10-year-old has probably $25 to $30 stashed at home and a couple hundred dollars in the bank, all of which she may tap for a big purchase, although usually only with parental agreement.

It's significant, too, that virtually all of children's money is discretionary and can be spent on anything they desire. Moreover, and very important, most kids don't have to exhaust their own funds to get the things they want. They can ask for them and receive them much of the time. Given that kids have relatively good financial resources and that many things they want probably cost less than $20, and even less than $5, it's understandable that marketers might view them as unconcerned about price. Yet this is a myth.

How and What Children Learn About Price

Children become aware of the concept of price before they enter elementary school. The median age of their first purchase with parental assistance is 5-1/2 years. At this initial stage of consumer behavior, children perceive price in terms of units of money or numbers of coins—it takes this many coins to get that. But by the median age of 8 years, when kids make their first independent purchase, they understand price as the amount of money they pay for a product.

Concurrently, children may develop a negative view of price as a barrier to obtaining the growing number of things they want. Somewhere around age 8, kids begin cataloging prices of products they desire and commonly buy with their own money. At this time, also, they may begin to assign evaluative criteria to prices of offerings such as "too high," "okay," and "good deal," as some remarked when asked about prices at certain retail outlets.

Take a look at the drawing in **Figure 11-1** rendered by a 9-year-old asked to: "Draw what comes to your mind when you think about going shopping."

> • • • • • •
> *Somewhere around age 8, kids begin cataloging prices of products they desire and commonly buy with their own money.*

FIGURE 11-1

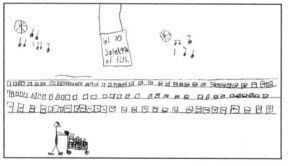

The young man tells it like it is—a jungle of sorts, with just about everything bigger than he is. There is little distinction among store elements except for a sale sign: "99¢ fish." Out of all the hundreds of fixtures and thousands of products, their brands, and promotions, price stands out.

Let us look at some details of price in the context of kids' cognitions and marketers' responses to them. Many marketers claim kids "don't care anything about price," but if that is true, why do many go to so much trouble to avoid the topic of price in promotion and selling efforts and even conceal prices from young consumers?

Price as a Negative

Marketers who say children don't care about price imply that children generally ignore price as a factor in their purchases and requests, focusing only on products' satisfying attributes. It follows, therefore, that sellers can charge whatever they think is a fair price. This assessment may be somewhat true for low-priced products such as gum or candy, but price usually becomes a concern for kids, and often a negative concern, when they consider the purchase of a product with a relatively high price—be it a candy bar or a computer.

Children's naturally self-centered reaction to negativity is to avoid it—like they do spinach—rather than try to understand it. Price is often a negative when it:

• prevents them from buying things with their own money,

• prevents parents from buying things for them,

• is something their parents complain or argue about, and

• is something sellers try to conceal.

Thus, marketers may mistakenly interpret children's tendency to avoid price when it is negative as a lack of interest. But children typically are concerned about price, and this concern grows with age and understanding.

In the case of candy bars, 75 cents appears to signal "high price" to many children.

Price Knowledge Leads to Price Sensitivity

Marketers and parents are not completely off-base when they discount children's concern with price. The myth that children are not price-sensitive was more or less true just a decade ago. But that has changed. One of my qualitative studies in 1989, for example, showed that about 20 percent of children were price-conscious regarding the products they were interested in—they regularly used price as a purchase criterion. Perhaps twice that many were price-conscious specifically about toys and clothing.

A similar study a few years later suggested that almost half of kids generally demonstrated price-consciousness. By 1995, price-consciousness appeared among almost three-fourths of kids according to a study by Kurt Salmon Associates for Lisa Frank, a branded school-supply firm. While the latter study was among older children aged 8 to 17, and the two former studies were among 7-to-11-year-olds, they all demonstrate that children do indeed care about price and that this concern grows with children, or more correctly, with the development of their cognitive processes.

Even among lower-priced products such as confections, children seem to possess a degree of price sensitivity that causes them to set upper limits on prices they will pay. Research reveals these ceilings. For example, in the case of candy bars, 75 cents appears to signal "high price" to many children unless the producer or retailer modifies the product to satisfy additional needs. Kids buy Snickers candy bars mainly because they taste good. But add a premium such as a toy whistle that satisfies the play need and maybe achievement need, and the upper limit will go to a dollar, even two.

Likewise, kids usually perceive 75 to 80 cents as a high price for a fountain drink unless, again, it has added value such as a collector card or chance to win an accompanying contest. These upper price limits for certain products seem particularly common among kids who are consumers of the same brands, suggesting that children are very brand-aware, use brand as a general indicator of quality, and place similar evaluations on the same brands. I believe these upper limits would be applied also to new brands of similar products, perhaps more severely.

Children tend to have less experience with and knowledge about more costly items, which contributes to decreased price-sensitivity.

Upper-price-level sensitivity seems to exist even more for moderately expensive products—a Barbie doll set or video game software. But it's less in evidence for the most expensive items—running shoes or video game sets. This pattern suggests a kind of inverted U-shaped price-sensitivity curve.

Children's motivation, experience and knowledge regarding products and brands, and their available wealth interact to determine the shape of the curve. Generally, as one progresses up the cost scale, items are also more complex, yet offer more potential satisfaction for a wider range of needs. The increasing potential for satisfaction encourages children to ignore an upper price limit. Children also tend to have less experience with and knowledge about more costly items, which contributes to their decreased price-sensitivity.

In the case of very expensive items, however, the upper-limit price sensitivity of parents, which may be different from that of kids, often kicks in and provides a final purchase decision. Parents may be willing to spend more of their money on desired items that appear to be good value, perhaps things that satisfy the needs of both child and parents, such as "edutainment" software. Or parents may veto a purchase if they feel the purchase price is too high or isn't vital to the child's well-being, thus taking the decision entirely out of children's hands.

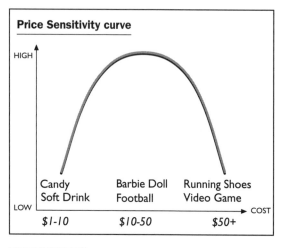

FIGURE 11-2

Much of the price-sensitivity children demonstrate is learned from parents who indirectly and directly impart it. Parents of today's kids survived the recessional years (depending on the part of the country where they live, somewhere between 1986 and 1992), but not without some scars. They are more price/quality conscious, less trusting of pricing by marketers, and more discerning of price differences among stores and brands than their predecessors of the 1970s. They buy more store brands, for example, than they used to.

As parents talk about and act on these matters, children hear them and imitate their thinking. Parents also take advantage of teachable moments during shopping visits to deliberately impart price shopping skills to their kids. As noted elsewhere, today's parents fear their kids won't have it as good as they did. Many parents perceive helping kids spend money effectively as one way to help them compete with others and cope with a less friendly economic and social environment.

As children learn the prices of products, they realize they are different from store to store and tend to watch for the differences. Bear in mind that seeking and finding lower prices satisfies children's achievement need as well as the need to please their parents.

Most children born from the mid-1980s on are aware that some stores have lower prices than others. Given the chance, they will buy at stores with the most attractive prices.

Breed Loyalty Not Suspicion

Merchants have claimed discounts for so long, and all too often deceptively, that people have become insensitive to them. There was a time when Weber's Law would dictate that markdowns had to be at least 15 percent to attract consumers to sales. But for today's parents, and probably for their children too, the threshold appears to be at the 25 percent level or higher.

Children probably respond more favorably to shouts of "sale" and psychological pricing than their parents do, but both groups are increasingly skeptical as a result of frequent deceptions and insults by merchants. Pricing such as three for $3 and four for $4 may not only be deceptive—it may imply a sales price that doesn't exist—it insults the intelligence of even children—"Everyone knows that one's a dollar," said one kid.

Research among consumers of all ages has shown that when they are emotionally positive about certain brands or brands of stores, they are more receptive to price increases—they show more understanding and complain less.

Raising a New Generation of Price Shoppers

At the beginning of the 1980s, probably around one-third of consumers were price shoppers, in that they attempted to shop at stores with the lowest prices on products they sought. But by the beginning of the 1990s, perhaps two-thirds could be described this way.

Children of price shoppers also tend to be price shoppers—acorns do not fall far from the tree. So, yes, probably most children born from the mid-1980s on are aware that some stores have lower prices than others, and given the chance, they will buy at stores with the most attractive prices. Today's children don't yet have the experience or opportunity to be the price shoppers their parents are. By the time they become young adults, however, there's a good chance they will be even more intense price shoppers than their parents.

Price shopping is a learned behavior derived from several major sources: parents' direct and indirect teaching, peers sharing information with other peers, stores communicating information about prices, and children's own consumer experiences. Let's consider the role of each factor in children's price shopping.

Parents' Teaching

Children may learn price shopping by simply observing their parents. But parents of the 1990s tend to be deliberate about teaching children how to "stretch" their money, get the "best buy," and "watch prices."

Sometimes parents teach a simple price/quality decision rule—"Oscar Meyer is the best brand of hot dogs; you've just got to get them at the best price," or "Try to buy name brands, and try to buy them at Kmart." Sometimes the concept is a bit more complex—"You just don't buy fruits unless they are in season," or "Buy the one with the lowest unit price."

Some parents do not teach price shopping to their kids. Poorly educated mothers are less likely to do so, which is ironic given that this lower-income group could benefit most from the practice. But lack of access to transportation may inhibit them from doing so, as may the complexity of the endeavor.

As kids get older, they tend to shop where their friends shop or where they can be with their friends, such as at a nearby convenience store. The need for affiliation with peers gradually outweighs the need for affiliation with parents. The net result is that satisfying the achievement need by obtaining the lowest price becomes secondary to satisfying the affiliation need by purchasing what and where peers purchase.

Peer Influence

Until around age 8, parents' influence on kids' consumer behavior is paramount. But by age 10, peer influence becomes as strong as parental influence.

* * * * * * *

Satisfying the achievement need by obtaining the lowest price becomes secondary to satisfying the affiliation need by purchasing what and where peers purchase.

Kids permit peer influence because of the strong need to conform to reference groups. Conforming means acting and thinking like significant others.

Kids do not disregard everything their parents have taught them, of course, but as these tenets come into conflict with those learned from peers, parental teachings may fall by the wayside. Peers may reinforce price-shopping behavior, or they may discourage it.

Peer influence on purchases may focus more on style and brand, and less on price. However, several studies suggest that when tweens and teens shop together, the topic of price often enters their discussions.

Price-Related Marketing Communications

As consumers grew value-oriented during the recessional years of the late 1980s and early 1990s, many producers and retailers responded with value pricing. The value pricing of Taco Bell really put it on the fast-food map for consumers of all ages. Shouting "low price" is popular today—price being the measure of value to most consumers.

Children generally respond to these shouts. The louder the shouts, the more the children tend to believe them, at least until ages 10 to 12. When asked where the lowest prices are for kids' products, they are likely to answer according to the loudest shouter. Kids also use such information to persuade parents to buy relatively expensive products—"It's on sale at Target. You wanta save money, don't you?" In a kids' magazine advertisement for its Pinocchio video, New Line Home Video stated the price as "$19.95 or less," information for kids to convey to their parents.

But most producers and retailers seem to avoid price, even conceal it if they can. The logic of this escapes me, since price is generally important to today's consumers, and all elements of the marketing mix should aim to satisfy consumers. Ironically, producers and retailers who practice price avoidance may unintentionally communicate negative price information to children. Ads without price information and clothing with hidden price tags convey to kids, in effect, "our prices are high and we are trying to hide them."

Children's Price Experience

Interactions with parents often provide price lessons—"That's too much;" "Let's look around before we get it at that price;" and "I never pay that much for mine." Peers may make similar statements and add other evaluations such as, "Boy, are you dumb if you paid that much for those shoes!" Given that parents and peers are credible sources of information, such remarks

When asked where the lowest prices are for kids' products, they are likely to answer according to the loudest shouter.

can have a lot of impact, both at the time they are made and in the future.

But firsthand experience with price at the point of purchase probably produces the most used information. Shelf prices, tags, and point of purchase banners provide children with actual prices. Children have a relatively "empty tablet" and can absorb a large number of prices. Furthermore, at this time in their life, they like numbers. Teachers often use money and prices to teach arithmetic principles. And when children actually buy things themselves, they become keenly aware of prices, just as an adult who is driving takes more note of the route than passengers are likely to do.

Question: How Should Marketers Price to Kids?

Answer: Honestly, forthrightly, enthusiastically. Marketers should treat price as very important information for the child consumer and present it correctly, conspicuously, and proudly, whether in ads, catalogs, or stores.

Honestly

To deceive a child is the lowest form of deception. Anyone can do it. But deception is not a viable marketing strategy. Being honest with children is absolutely necessary if a long-term relationship is to develop. Making children suspicious of price only keeps them at arm's length and perhaps out of sight.

So hang price tags on clothing and other items where kids can see them. Design them in candy stripes or neon green so kids know the products are meant for them. Don't use adult terms—"10% off when you open an account." Don't use vague terms—"25% off" should be "25% off the tag price." Make the price complete—"$5.98" should be "$5.98 plus tax," or better still, include the tax in the price. The same goes for shipping and handling, where applicable. Keep it honest by keeping it simple.

Forthrightly

In-your-face pricing is much better. Always. Prominently displayed prices are more appropriate and informative. If a merchant is ashamed of a price, he shouldn't hide it, he should reduce it. Big signs are the answer.

Better still, give kids better prices on kids' products and demonstrate that kids' business is important to the store. For example: "$2.98, special price of $2.69 for kids." What better way to show sincerity towards the kids' market, to make sure Mom brings the kids with her, and to make sure

Supermarkets practice leader pricing with adult products such as coffee, flour and sugar, but rarely with kids' products such as candy bars, toys, and frozen novelties.

the kids bring Mom with them? Being forthright with price is being kid-like—and kids like that.

Enthusiastically

Supermarkets practice leader pricing with adult products such as coffee, flour and sugar, but rarely with kids' products such as candy bars, toys, and frozen novelties. What a way for a merchant to show enthusiasm for wanting kids as customers, by lowering the price on kids' items just as they do for adults and advertising them in weekly flyers in a separate "KIDS' SPECIALS."

Coupons are another way to enthusiastically promote price. Coupons have never really caught on with kids, but that's not the kids' fault. They know what they are, and they like the concept. But most coupons are not designed for kids. Even adults find their "legalistic" language confusing, what with expiration dates, specific package sizes and flavor combinations, etc. A kids' coupon should use extremely simple language. For example, "this coupon gives kids 25 cents off the price of any Hershey chocolate bar," or even better, "any can or bottle of Pepsi-Cola costs 25 cents with this coupon."

Stepping forward with prices on kids' products makes good sense. For instance, a retailer could do this by providing a price list of school supplies to elementary-school teachers for use in math lessons. A manufacturer could place publicity pieces in kids' media that talk about price, informing kids about prices and factors that contribute to them. Enthusiastically presenting price to children is far better than avoiding the topic.

A kids' coupon should use extremely simple language.

In Sum

During children's earliest formative years, price does not play a significant role in children's purchase requests. When a 2-year-old child, for example, asks for a product, Mom doesn't typically say, "It depends on the price." But by first or second grade, price does become a factor, partly because children's requests tend to become more expensive, and also because parents feel they are old enough to learn some fiscal responsibility. By the time children are 10 or so, parents usually expect them to reason about price.

The economy at large also affects the way children learn about prices. The recession years made parents more price-sensitive, and they are passing this on to their children. Kids born in the 1980s are therefore more price-sensitive than those born in the 1970s.

Marketers must treat price as a significant factor in marketing to children. This means honest, straightforward price tactics in forms and language children understand. Prices should be presented with enthusiasm if they have been worked out with the child consumer in mind. The best way for marketers to feel confident of prices on children's products is to help children understand them. A product will always have a price; everyone knows that. So why conceal it or mislead with it? Present it as a normal part of the product, as it is, and children will accept it.

CHAPTER 12

Advertising to Children: Pervasive, Perturbing, Propelling

Myth: "Children are the object of far too much advertising."

REALITY: Children are the object of far less advertising per dollar value than adults, accounting for only around 3 percent of TV advertising, and less than 1 percent of all advertising.

MYTH: "To reach kids most effectively, advertise on Saturday-morning TV."

REALITY: It depends on your goals for reaching them. It may be more effective to advertise during prime time, or in print, or outdoors, or at the point of purchase, or ....

A Possible Explanation for Both Myths

Consumer goods from amusement parks to zoos, from autos to zinnia seeds, advertise to kids, along with charitable organizations, social and environmental causes, professional sports, and financial services. During the past decade, advertising to kids has grown rapidly, absorbing new inventory in existing media, spreading to all new media, increasing specialization in the industry, and in general taking on a life of its own, a genre that we might term, "kidvertising." Marketers probably spend no more than $1.3 billion annually on all advertising to U.S. kids. While that may seem like a lot—and the expenditure is growing faster than that for adults—it's a small slice of the total advertising pie.

Yet complaints and criticisms from the adult world—parents, consumer advocates, and regulators—about advertising to kids would cause one to think it is much more extensive. Maybe kids appear to be the objects of too much advertising because of the increasing amount targeted to them in places other than conventional media, such as school buses, video games, and the Internet. Yes, "kidvertising" is ubiquitous, because it goes wherever kids go.

This spread of advertising to children beyond Saturday morning TV is what has created the second myth. Reaching this new generation of kids— what The *Wall Street Journal* calls "Generation Y" and what *Advertising Age* magazine calls the "Net generation"—is increasingly difficult because of their changing lifestyles. Consequently, standard Saturday morning kidvid alone just doesn't cut it anymore.

Currently, kids' viewing of Saturday morning network programs that target them is down—10, 20, 30 percent or more. The drop is so severe for CBS, for example, that it is reportedly considering getting out of the kids' Saturday morning business much as NBC did a few years ago. Fox, a network that has done a good job of growing the kids market, is even losing some of its young viewers, and is looking at cable to remedy this. It has begun 11 hours of daytime kidvid on its remodeled Fox Family Channel.

Cable for kids is doing better than networks that target kids, particularly the leader, Nickelodeon. In fact, cable revenues surpassed broadcast revenues for the first time in 1997. Cable continues to add new offerings for kids— Cartoon Network, Discovery Kids, and Fox Family Channel, for example. And in spite of the reported decline in network TV viewing by kids, advertising rates for children's TV continue to grow, usually by double digits.

Contrary to what *Broadcasting & Cable* magazine suggests, not all network losses have gone to cable. Some children have switched some of their TV viewing to the new networks, Kids' WB! and UPN, which is teaming up with Disney for two daily hours of kids' programming. They are watching public television—Barney and his new competition, Teletubbies, are capturing the heart of the preschool set. Pay TV is a small price to pay, according to some parents. Kids also watch videos from their growing libraries, including homemade ones, over and over and over.

There are many more kids' magazines than there used to be, as well as some kid-specific radio programming. These are capturing more of some children's media time. And more and more kids are shifting some attention and time to cyberspace. Advertisers follow kids wherever they may go, which is why we see more advertising to kids in more places beyond conventional media. There's a good chance that it is this pervasive nature of advertising that incites some of the complaints against it; advertising seems to be everywhere kids are.

Why do advertisers spend so much money on the kids market? Should they spend more or less? Should they spend their advertising dollars differently? How effective are they in achieving their advertising goals? What are

In spite of the reported decline in network TV viewing by kids, advertising rates for children's TV continue to grow, usually by double digits.

the complaints and criticisms about, how valid are they, and what can be done about them? Let's start with the first question. Before we do, however, we should preface it with some parent-related realities that always seem to fade into the background during such discussions.

- Parents brought pizza into the house and put it into their kids' hands and mouths before pizza companies ever thought of suggesting to kids that their parents buy some. This is equally true of most foods and beverages, particularly those that are sweet, salty, and fattening, and just about any other kind of product that children may request.

- Parents introduce TV to their children; children don't start watching it in the hospital nursery or start flipping channels from the crib. Thanks to parents, it has been a trusted babysitter for 40 years.

- Parents take kids to stores long before stores contact the kids and invite them. Through stores, parents introduce their kids to endless product offerings, and teach them how to ask for and buy products.

- Parents make "free" a stock word in their children's vocabulary long before TV or packaging does, and demonstrate to children their own warm response to the word.

- Parents introduce the concept of brands to their kids before brands introduce themselves to kids through advertising and displays. Kids learn early to give names to things they like and want.

> *Through stores, parents introduce their kids to endless product offerings, and teach them how to ask for and buy products.*

These realities about parent-child relations should serve as reminders of parents' role in teaching their kids most basic consumer behavior patterns including children's interactions with marketing and advertising. They should remind us that parents too often give advertising far more credit than it deserves and much of the credit for their own accomplishments.

Advertising Spending on the Kids' Market: How Much and Why

Nobody knows precisely how much is spent on advertising to kids, but bits and pieces of information permit an estimate. The amount appears to be growing faster than that for adults, and there are also hints that advertising dollars targeted to families—parents and kids simultaneously—are growing rapidly, too.

Why the sustained growth of advertising to kids? It's that simple formula: People x Dollars = Markets. The number of children born in the U.S. has been about 4 million a year for the past decade, the highest since the original baby boom. Their incomes and influence on parental spending have been growing, too.

At the same time, marketers have recognized the power of the kids' market. Media are responding with more inventory of advertising time on television and radio, more space in kids' magazines, and more access through new or less traditional media—Web sites, school buses, bulletin boards, direct mail, and movies, to name a few.

TV Spending

One fairly reliable bit of information published each year is expenditures on advertising time on TV programs in early spring before the fall season begins. Its growth and changes in rates are good indicators of the value of the kids market to advertisers. Traditional buyers have been producers of play items, ready-to-eat cereals, and confections, but the list now includes fast food, clothing, toiletries, and hospitality industries, plus social "products" such as public service announcements regarding drug abuse, AIDS and so on.

In spring 1997, *Advertising Age* magazine reported up-front sales of ad time on kidvid for the 1997-98 season of about $840 million, up 15 to 20 percent over the previous year. Total advertising revenue of broadcast and cable was estimated at $923 million for 1997. I assume this figure does not include most spot advertising, which runs around $225 million a year.

This does not include the advertising targeted at kids, along with their parents, during prime-time. The problem is that we don't know how prime-time advertising dollars are earmarked for kids. So, we will omit prime time kids advertising from our estimate and conservatively—very conservatively—conclude that advertisers spent somewhere around $1.2 billion in 1997 on TV time directed at kids. That compares with $36 billion in total TV ad spending in 1997. Thus, around 3 percent of TV advertising is spent on the kids' market, a market valued at somewhere around $500 billion (as a primary and influence market).

The increase in spending is significant since TV viewing by kids is down a great deal on the networks. Why should advertisers pay more with fewer kids watching? That's a good question that only Mattel, General Mills, or other major buyers can answer, but it does suggest the increasing value of the kids' market to them. The increase also reflects more competition for time slots. More businesses are coming into the market, which drives up the price of a 30-second commercial. Starting in late 1997, the Office of National Drug Control Policy entered the field with a substantial amount of hard money—not just donor money as before—to target kids with anti-drug messages. Other social causes are likely to follow suit, thus driving prices even higher.

Print and Other Media Spending

Magazines for kids are having a heyday in the late 1990s. There are more of them, probably around 100, that contain advertising. *Sports Illustrated for Kids*, with a rate base of around 1 million, reported nearly 25 percent growth in advertising pages in 1996. *Disney Adventures* with a similar rate base had a 7.5 percent increase, and *Nickelodeon* magazine raised its rate base from 550,000 to 700,000. Together these three leading kids' magazines probably had at least $30 million in 1997 ad revenue. Several new magazines appeared, including *Muse* and *Dinosaurus*, but others folded, including *Outside Kids* and *Popular Science for Kids* (now a TV program). In total, magazine advertising that primarily targets kids probably amounted to more than $40 million in 1997.

Newspapers for kids and kid-oriented inserts in newspapers come and go. They are apparently unable to escape the dull adult image the industry has created and perpetuated. Coming up with an estimate of advertising spending in children-oriented newspapers or newspaper inserts is difficult, but minimal in any case. It could range from zero to maybe $2.5 million, which was my estimate in 1990.

Radio for kids seems to be off the ground now, perhaps best indicated by Disney's entry, Radio Disney. But with the shutdown of KidStar, former leader in the field, caution is in the air. In total, Children's Broadcasting Company, Fox Kids Countdown with its Sunday 2-hour program, Radio Disney in 36 markets, and a bit of local programming here and there, probably generate advertising revenues in the neighborhood of $5 million.

Radio advertising to kids sounds logical since most children have radios and listen to them. But the fact is that radio ad revenues have never soared since the advent of TV. I think radio suffers from inadequate objective measures of its youth audience. On the other hand, rates on kid radio are probably suppressed and represent a good buy.

Advertising to kids on Web sites is increasing, but remains in the initial stages. Web sites that require kids to register and provide personal information are slowing the growth of what otherwise could be a shooting star. And of course they infuriate parents. Can you imagine what would have happened if 1950s' TV programming had required registration? In any case, advertisers in search of the kids' market are lining up to buy if "webcasters" can tell them what they will get for their money. Probably the brave ones spent $1 million or so in 1997.

Direct mail to kids, which is 100 percent advertising, continues to blossom. Product placement in movies for kids is maturing, as is pre-movie in-cinema advertising. Advertising via school venues is booming as school administrators find it a great source of operating funds.

These "other media," along with print, add at least $75 million to the $1.2 billion generated by TV, resulting in a total of around $1.3 billion in advertising targeted at kids. Not an enormous amount—about 1 percent of the $160 billion spent on advertising in the U.S. in 1997.

What's All the Complaining About?

The belief that children are the objects of far too much advertising—the first myth—stems in part from Americans' ongoing love-hate relationship with advertising. The complaints, charges, criticisms, and generally negative remarks regularly expressed about advertising to kids result from three sets of closely intertwined attitudes.

1. Attitudes toward advertising in general.

Americans harbor a widespread mistrust of advertising in general. A 1998 Roper Starch Worldwide study shows that 66 percent of adults agree advertising encourages people to use products that are bad for them. Furthermore, 69 percent feel it encourages people to buy things they don't need. Even more, 78 percent feel that advertising to children often has both of these negative effects, presumably because they feel it exploits children's greater naiveté.

Members of the advertising industry—and not just a "handful who spoil it for all"—often perform in inappropriate ways that attract public suspicion, disbelief, and avoidance. For example, ads in family-focused magazines designed to deceive by looking like editorial material eventually take on a deceiving demeanor and produce mistrust in moms' minds. Moms, in turn, generalize their mistrust to other advertising including that which targets their kids. Kids gradually absorb and adopt parents' opinions of advertising.

An example of this kind of deceptive practice appeared in the comic section of a Sunday issue of *The Houston Chronicle*. It consisted of a full-color, six-frame comic strip titled "Weinerman." The "strip" was in fact a joint advertisement by Nike and Weiner stores. Reflect on the time, effort, and money

• • • • • • •
A 1998 Roper Starch World-wide study shows that 69 percent of adults believe advertising encourages people to buy things they don't need.

it took for the manufacturer, retailer, ad agency, and newspaper to execute this attempted deception. Just think how much more this joint effort could do for these firms and advertising in general, if ads were properly and tastefully developed and strategically placed.

The advertising industry is well aware of the public's long-standing mistrust of advertising and how that mistrust erodes advertising's effectiveness. From time to time, its trade associations develop programs to counteract it. Typically these programs consist of an advertising campaign on behalf of advertising that in effect says to the general public, you can trust advertising, it is good and good for you. It's difficult to say how much this helps. Americans aren't entirely anti-advertising. Roper data indicate they value the information it provides, but they evaluate it on their own terms, and those terms are increasingly skeptical in many ways.

TV ads that show toys doing things they can't do and foods giving children super strength, incite anger, doubt, and wariness.

2. Attitudes toward the advertising message.

Repeated deceptive styles of advertising messages eventually generate dislike and mistrust of those styles. Their use in children's advertisements attracts doubt and even anger of parents and children advocates. Ads that promise "Your first issue free when you subscribe for a year" or "Absolutely no obligation," and TV ads that show toys doing things they can't do or foods giving children super strength, incite anger, doubt, and wariness. Yet, such practices continue, and many advertisers even wear them like a badge.

Another message style that produces mistrust, anger, even outcries from parents and children advocates teaches children socially undesirable values—defiance of parental authority, dishonesty, violence. Television programming is loaded with gratuitous violence copied without regard for right or wrong by advertisers who seem to think that if kids like a little violence, they'll love a lot. I have heard advertising agency executives defend ads that contain gratuitous violence with the phrase: "Kids love it!"

3. Attitudes toward the advertising source.

The reputation of the message source naturally influences attitudes toward its advertising. This is a given. When advertising for trustworthy Kodak features spokespeople with questionable credibility, such as Dennis Rodman, people may come to mistrust Kodak as they do the spokesperson. Parents may then generalize this mistrust to all ads that target kids and use professional athletes as spokespeople. The credibility of celebrity spokespeople in general is declining, anyway, so marketers targeting kids should be especially cautious when using this approach.

It doesn't take a spokesperson to reduce the believability of companies and brands. Some companies can be their own worst enemies. Firms that receive negative publicity from, for example, bad packaging, bad products, or being bad community members, hurt their image and consequently may have to spend a fortune on public relations to correct the image if that is possible. Otherwise, its advertising and communications will not be trusted as much, and they will not be as effective. This is as true for those targeting kids as those targeting adults.

● ● ● ● ● ● ● ●
The mere fact that an advertisement reaches its intended audience and people remember it does not mean it is effective.

Bad Advertising to Kids Produces Bad Results

As described above, and as shown in **Figure 12-1**, kid-targeted advertising with objectionable messages produces mistrust of the advertising and advertiser, contributes to mistrust of advertising in general, and eventually leads to defensive and avoidance behavior among children and parents. It also generates public criticism of ads that target kids with objectionable contents such as untruths, deceptions, gratuitous violence, or sexual connotations. The mere fact that an advertisement reaches its intended audience and people remember it does not mean it is effective. It must be accepted and believed. Eventually, it will be neither believed nor received—the consumer will just block it out.

FIGURE 12-1

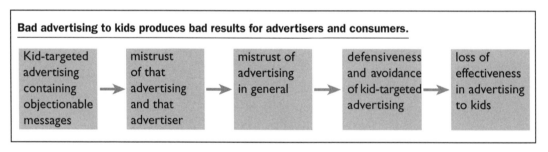

Bad advertising to kids produces bad results for advertisers and consumers.

| Kid-targeted advertising containing objectionable messages | mistrust of that advertising and that advertiser | mistrust of advertising in general | defensiveness and avoidance of kid-targeted advertising | loss of effectiveness in advertising to kids |

Thus, bad advertising, that is, advertising with objectionable messages, including messages from unreliable sources, loses its intended effectiveness. The solution is not to try to convince consumers that objectionable advertising is acceptable. The answer is more good advertising.

Turning Bad Ads into Good Ads

Guidelines from how-to-do-it professionals notwithstanding, how can advertising to kids elicit less criticism and become more effective? All the criticism won't go away. Some will protest any advertising to kids on principle. But these watchdogs serve a purpose, too, to remind advertising to regularly take inventory of itself. Likewise, advertising can't or won't completely change its stripes. Its inherent purpose is to be persuasive.

The starting point for improving the image of kids' advertising and advertising in general, and consequently the effectiveness of advertising, is the message. Correcting messages that target kids eventually builds a better image for advertising by breaking the chain of doubt and skepticism. Here are some suggestions for improving advertising that targets kids and, indirectly, their parents.

Undersell

I know this sounds a bit like "Lay down your weapons," but it will help, and if done right, will make "kidvertising" more effective. It's not cowering and it is competitive. Some supermarket chains, for example, compete by having unadvertised specials on their shelves. Some are not even denoted at the shelf but left for customers to discover as a reward. There ought to be some excitement and satisfaction for kids to discover after they respond to an ad. No one, and I mean no one, loves to uncover a surprise more than kids do. Why not emphasize one special feature in an ad and tell the kids, "There's more," or to "Watch for the surprise," even allude to additional value that awaits them? Compare this type of ad with ones that oversell, promise more than products can deliver, and raise children's expectations beyond reality, thereby producing disappointment. A rule of customer service applies here: don't merely meet people's expectations, exceed them.

Understate

There's a notion out there in advertising land that goes: "Whatever you have to say to kids, shout it." Presumably it is a way to overcome clutter and garner more attention among competing messages. The result is a great deal of annoying advertising. (I wonder, too, how much it reminds kids of angry parents or teachers?) Advertisers seem to increase their volume when they are touting an inferior or parity product. They may also be under the impression that kids like loud. Whatever happened to, "Walk softly and carry a big stick," which in advertising parlance means you don't have to be loud, coarse, or boisterous when you have a superior product. Publicity (discussed in a later chapter) may even perform this "velvet hammer" kind of communicating better than advertising, and

· · · · · · · · ·
No one loves to uncover a surprise more than kids do. Why not emphasize one special feature in an ad and tell the kids, "There's more," or to "Watch for the surprise," even allude to additional value that awaits them?

should at least be included in the communications mix along with advertising. But advertising can learn to do it.

Undercommercialize

Parents tell us that they get a little tired of advertising trying to sell everything to their kids. The word sell is often underlined with anger. Ads that target kids do seem to be perceived as more sales-oriented than those for adults. Why? Probably because they are. Today a majority of "kidvertising" is driven by promotions, and as often as not, promotions for other products in addition to those of the sponsor—two commercials in one, so to speak. A mother might wonder if some fast-food restaurants are not also in the toy business. Ads that loudly connect with Star Wars or other movie tie-in premiums, are good (or bad) examples of overcommericialization. Add to these all those branded-character commercials that already dominate the children's world such as Garfield, Barbie and Power Rangers, and you have the overselling of kids. Why don't fast-food chains and others take a page out of the Coca-Cola advertising book and build their own brands instead of other companies'? And why don't the big "kidvertisers" such as Mattel and General Mills do more marketing, and less selling, to kids?

● ● ● ● ● ● ● ● ●
Respect for the family in advertising to children will win over the child, the parents, and the critics, and ultimately sell more merchandise.

Underline the Family Concept

Kids belong to families. Families are receiving more focus again, as evidenced by a half-dozen new magazines with the word family in their titles. Realistically, the family should be the backdrop of much of kids' advertising. Ads for foods and beverages might show kids having meals with parents and siblings—families are now part of a complete breakfast, too. Ads for entertainment might show them watching TV with members of their households, since they actually do this. Ads for hospitality businesses might show kids vacationing with parents, even grandparents, as they increasingly do.

Many ads for kids disparage parents and spit in the eye of adult authority. Paul Kurnit, head of Griffin Bacal, and surely the most noted kids advertiser and advertising agency out there, offered some tips for effectively advertising to kids, in an issue of *Advertising Age*. One of them was: "Poking fun at authority figures is fair game." I don't think it is a game at all, but detestable. Common sense says that ads that deeply insult parents will reap the ire of those parents. Further, I'll bet that ads with this defiant tone even make some kids a bit uncomfortable.

I recall a couple of years ago when Bob Garfield, the well-known advertising critic who writes for *Advertising Age*, gave his lowest rating to a kid-targeted Nintendo TV ad developed by Leo Burnett because of its in-your-face ridicule of authority figures including parents. Garfield described the ad much better than I could when he said it was an "... exercise in craven cynicism and moral abdication...." He went on to say "kids are mediawise enough to realize that this message was brought to them by the very same adult world they are being incited to disrespect." I would be remiss if I did not repeat Garfield's closing remarks. He said, "Nintendo, of course, is by no means the first advertiser to take the make-fun-of-grown-ups tack, and maybe people are getting inured to it. But at some point someone has to take a stand. These people have no right to speak to our children this way, and they had damn well better stop."

It's not necessary, either. Respect for the family in advertising to children will win over the child, the parents, and the critics, and ultimately sell more merchandise.

Undo the Dishonesty

As mentioned earlier, Roper data find 69 percent of adults believe advertisers regularly mislead or exaggerate product benefits. This and other data prompted the research firm to conclude in an issue of *The Wall Street Journal*, "Business get low marks for failing to give good, accurate information about products in advertising and not respecting consumers' intelligence."

Dishonest advertising to kids is easy to execute. Even so, I am surprised it exists when you think about the deterrents, in addition to many laws, intended to prevent and correct it before it reaches its intended audience. In total, I call these deterrents the SCITAM screen. As shown in **Figure 12-2**, its structure consists of the following members:

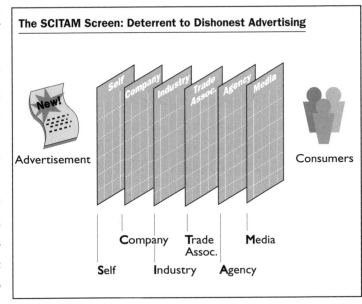

The SCITAM Screen: Deterrent to Dishonest Advertising

Advertisement — Self / Company / Industry / Trade Assoc. / Agency / Media — Consumers

FIGURE 12-2

Self—The person responsible for developing an advertisement possesses values as part of a self-concept that forbid him or her from creating an ad with socially undesirable elements. They are the same values that keep a person from running a stop sign or damaging a library book.

Company—Many companies police their advertisements and require they be internally and externally approved from an ethics standpoint. In effect, the values of those in leadership positions are applied to the work of their subordinates.

Industry—Within the limits of anti-trust laws, companies within industries often come together and develop ethical boundaries for advertising, putting them in the form of codes of ethics or other kind of statement.

Trade associations—Several thousand trade associations represent several million businesses in the U.S. These associations assist members with mutual problems such as unethical advertising practices. Trade associations develop codes of ethics, too, agreed upon by member firms.

Agencies—Virtually all large businesses use advertising agencies to plan and develop advertising campaigns. When an ad agency develops ads for a client, the agency is guided by the values of its personnel, its own code of ethics, and that of its trade associations, as well as those of the client.

Media—Finally, most media have rules regarding the type of advertising material they will accept, and may ask a potential advertiser to make adjustments to remove materials believed to be undesirable.

When one steps back and observes these deterrents to dishonest advertising—in addition to the many formal regulations that govern advertising—it is hard to believe ads that target kids would be anything but squeaky clean. But an ad in a current kids' magazine for a club for kids and parents prominently states "entirely without obligation" and "no obligations." Of course there are obligations, major obligations, because the club is a negative option type that sends merchandise regularly to the household, which has to be paid for or bundled up and returned. TV ads that misuse camera angles to make toy cars look as if they are going faster than they really do, magazine ads for trading cards with tiny print to describe the odds of finding a valuable card in a pack, and so on simply contribute to record-high levels of mistrust by the public.

Should Advertisers Who Target Kids Spend More, Less, Differently?

Yes, yes, and yes. Virtually all marketers, and particularly all retailers, should spend more on brand building, that is, on targeting kids as a future market. They should spend more on targeting kids as current and influence markets. They should spend less on short-term joint efforts that often build brands for promotional partners. And they should spend some advertising dollars differently—in different media on different messages.

A large part of TV advertising aimed at kids is promotion-driven and therefore has short-term objectives. Such efforts make good sense in the short run—it is a great way to temporarily increase sales for a brand or a store. But they can come one after the other until a firm's advertising consists of nothing more than meeting a series of short-term objectives. Whoa!

It is McDonald's, for example, tying its wagon to Disney. If Disney stumbles, and it sometimes does, McDonald's will experience a similar blip. It is *Sports Illustrated for Kids* magazine tying its wagon to Nike. If Nike stubs its toe or shoots itself in the foot, the pain may be felt all the way to the subscription department in the Time-Life building. Joint promotion efforts between kid marketers make sense, but they mean risks for both if one falters.

All this short-term stuff is high risk and should be covered by long-term brand building. It is what most fast-food chains such as Hardees and Wendy's have failed to do very well. This is no less true of many supermarkets, department stores, drug stores and a whole host of manufacturers. This I-don't-care-how-I-get-to-the-bank-as-long-as-I-get-there-often thinking saps the fundamental strength from a company. Along with short-term efforts, firms should pair their basic strengths with their brands and present them to children in messages designed to keep a steady stream of new customers coming on line.

Delta Air Lines, for example, has joined such youth marketers as Disney and the NFL over the years to target kids with various short-term advertising and promotion programs. But the airline also has advertising and promotion strategies intended to grow future customers. I witness such retailers as Service Merchandise, Best Buys, and J.C. Penney offering a wide range of mer-

Promotion-driven makes good sense in the short run—it is a great way to temporarily increase sales for a brand or a store.

chandise for kids, but doing little, at least in a consistent manner, to grow future customers from this market. Hardees recently announced a $100 million ad campaign to rebuild its brand. It should be sure to take a small portion of its advertising budget, or slightly increase its advertising budget, to specifically target kids as primary, influence, and future customers.

Targeting kids does not have to be done at expensive TV rates, although proper partnering can make TV a viable option. Magazines are a great medium for brand building, since kids tend to collect them and read them several times. Catalogs and letters also tend to be saved and read more than once. When magazines and mail are from kids' clubs, they tend to receive more than casual attention. Advertising to kids jointly with community partners such as schools, museums, and theaters is a great way to build relationships with kids (and their parents).

Stores that get family traffic should set aside some of their point-of-purchase advertising dollars for kids. Kids' in-store influence on family purchases has grown so much so quickly that a store probably would not go wrong if it converted a significant portion of media dollars to POP advertising. Supermarkets and mass merchandisers, for example, would be very smart to put some in-floor advertising dollars at work to target kids, literally—since the floor is where kids' eyes often rest.

Figures 12-3 and **12-4** reveal the importance of floors to children. The first is by an American 3rd-grader, the second by a Chinese 3rd-grader. Although an ocean apart, they still assign great significance to store floors. And for good reason. They have fond memories of many fun hours on the floor. It's their playground at home, and probably at day care, too. And since they are still close to the floor, they give it a lot of attention. Thus, placing ad messages in floors—tiles, carpet, whatever—is a logical way to target children at the point of purchase. In fact, if done properly, it could assist children in finding merchandise in large, complex and changing shopping environments, such as large mass merchandisers.

FIGURES 12-3

FIGURES 12-4

In Sum

The guidelines here suggest ways to improve the effectiveness of advertising to children by improved development and execution. Some of these recommendations may be revolutionary in nature. Asking advertisers to reduce the commercialization in their ads surely sounds like asking them to "roll over and play dead." Asking them to understate probably sounds like asking a carpenter to give up his hammer and saw. To underline the family concept surely sounds contrary to offering kids the independence they seek.

Asking advertisers to be completely honest almost seems to deprive them of some basic tools of their trade. But I truly believe that good, even great, advertising can result from adherence to these guidelines in the hands of skillful advertisers. The result, ultimately, will be more effective advertising, more positive responses to advertising in general, and more sales and profits for those firms that subscribe to these practices.

CHAPTER 13

Kid-Targeted Promotions: Why They Work So Well

MYTH: "Promotion lessens the chances of developing brand loyalty."

REALITY: Promotion can create a bond with children that looks very much like brand loyalty.

MYTH: "Children are not grateful when they are given things."

REALITY: Children may not show their gratitude like adults, but they tell us they like those who give them things and are fondest of the biggest giver.

MYTH: "Children would rather have a free bicycle than a free baseball."

REALITY: It depends on the time. If the children have to wait 100 UPCs for the bicycle and 5 UPCs for the baseball, most of the time they will opt for the baseball.

Children, parents, and marketers who target children all love promotions, particularly premiums. Promotion, properly called sales promotion, provides children with satisfying products and services at little or no perceived cost. It pleases parents because it pleases children, at little or no perceived cost. It can grow business for marketers who use it correctly. Testimony to the importance of promotion to kids was a 1974 Federal Trade Commission request that marketers voluntarily remove premium offers from television advertising to children. The FTC's concern was that premium offers distracted children's attention from host products' attributes.

Children key in on promotion opportunities. Their most common interest is in premiums—something free with a purchase or store visit—but they also show enthusiasm for contests and sweepstakes that promise opportunities to win free products. How do children learn to love promotions? Probably through the love and help of good old Mom.

Mothers have fond memories of premiums they received from fast-food chains, gas stations and other retailers in their youth. They may have saved some favorites, or even collect current series. More than one adult woman has been spotted going from one drive-through to another in hopes of completing a Beanie Baby collection. Mothers also participate in contests and sweepstakes, take advantage of special premium offers, and use coupons. Kids naturally learn these consumer behaviors.

Therefore, kids and parents often are on the lookout for promotional programs. These programs give them "something for nothing," they believe. Very early in childhood, parents communicate to children the economic implications of the term "free." Children take the cue and often use promotion offers as leverage: "Let's stay at Days Inn. They have lots of good free stuff." Parents, in turn, think to themselves, "We've got to stay at some motel tonight, so we might as well stay at Days Inn since the kids like it and it likes kids."

Marketers are equally enamored with promotion as demonstrated by the increasing share of budgets devoted to it. Today's consumer package goods firms may spend 75 to 80 percent of their marketing communications budget on promotions to kids and families compared with around 25 or 30 percent a decade ago. These growth figures reflect marketing's recent recognition of kid-targeted promotion as a marketing tool that produces great results. Many consumer companies have established promotion departments with the stature of advertising departments and spend lavishly on incentives such as premiums, contests, and sampling.

This spending has prompted growth in promotion-services businesses. One of the largest promotion firms, Frankel & Company of Chicago, for example, has experienced much of its new growth in kids' promotion. Strottman International, with offices in Irvine, California, and Atlanta, is a relatively small firm that has garnered industry recognition by specializing in the kids market. While Strottman serves such diverse industries as fast foods and entertainment, it surely can take much of the credit for convincing the hospitality industry of the benefits of kid-oriented promotions. In this era of integrated marketing, many advertising agencies also have developed separate promotion shops.

Expenditures on Kid-Targeted Promotions: Growing Fast and Paying Off

I do not know of any person or organization that keeps track of promotion expenditures in the kids market. But the figure appears to be several times greater than advertising to kids and is growing much faster. As noted above, as much as three-fourths of marketing budgets are reportedly allocated to promotion. We tracked published estimates of major expenditures on kid-targeted promotion for a year in hopes of getting a handle on how much is actually spent, but there are many problems with this approach. For example, it is not clear how many dollars go strictly to promotion because there are also packaging, advertising, and publicity dollars spent to expose the market to the promotion, as well as administrative and operating costs.

• • • • • • •
Very early in childhood, parents communicate to children the economic implications of the term "free."

Since advertising expenditures for the kids market are better tracked and reported, we used a commonly reported 3:1 ratio of promotion-to-advertising expenditures to estimate total promotion dollars. Since we estimate advertising spending for the kids market somewhere around $1.5 billion annually including media costs and production costs, we estimate promotion spending to be three times as much, or $4.5 billion. This includes spending on kid-related premiums, sampling, contests, games, sweepstakes, coupons, price packs, cash refunds, advertising specials, patronage rewards, and point-of-purchase promotions such as demonstrations. It does not include millions of dollars in slotting fees paid to retailers to stock items for kids.

While $4.5 billion sounds like a giant expenditure, it is probably an understatement given recent promotions by major players in fast food and hospitality. For instance, Burger King made a deal with Turner to offer $5 mail-in rebates on five new Scooby-Doo videos and also to include Scooby-Doo characters with 60 million Kid's Meals during the summer of 1996. It may be no accident that both kids and their parents are fond of this character. Across the street, Wendy's offered a competing dog-related promotion built around the PBS Wishbone TV show. Taco Bell was ringing in kids with offers related to The Tick, an offbeat, mock-superhero from Fox kids' television. McDonald's joined its Happy Meal with Disney for the umpteenth time, with nine Disney characters in mini "video" boxes.

At the same time, Delta airlines was pleasing kids with its Fantastic Flyer Funfeast meal tied in with Broderbund Software's Carmen Sandiego character. We should also mention the Mom-pleasing "free vegetable side dish" deal at Boston Market, special deals with kid meals in the food-service areas of thousands of Wal-Mart, Kmart, and Target stores, and children's gifts at many regional sit-down restaurants such as Bob Evans, Sonny's Real Pit Bar-B-Q, Tanners Chicken Rotisserie, and Lettuce Souprise You.

Many families who take restaurants up on these offers are vacationers staying at nearby Days Inn, Ramada Inn, Best Western, and Howard

Johnson motels, where they also receive a wide range of premium offers. Howard Johnson has been promoting its Kids Go HoJo for years, giving away millions of Kids Go HoJo Fun Packs and tying in with Sega of America's Sonic Hedgehog. During the summer season when family visits peak, Howard Johnson offered a Sega game tips videotape. Days Inn has had a long standing tie-in with Fred Flintstone, with a Flintstones Fun Days family fun travel kit containing toys, maps, games, and crayons, as well as plush Flintstone dolls for $2.99.

Many other motel and hotel chains have duplicated such kid-based promotional activities to capture a share of the family market. Holiday Inn Worldwide currently offers an innovative Kidsuite. This concept consists of a standard room that contains a separate kids' area decorated by sponsors such as Coca-Cola, Little Caesars Pizza, and Sea World, which pay for the remodeling and decorating and also supply hotels with an annual fee of $5,000 in cash or bartered goods.

These few examples help explain the $4.5 billion-plus in spending on kids' promotions. Other sectors of the retailing economy do big spending on kids promotions, too, but may be less apparent. The banking industry's promotion spending on kids is big and getting bigger, including credit-card business. Industry mergers and competition are spurring major players and a lot of small banks to launch kids' saving programs that include heavy use of premiums, contests, and sweepstakes.

Television and radio broadcasting stations and networks are courting kids on a daily basis with all kinds of promotion efforts, as are theme parks and cinemas. Major retailers in clothing, shoes, sporting goods, toys, and computers also see the children's market as worthy of promotion dollars. Even auto dealers have joined the competition for the kids' influence market with promotions of their own.

What is the payoff from all this promotion targeted to children? What does a firm hope to accomplish when it underwrites a $50-to-$100 million promotion to kids? It must be substantial. Yet the failure rate for these kinds of promotions is very great.

We can get some idea of the payoff of big promotions from the restaurant industry, which sometimes reports results of efforts. Burger King management believes it can out-compete McDonald's in the arena of promotion, and its joint efforts with Disney, a long-time partner of McDonald's, seem to indicate this. Burger King reports its $1.99 kids' meal generates an average family check of $8-10. When it tied in with Disney's Toy Story, its Kids Club

We estimate advertising spending in the kids market somewhere around $1.5 billion annually including media costs and production costs, and we estimate promotion spending to be three times as much, or $4.5 billion.

meal sales doubled to over 1,000 per store per week. Less dramatic but similar sales successes are recounted by other major chains and many smaller ones. For O'Charley's of Nashville, Tennessee, offering a "kids eat free" promotion has quadrupled the number of kids meals served, and of course, the number of family meals served, and has kept the likes of McDonald's and Burger King from taking over its family business.

• • • • • • • •
Bank-industry mergers and competition are spurring major players and a lot of small banks to launch kids' saving programs that include heavy use of premiums, contests, and sweepstakes.

Does Promotion Keep Kids From Forming Brand Loyalties?

Despite the clear and measurable benefits, kid-related promotions give rise to three myths we need to clarify and correct. The first says promotion reduces the chances of children forming brand loyalties.

We need to define what we mean by brand loyalty before we dissect this myth. The broader interpretation is a preference or liking for a particular brand over brands of similar products that results in the purchase of that brand much of the time. It is an "AB" definition in the sense that it assumes people have favorable attitudes (A) formed toward a brand that result in consistent purchase behavior (B) toward that brand, including brand extensions. A narrower interpretation says brand loyalty is simply the frequent purchase of a particular brand. There is no attitudinal explanation for the purchase; the behavior speaks for itself. In the first case, brand loyalty is measured on a scale of liking, in the second, on a scale of purchase.

For the purposes of discussing children, we assume the broader interpretation. This recognizes it is possible, and not uncommon, for a child to like a brand very much and not purchase or request it very much or at all. This is the brand loyalty that automobile makers and gasoline refiners can create in childhood, for example, but does not produce significant results until youngsters reach adulthood.

What causes children to prefer specific brands? It begins long before purchase behavior does. It appears to be primarily a function of two factors:

(1) children's positive experiences with a brand; and

(2) parents liking that brand (a positive experience of another kind).

The primary cause of brand loyalty appears to be children's positive experience—i.e., receiving satisfaction from a brand.

The fact that parents like a particular brand creates a comfort level for children. It also means parents will understand and hopefully comply when children make requests for that brand. Research over the past 40 years has indicated that children like the brands their parents like. Children may hear their fathers say, "I'm a Ford man," and that's good enough for those who place total trust in their fathers. They may not understand exactly what their father means when he says, "Let's pull into this Shell station and get some gas; I get good mileage from it." But it sounds like a brand they can trust. In fact, Jacques Chevron, head of his own brand development firm, refers to brand loyalty as "a covenant," suggesting a trusting relationship.

We can theorize that the more a brand satisfies children's high-priority needs, the more they will like it and seek it out. They will ask parents to buy it until they are old enough to buy it themselves, a period that may last a few short years or until adulthood.

If brand loyalty mainly results from children's good experiences with a product, how does promotion threaten this process? Advocates of this myth would say premiums are so desirable that children seek them without regard for the product they promote. In other words, children go whereever the premiums are, switching willy-nilly from brand to brand.

It is possible, and not uncommon, for a child to like a brand very much and not purchase or request it very much or at all. This is the brand loyalty that automobile makers and gasoline refiners can create in childhood.

This may be true in the case where children perceive two or more brands in a category as equally satisfying. Where one brand is perceived as better than another, premiums may be useful to stimulate additional purchases of the preferred brand. Less-preferred brands may use promotion to elevate their value in the eyes of children, particularly when the promotion offers a play object which is usually a more important need than, say, food.

Many brands within categories are "peas in a pod" in the sense consumers perceive them to have few or no discernable differences. Children in particular do a great deal of generalizing because of their relative inability to discern differences in similar objects. With such "parity" products, children may hold preferences for a set of two or three brands and choose the one most desirable at the time, measured in terms of availability, price, or promotional offers. Therefore, promotion doesn't erode brand loyalty; producing and marketing parity products does.

In fact, promoting children's products can create bonds that look very much like brand loyalty. Ironically, the goal of many promotions appears to be an increase in short-term sales rather than an increase in brand awareness and loyalty.

The Fast-Food Example

Several examples exhibit how promotion may either decrease or increase brand loyalty. McDonald's is children's favorite brand of fast food. Study after study has shown this. What explains it? We would say it comes down to children's good experiences with its restaurants and consistent satisfaction of children's needs. Advertisers might take a lot of the credit by saying they create a great image for the firm. They should; they do. But McDonald's is the king of promotion when it comes to kids, and adults, too, and those promotions, at least the good ones that target kids, increase children's liking for McDonald's.

• • • • • • •
You often see children drinking the soft drinks and eating only the french fries in Happy Meals, not the hamburgers.

As stated in the chapter 10, research shows that children's favorite fast food is pizza. Does this mean McDonald's sells the wrong food? To some extent, it does. If you doubt it, take a look first hand. You often see children drinking the soft drinks and eating only the french fries in Happy Meals, not the hamburgers. In fact, they may eat very little and just play while parents urge them to eat.

That's the key, the four-letter word p-l-a-y. Play is children's number-one need, and no restaurant chain offers more. While parents teach, "Don't play with your food," McDonald's says, "Come PLAY with your food." The playground—the biggest permanent premium of any food retailer—the premium and Happy Meal bag, other children, even the process of eating french fries, offer a multi-play combination that makes McDonald's children's most preferred restaurant. It's not the hamburgers.

Does this mean McDonald's promotions may be hurting its opportunities for even greater brand loyalty among children? Perhaps. Do tie-ins such as those with Disney movies help create brand loyalty among children? Yes and no. Yes, if they sense it is a McDonald's offering that comes from the heart of McDonald's. No, if they feel it is a Disney offering.

An issue of Delta Air Line's *Fantastic Flyer* magazine had two promotional advertisements. An entertaining one for Alamo car rentals in comic-strip form offers children an opportunity to win an IBM computer. But this is more likely to build brand relations with IBM than the lesser known brand, Alamo. The other ad is for Coca-Cola. It is also entertaining, also in comic-strip form, and offers children a chance to buy a football at a low price. The football is decorated with Coca-Cola's familiar red and white colors and logo. Will this build brand relations with kids? You bet. Good brand-based promotion helps build, not lessen, brand awareness, preference, and loyalty.

Taco Bell, part of Pepsico at the time, participated in what purported to be the largest promotion campaign ever. Pepsico reportedly spent in the neighborhood of $2 billion globally on promoting the Star Wars trilogy through its various divisions, including Taco Bell. Taco Bell is not your standard fast food; it's not hamburgers, chicken or pizza. It is, in fact, very young adult in image—its food offering, interiors, exteriors—and only recently began to seriously target kids. It needs a young following to become its next generation of young-adult consumers. Will the enormous Star Wars promotion do it? Or will Taco Bell build temporary traffic—the narrow meaning of brand loyalty—while acting as a middleman for Lucasfilm and its merchandise?

Back to McDonald's one more time. It has been very successful with its Beanie Baby tie-ins. Its fall 1998 promotion made headlines and increased sales 70 percent in a two-week period. People who rarely visit a McDonald's restaurant went there to grab these popular collectibles. But after the promotion was over, McDonald's had fewer customers—6 percent fewer—than before the promotion, according to a study by Consumer Aptitudes Inc., a research firm that examines restaurant patronage. This suggests novice customers didn't get anything more than the premium out of the experience and had no reason to return, and that regular customers were also taking a break. And it suggests promoting another well-known brand will not build permanent business for the restaurant chain.

> • • • • • •
> *McDonald's says, "Come PLAY with your food."*

The real question is whether kids (and their parents) come back after the promotion is over. The critical element in kid-based promotions—premiums, contests, sweepstakes—is satisfaction of needs and particularly the need for play. After the typical premium offer from McDonald's is over, there is still lots to come back to.

In sum, then, promotion can either increase or decrease the chance of developing brand loyalty. Promotion that makes a particular brand for kids even better—more fun is most important—and directly identifies with the brand is most likely to enhance the brand's relationship with children. If a brand emphasizes another's brand with a promotion, as is often the case, the promotion is not likely to encourage brand loyalty.

Children are Ungrateful—Not!

Adults often feel children lack the basic etiquette that maintains a civil atmosphere. In other words, they are self-centered and don't know how to say thank you. They often appear ungrateful when given things such as premiums and patronage gifts. But in various ways through various research methods, children clearly inform us they like those who give them things and are fondest of the biggest givers.

For example, when asked to analyze their family life, they often tell us one parent is kinder than another, meaning one parent gives them more, gives in to their requests more, and in general is more sensitive to their needs (wants). They relate similar evaluations of one or more grandparents around 20 percent of the time, and in a few cases even suggest grandparents are kinder than parents. The criterion of evaluation is almost always generosity.

The critical element in kid-based promotions—premiums, contests, sweepstakes—is satisfaction of needs and particularly the need for play.

This taker/giver thinking is fairly logical, although some in the promotion business seem not to understand it. Children learn even before they talk that others are givers, they are takers. That is, if they want anything, they are supposed to ask for it. As they discover more objects to want—always in the possession of others—they make more requests to parents, and also to grandparents and others. As children become acquainted with the marketplace with its endless offerings, and understand they can make requests to parents to get things, only a short leap is required to expect the marketplace will give them things, too. So when merchants offer premiums and opportunities to win things for visiting their stores, for instance, such behavior fits right in with children's expectations. They only hope the merchants will give them more, and more frequently.

Figure 13-1 was rendered by a third-grader based on the instructions: "Draw a cereal box." (The study is mentioned in more detail in the discussion of packaging in Chapter 16.) The researchers were curious to know if children would provide a brand name. In general, the answer is yes, at least for older children. But it also elicits other information. A significant portion of children who drew a branded cereal box also included some reference to a promotion.

Figure 13-1 displays two promotions, both in the center of the drawing and both connected to the brand name. The position of these two promotional statements indicates how important they are to the child. The one just below the brand name states that "Theres a pussle on the back," probably referring to a game printed on the back panel. This is part of the cereal's play offering to children. The second promotion in even bigger print says, "Free toy inside." Again, a promotional offer related to play. Thus, the cue word cereal elicited a rendering of a brand name cereal, Lucky Charms, and also a dual offer of two play items—all from the mind of a child who expects something, in fact, multiple somethings.

FIGURE 13-1

Marketers should not be misled by the fact that children have trouble saying "Thank you." They take careful note of who gives what. This is well summarized by one 11-year-old girl who told us, "If my dad doesn't give it to me, my other dad will." It's all in the numbers.

Would Children Rather Have a Free Bicycle or a Free Baseball?

Children are impatient and impetuous. They hate waiting, and the way they cope is to fidget, play, and whine "Are we there yet?", all of which can be extremely annoying to adults who have learned to mask their own impatience. This is pretty common knowledge, yet marketers sometimes ignore it. Contests that don't announce winners for months, savings accounts that don't pay off until Christmas, and premiums that require large numbers of donations or UPCs or store visits are not calculated to bring out children's best behavior.

If a free bicycle requires the accumulation of 100 UPCs and a free baseball only 5 UPCs, most kids will opt for the baseball even though the adult marketers who put together the offer perceive the bicycle as a good deal worth waiting for. Kids don't necessarily understand time, but they have built-in alarm clocks. They may not know when it's lunchtime, but they know when they're hungry. A promotion truly targeted to kids will take their unique time perspective into consideration.

It isn't that children won't take an interest in a more costly premium or contest with greater awards. They will if all the pieces fit—if the promotion awards are highly desirable, if the communications are in kids' language, and if the sponsor is popular with kids. But time can be an enemy of their enthusiasm and ultimately cost the promotion some effectiveness. At some point, interim awards may be necessary to keep children's interest. For example, a long-term game at a fast-food restaurant should award many small prizes, such as french fries or beverages, along the way.

Tips for Successful Promotions to Kids

In our discussion of these three myths, we have pointed to some promotions that work with kids. Let us put these thoughts together along with some others to suggest what characteristics of promotions might work best with kids and meet marketing goals.

Satisfy Kids' Significant Needs

Kids' most important need is **play**. Most promotions should focus on it. But children have other important needs. They are:

Sentience: the need for sensory experiences such as taste and touch,

Affiliation: the need for cooperative relationships with others, and

Achievement: the need to overcome obstacles.

McDonald's, for instance, satisfies the first three of these needs well when it focuses on fun, food, and family. A whistle made from tart gum or candy might satisfy play, sentience, and achievement.

Satisfy Parents' Needs for their Kids

Promotions should primarily satisfy kids, but they are likely to go into the failure column if they don't also satisfy parents. Parents need their kids to be happy, healthy, and coping with life. For example, they like snack items used as premiums to be more nutritious. They also want their kids to be able to cope with what life hands them and view education as the best solution. Therefore, a fun game that teaches geography is better than a game that is merely fun. The operative word today is "edutainment"—the promotion should entertain and educate.

Satisfy Kids' Time Perspective

We often hear the term immediate gratification when referring to kids. It's a good term. Make kids "instant winners;" give them something now. Kids aren't good at waiting. However, stringing out a premium by awarding parts or pieces each week or with each purchase may be fine if the promise is clear.

Identify the Promotion with the Firm and its Brands.

There is great opportunity to build brand loyalty with promotions, but many marketers seem to ignore it. For example, at one time Taco Bell offered its own Nacho Dog and Cat figurines as premiums to children. Each item has the Taco Bell name on it and the name Nacho, which also suggests Taco Bell food. This premium offer should help build brand loyalty.

Practice the S Principle and Use Numbers

The operative guideline for marketers who promote to children is the S principle—that is, emphasize the pluralS. When announcing their offering, the object's name should end in S—not "Free action figure," but "Free action figureS," not "Win a pass to the movies," but "Win passeS to the movies." Children love the biggest giver and the biggest giver is symbolized by consistent use of Ss.

- - - - -
Kids don't necessarily understand time, but they have built-in alarm clocks.

Another way to emphasize quantity in marketing communications to children is to use numbers—"Collect all 7," not "Collect them all," and "Trading cards of all 45 players," not "Trading cards of the entire team." Children want things and they want a lot. Specific numbers such as "a deck of 52 cards," rather than a "deck of cards" get their attention. It seems, also, for unexplainable reasons, that S numbers—six and seven—convey large quantities to children. Perhaps it is because the letter S is so complex to children, but it may be that their minds focus on it because it is a symbol of the plural form—gifts rather than gift, prizes rather than prize.

In the case of contests and sweepstakes, sponsors tend to offer one big first prize and several smaller awards for other winners. Even with one first prize, Ss and numbers should still be emphasized if possible. For example, rather than "First prize is a trip around the world," it could be, "First prize is a visit to 10 countries around the world." Several first prizes might be even better. Instead of one "First prize of $10,000," there could be "Ten first prizes of $1,000 each."

Marketers should not be surprised that kids expect promotions from them. Just about everything kids have is given to them. They expect marketers such as fast-food restaurants to give them something and may even ask for it—"Got anything free?" The answer should be "Yes."

Children love the biggest giver and the biggest giver is symbolized by consistent use of "S"s. It seems that S numbers—six and seven—convey large quantities to children.

In Sum

Promotion is only one element of the marketing communications mix, along with advertising, publicity, packaging, event marketing, direct marketing, and personal selling. But promotions seem to work exceedingly well to persuade children to buy and to buy by brand. This is particularly true of premiums. However, opponents voice concern about promotion lessening brand loyalty in the sense that children will focus on the promotion—on the free toy in the Cracker Jack box or kids' meal—rather than on the product or store that provides the promotion.

But it appears that the lessening of brand loyalty via promotion, to the extent it occurs, may be the result of badly executed promotions rather than promotions in general. If children believe free items are gifts from a particular seller, they will be grateful to that seller, like that seller, and tend to go back to that brand or store. If the premium possesses the brand name and/or symbols and colors of the product or store, it will help elevate the image of that brand in kids' minds.

If on the other hand, promotions focus on a brand other than that of the promoter, and the other brand has a good image in the minds of children, the other brand is likely to benefit from the promotion at least as much and possibly more than the promoting business does. The latter is common today. It generates short-term sales, thus fulfilling the goal of brand loyalty as defined by purchases, but not necessarily long-term allegiance. A suitable promotion should not seek the latter goal in place of the former one, but to accomplish both goals at the same time.

CHAPTER 14

Public Relations for Kids: Talking Instead of Shouting

MYTH: "Public relations is not an alternative to advertising when it comes to the kids market."

REALITY: Public relations is not an alternative to advertising when it comes to kids; it's an absolutely necessary companion.

In early 1994, Ty Inc. introduced Beanie Babies—73 different palm-size plush animals. By Christmas 1996, they were a hit with the preschool crowd and their parents. While monster hits in the toy business are news, what makes this toy story really news is the fact that it succeeded without advertising behind it. In this day and time when a play item for kids succeeds without advertising, particularly without television advertising, one almost suspects a miracle. This was no miracle. It was public relations.

Ty Inc. chose an uncommon marketing strategy of scarcity to provoke intrigue. This got attention in the press. The toy industry rarely goes for this tactic, preferring to blanket the nation with new products. Ty's publicity reached both retail buyers and consumers and stirred up interest—and sales. I don't mean to suggest Beanie Babies would have succeeded on PR alone. They offer tangible benefits, too. The product has play appeal; it also appeals to the acquisitive need, the need to collect things; and at a time when toys are getting very expensive, it is refreshingly inexpensive.

Does this situation or others like it suggest that publicity—"free advertising" as it is sometimes called—is an alternative to advertising when it comes to the kids market? No. Public relations is not an alternative to advertising; it is a necessary adjunct if advertising is to fully accomplish its goals. In the case of Beanie Babies, one wonders how much more successful they would have been and how much faster they would have caught on had advertising been employed in tandem with a carefully programmed public relations campaign.

Kid-Targeted Advertising Needs PR Help

The myth that PR is not a substitute for advertising surely originated in the advertising industry many years ago. The industry created this assertion as a means to counteract the increasing use of other marketing communications, particularly public relations and promotion, by marketers as their satisfaction with traditional advertising results continuously declined. Consumers have also become more critical of advertising, as discussed in Chapter 12.

These problems may seem to justify substituting public relations and other marketing communications types for advertising, but they are even better justification for using PR in conjunction with advertising. Properly planned and executed advertising has plenty of power to inform and persuade. PR can substantially enhance these goals in an integrated marketing strategy that uses both types of communications. How?

1. Because of public relation's relatively high credibility, it can enhance the credibility of advertising in general, advertising messages, and advertised brands and products. This is particularly important for parents who are more skeptical than kids.

2. When public relations joins with advertising, it synergistically increases the intended effects of each. It gets the total job done better, in the manner of a "whole that's greater than the sum of its parts."

3. Public relations reaches people that advertising might not reach simply because a lot of people ignore or even avoid advertising. Parents tune out more advertising than kids do, but kids are increasingly dodging television advertising by zapping it and spending more TV time playing video games and watching videos.

4. Using public relations along with advertising is a low-cost way to up the power of advertising. Adding a layer of public relations is much cheaper than adding another layer of advertising.

If a business has only a small amount of money to spend on marketing communications, spending it on public relations is probably wiser than spending it on advertising. So, yes, there are situations in which PR is an alternative to advertising. I am sometimes asked by belt-tightening firms that market kids' products which advertising dollars they should cut: those spent on kids or those spent on parents. There is no easy answer to this question. It's like asking, "Which shoe should I not wear today, the left or right one?" I usually suggest reducing advertising expenditures for both groups and adding a small layer of public relations that targets both, or cut some ads to parents and add a small layer of lower-cost public relations that targets them.

It's important to note that not all PR practitioners are suitable to be paired with advertising, for at least two reasons. Some public relations practitioners have a narrow view of their profession that says, in effect, when things are going bad, it's time to call in PR—for example, when a politician is losing a race or when a manufacturer has to issue a recall. Second, some practitioners hold another narrow view that says to clients: tell us what is good about your firm and products and we will tell others; that's our job. Neither of these views fits very well in today's integrated marketing efforts. Add to these narrow views some people's attitudes that PR is PR regardless of the target—kids or adults—and you have a recipe for disastrous results. So, fitting public relations—not some people who practice it—into the marketing communications mix is strongly recommended.

What Kind of PR Efforts are Most Effective in the Kids Market?

Public relations as a marketing communications function is relatively new in the kids market, but certain types are already proving themselves. The manner in which public relations—whatever type—is used with advertising in the kids market varies among users and practitioners. **Figure 14-1** illustrates four common strategies, all of which are intended to enhance advertising.

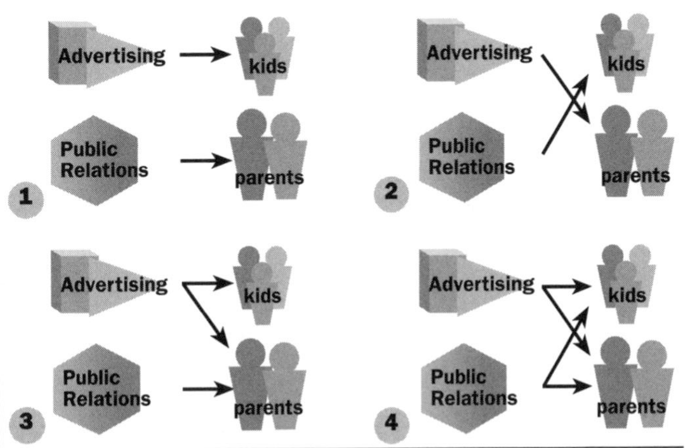

In strategy (1), advertising is targeted to kids; public relations to parents. In strategy (2), public relations is directed to kids, while advertising is targeted at parents. The thinking underlying strategy (1) is that advertising is effective in persuading children to want a product and

FIGURE 14-1

Communication Strategies Jointly Utilizing Advertising and Public Relations

public relations serves to convince the parents of the product's worth and suitability. In strategy (2), advertising is intended to inform and persuade parents who are viewed as the primary decision maker for certain products, while public relations targets kids to create product awareness and acceptance.

In strategy (3), advertising is targeted to both kids and parents to inform and persuade them because they are both decision makers for a product or service, while public relations is targeted to parents to convince them of the integrity of the producer or brand. In strategy (4), advertising and public relations are targeted to both parties to convince them of the value of specific products for kids and the integrity of producers who make them. This latter strategy may be more appropriate when the producer (seller) is new to the kids market. For the sake of brevity, I have not mentioned grandparents, teachers and day-care personnel as targets of advertising and PR, but they are important—for some products, as important as parents.

Aside from these strategies, I feel four specific types of PR are useful in the kids market: publicity, public service activities, school relations (in-school marketing), and special events. These four types are not mutually exclusive, and businesses often use two or more in tandem with other marketing communications to the point they are inseparable.

> • • • • • •
> *Publicity is particularly useful for introducing new products and services simply because the press finds them newsworthy.*

Publicity

"Marketing's velvet hammer" is how publicity has been described because of its ability to communicate about products and stores while being unknowingly persuasive. Publicity to kids and parents may appear in any news media—TV, radio, magazines, newspapers, Web sites, books, cinemas, and newsletters. It may, and should, appear in many simultaneously.

Publicity is particularly useful for introducing new products and services simply because the press finds them newsworthy. For example, during the past couple of years a host of new software titles have hit the kids market. Most are from relatively small producers that cannot afford national television advertising. But these firms may be successful in informing the market through magazine advertising, along with articles and product descriptions prepared specifically for certain magazines and circulated as press releases.

In any family-oriented magazine you will find articles on topics such as how to select software for children, accompanied by pages of descriptions of new software and where to obtain them. It is difficult to overstate the credibility of most media publicity compared with that of advertising. Add the "multiplier effect" of publicity on advertising, and one begins to appreciate why advertising should never go out without a publicity "chaperone." For example, children love to read about new attractions at theme parks, and parents love to read about vacations that incorporate theme-park side trips. The two stories, properly placed, can do wonders for a modest advertising program.

"When properly placed" is the tricky part, because marketers have no control over what media people will deem newsworthy. Newspaper editors and others are inundated with press releases. One way to boost the chance of getting "picked up" is to have publicists involved with product development and marketing. This way, they are more likely to sense what's newsworthy. Relationships with key media contacts are another necessary asset for public relations professionals. It doesn't take a Disney to get publicity. It can be a smaller firm such as Ty Inc. that introduced Beanie Babies to the world of kids. The point is that there must be story value for broadcast news and print media. The product must be "sold" to editors and producers before it can be sold to the public.

Two in three adults sometimes consider a company's involvement in social causes when making purchases.

Public Service Activities

Many businesses attempt to build a favorable public image by lending people a hand. This is often called cause marketing. Such public-service efforts endear firms to families, communities, and service organizations. Americans believe corporations have social responsibilities to their communities and the public at large. It is possible to meet these responsibilities while enhancing corporate image.

A 1996 study by Roper Starch Worldwide found that two in three adults sometimes consider a company's involvement in social causes when making purchases. About one in five refuses to buy even best-quality items when they don't like the companies that make them. A "good guy" reputation can have substantial favorable impact on the bottom line, especially when it comes to kids.

The list of possible public-service activities related to children and families is endless. It includes school improvements, education, neighborhood improvements, playground development and remodeling, children's health matters, nutrition, day care, and safety.

Related to safety, for example, Blockbuster Video annually joins with the National Center for Missing and Exploited Children to battle kidnapping. Parents can bring their children to any of the 3,400 Blockbuster Video stores and have their children "kid-printed"—have a video made of the children that shows their physical features and mannerisms. Additionally, children receive a *Safety Activity Book* with stories about child safety and coupons for free video rentals. This program builds a good image for Blockbuster among families—its prime market—in thousands of communities across the nation. That's meeting one's social responsibility and that's good public relations—doing well by doing good.

Just about every business firm has taken on some kind of cause marketing, and that's good. But cause marketing is one kind of public relations that can lose some of its inherent credibility if not handled carefully. It's vital to be genuine. If people suspect a company is only giving lip service to a social or environmental problem, they will be insulted rather than impressed. Bragging too much about involvement in social issues can also backfire. Such behaviors are commonplace and cast suspicion on the players. In turn, advertising and PR efforts directed to a cause lose some of their ability to persuade.

Moral: Public service PR is effective for good-doers, ineffective for do-gooders.

School Relations (In-School Marketing)

Why target schools? To paraphrase Willie Sutton when asked why he robbed banks: "That's where the kids are." It is also a place to reach teachers, school officials, and parents. Promotional messages presented to children in school settings generally have greater credibility than those presented in a commercial environment such as a television program or restaurant. So not only does in-school marketing reach children with high efficiency, it does it with high believability.

FIGURE 14-2

McDonald's has been a huge success in China, and as in the U.S., particularly with kids. A lot of that success has resulted from public relations, and specifically, school relations. For example, McDonald's personnel visit elementary schools in China and teach children how to write English, including how to write its famous Golden Arches logo, not an easy task for Chinese youngsters. **Figure 14-2** illustrates, in part, the results. This drawing is from a 3rd-grade Beijing child who, along with his classmates, was asked to draw what comes to mind when you think of the new "long" two-day weekend. This child perceives the long weekend as a time to play, and a time to put on your favorite jogging suit and run with your friends to a McDonald's breakfast. Note the accuracy of the Golden Arches sign. It probably doesn't hurt that the color gold is revered in Chinese culture.

Building relations with schools builds brand and/or store image. Most schools are in great need of financial assistance because many programs are poorly underwritten by government. Business can provide many services to schools by supporting programs such as music or athletics, providing teaching aids and materials, paying for physical facilities, and offering to be a partner in special events that improve children's fitness and safety.

Just being a source of information about an industry or product line can be valuable to elementary school children. For example, inviting classes to tour a restaurant to see how foods are prepared or a department store to see how the merchandise reaches the sales floor can be important first-hand information for children. These observations can be supplemented with in-class exercises on how to assess the nutrition value of restaurant meals or quality of clothing sold at department stores.

Sometimes a trade association representing an entire industry will put together a school relations program. For instance, the American Frozen Food Institute (AFFI) recently kicked off an educational program that targets kids in grades 1–3 in 10,000 schools. The intent of the program is to help children learn to make healthful food choices and develop good eating habits by integrating frozen foods into their diets. About 30,000 teachers received a complete set of teaching materials to help teach students about frozen foods' nutritional value and preparation methods, as well as how to cook safely. This effort appears to be a good example of helping teachers and students while enhancing the image of an industry among young children—its future customers.

Virtually every product category that targets kids uses school relations programs, but educational products are the most logical ones to promote through schools. Convincing administration and teaching staff to present product messages to students is a difficult task, but they understand and appreciate good educational materials and will invest time and energy in them. Southern Star Interactive, an educational software developer, distributed $5 rebate coupons to English teachers in 40,000 classrooms across the country. The idea was for Southern Star to get some hard-to-come-by shelf space in major book stores by demonstrating to these stores it had secured a core of customers for its literary classics. This program is in tandem with an advertising program in magazines that reach teachers, but it is unlikely that advertising alone could have accomplished the task.

When done right, school relations programs can benefit schools, students, and businesses. When done wrong, they hurt all three parties and invite the wrath of consumer advocates. Even when done right, in-school marketing may fall under fire. But many producers of children's products have successfully developed and implemented various kinds of school relations programs. Indeed, schools themselves are inviting businesses to partner with them in many kinds of projects—teaching materials, teacher development, improvement of physical facilities, and support of athletics.

One Colorado Springs school district has attracted attention with its "Revenue Enhancement Through Advertising" program, in which it invites companies to advertise on its buses for $2,500 per bus per year. The district uses the revenue to supplement regular funding for band, choir, cheerleading and other normal school activities. The program has been a big success and attracted major advertisers such as Burger King and 7-Up, whose ads are first approved by a review board. While the program is not without its critics, the school system generally sees the advertisers as good partners who are providing much needed funds.

Special Events

Special-events marketers usually target adults or perhaps families, but they are increasingly focusing on children, too. Marketers are recognizing that properly executed events are a natural for kids because of their (1) multisensory nature and (2) characteristic play and entertainment orientation. Special events usually involve all kinds of sensory experiences so vital to children.

Events are a great way to localize support for a message in a national advertising campaign. For example, KFC has a joint project with *Family Circle* magazine for a Mother's Day card drawing contest for 4th-to-6th graders at more than 65,000 schools. Hallmark produces the winning design and sells it in stores nationwide.

In this case, the venue is school, but there are other options—wherever the kids are. Shopping malls are a great location for kid-targeted events. They provide a controlled climate and safe environment. Hands-on events that appeal to children such as kite flying demonstrations, bicycle races, and fishing derbies are best held outdoors in parks and areas set aside for athletic events.

Local retailers find special events are a great way to compete with the large advertising budgets of national chains. Well-managed events require very little advertising, yet can generate much goodwill and lots of sales. Events are a wonderful way to break through the clutter of advertising and

Local retailers find special events are a great way to compete with the large advertising budgets of national chains. Well-managed events require very little advertising, yet can generate much goodwill and lots of sales.

develop a quality image that may not come so easily through typical advertising. Moreover, where marketers tastefully team up with schools, image building is likely to be even more effective.

When Marketing Social Products, Call the PR Guy

Beyond commercial products and services, many social "products" are targeted to kids. These include health, education, religion, environmental quality, and government, to name a few broad categories. Social products have been "sold" successfully to children for years. Smokey Bear began telling children in the 1940s that "Only you can prevent forest fires." Fifty years later, everyone recognizes that slogan because everyone was introduced to it in childhood.

Rather than changing behavior patterns in adulthood, it is better to attempt to mold them during the flexible preteen years.

What virtually all of these "products" have in common is the acknowledgment that general behavior patterns are developed in childhood and carried throughout life. Rather than changing behavior patterns in adulthood, it is better to attempt to mold them during the flexible preteen years. Interestingly, the responsibility for marketing social products is now usually assigned primarily to advertising. Not to knock the work of the Ad Council, which has been at the helm of social product marketing for years, the job calls for the credibility and persuasion power of public relations.

For example, the Office of National Drug Control Policy (ONDCP) is devoting around $200 million of hard money—for the first time—to the war on drugs. What a rare opportunity to accomplish the unthinkable. This is a war that has been fought forever by Partnership for a Drug Free America and many other groups including commercial firms, and hasn't been won. Far from it. So why does the ONDCP continue to put such enormous amounts of money—the $200 million is expected to be matched by donations—into advertising that has proven its inability to make much headway? Half this amount could buy unimaginable amounts of messages through a wide range of public relations activities such as those mentioned above. PR is a natural for social products, it can take on incredible odds with its credible armament, and combined with advertising and promotion, win any war.

In Sum

It is hard to explain the difference between the impact of publicity and advertising, or the difference between advertising with supporting publicity and advertising without supporting publicity. It is even harder to measure the difference. One publicity advocate has described it as talking versus shouting, while another says it is like getting a personal visit from someone compared with a greeting card.

Public relations is not an alternative to advertising to children; it is an absolutely necessary companion because of its high degree of credibility. Public relations efforts should accompany advertising campaigns because the public finds advertising less than believable. And even if an advertising campaign is credible, PR can provide additional credibility to the message and message source. Finally, PR may be where advertising isn't and thus extend the reach of the message. Publications that do not accept advertising, for example, may accept publicity with good story value. There's really no reason not to use it.

CHAPTER 15

Kids' Clubs: A One-to-One Relationship

MYTH: "Kids' clubs are a drain on resources."

REALITY: Over 80 percent of kids' clubs studied report that they
contribute to their company's bottom line while growing
new customers.

Kids' clubs have been around since the heyday of radio, but during the 1980s they had a comeback with the advent of database marketing. Business firms rapidly discovered clubs can be a marvelous mechanism for competing against traditional mass marketers. Done right, a kids' club can capture the purchasing power of the right children at precisely the right time.

But the more successful a kids' club becomes, the more it costs, and the more management becomes concerned about its impact on the bottom line. Membership, for instance, is usually a basic measure of success. As membership grows, costs of servicing the members grow. For example, if membership doubles, a company has to mail twice as many birthday cards, catalogs, and premiums. Such increased costs are not unusual; they are normal market development costs. However, in the case of kids' clubs, the short-run returns may be scarce.

One solution is to institute revenue-producing programs such as magazines that accept advertising from noncompeting firms. Another is to invite advertising in an ongoing club newsletter. Another common solution is to find partners who will share some club costs in exchange for access to club membership.

Overall, clubs have learned to pay for themselves and even make some money. Our in-depth research on the operations of about 3 dozen large and small clubs shows that over half of club managers report their clubs make a moderate contribution to profits. An additional one in four reports a significant contribution to profits. That's in addition to the long-term goals of growing customers for sponsoring firms! The latter, of course, represents not only future dollars but continued survival of a business.

What Makes a Kids' Club?

Kids' club is a generic term for many forms of relationship programs with children. There are probably on the order of 1,000 kids' clubs in the U.S. initiated by consumer goods manufacturers and retailers, broadcasters, banks, service marketers, and other profit and not-for-profit organizations.

Some kids' clubs are really frequency programs intended to capture the child as a customer and get the greatest share of his or her business.

They exist on a local, regional, and national basis. The Burger King Kids' club is a national program with more than 5 million members. Fox Kids' clubs exist in major markets, including one for station KCPQ in the Seattle-Tacoma, Washington area with more than 100,000 members. Local shopping centers and malls, radio stations, and banks may have relationship programs with just a few hundred members. For instance, the Navy Orlando Federal Credit Union in Orlando, Florida, has a Sailor Sams Club that provides special savings accounts for 2,900 kids, particularly those of parents stationed at the nearby naval base.

Through the aid of database technology, large and small businesses are forming one-to-one relationships with children through kids' clubs. These permit "mass" marketing on an individualized basis. Consequently, they have greatly improved their chances of satisfying each club member as well as the financial goals of their firms.

Some kids' clubs aren't really clubs, but standard marketing programs with names that imply they are clubs of some sort. Many banks, for example, design special savings accounts for children under the banner of an attractive descriptor that suggests a social organization. Some kids' clubs are really frequency programs intended to capture the child as a customer and get the greatest share of his or her business. For example, some banks offer savings programs embellished with frequency mechanisms that award children with premiums in addition to interest, according to the amount and frequency of deposits.

No specific features define a program as being a kids' club, but our research reveals several common features, including:

- An **offering** especially for kids, such as a saving or reading program, under a special name that 60 percent of the time includes the word **club**, along with a word or symbol suggesting a focus on children. For example, KeyCorp's Society Bank of Cleveland has a special savings program for children called DinoSaver Club, which employs kid-cool dinosaurs to communicate program features to the young set.

As a side note, some clubs have better names than others. Famous brand names can capitalize on their recognition factor, such as the Mickey Mouse Club, while the former Honeycomb Hideout Club lacked this advantage. Neither name, however, is very descriptive of the club's offering as is, for example, DinoSaver.

Furthermore, our research shows that the older children get, the less appealing they find the term "club." Therefore, if a kids' club includes a wide range of ages including tweens—kids aged 9 to 12—there is some wisdom in implying the club concept while avoiding it in name.

- A **sign-up** mechanism that obtains the child's name, address, age, and perhaps other information such as birthday and name of school. Children like the idea of "joining" an organization that is interested in them, wants to help them, give them things, and communicate with them.

- Sometimes clubs ask children to pay a **membership fee**, in exchange providing them with a variety of gifts such as hats and T-shirts. Such fees help cover administrative costs. They also help create a stronger bond between the club and the children. Fees suggest to children the club is worth joining. But most clubs charge nothing for membership and may in fact "pay" children to sign up. When children join the Thumbuddy Club at the Citizens National Bank at Charles City, Iowa, for instance, the bank contributes the first dollar to children's savings accounts.

- All kids' clubs offer children some kind of **inducement** to become a member. Initial inducements are often very desirable to the children and include items such as T-shirts, caps, snacks, games, money, posters, coupons, and even gifts for parents. Sometimes the gifts are more substantial, often because they are part of a cumulative program. Children who joined Delta's Air Line's Fantastic Flyer program during its first 9 years of operation received a poster and copy of *Fantastic Flyer* with a promise of future issues of the kid-treasured magazine. Today, the club costs $20 a year, but the gifts include discounted airline tickets.

The Fred W. Albrecht Grocery Company of Akron, Ohio, attempts to grow new business with its Fun with Fruit Kids' Club, which offers the children a free fruit each month. The Sierra Schools Federal Credit Union in Reno, Nevada, offers premiums ranging from pencils and coloring books to watches and sports bottles, depending on the size of deposits children make to savings accounts.

Some sign-up incentives are meager and dissatisfying, for example, a cap that a child must cut from a sheet of paper and glue together. Such mediocre offerings only produce a corresponding image of the club and its sponsoring firm—surely the opposite of the club's purpose.

- **Personal contact** is often a feature—an important feature—of kids' clubs that gives children a feeling of belonging. This personal contact may or may not be face to face and also includes mail, phone, and interactive media. Club members often receive personalized mail such as birthday cards, holiday greetings, newsletters, and questionnaires. Children cherish mail. It gives them stature in their households and shows they are people, too. The mail children receive from Delta's Fantastic Flyer program often prompts them to write back to one of the club's spokes-characters.

• • • • • • • • • •

Mascots are warm, fun, and engaging. They are literally good friends, someone who is in charge, so to speak, and yet not bossy and critical like parents and other adults can be.

Children also find it exciting to talk on the phone, even if it's to a recorded message. Local and regional clubs may contact members by phone, or allow children to contact them. Bank clubs commonly encourage children to call and ask questions or check balances in their saving accounts. Some clubs, such as the Club KidSoft, a California-based publishing company that markets software to children and their families, regularly conducts marketing research with its young members through unique mail questionnaires that personally involve the children. As more clubs set up Web sites, this admittedly less personal method of communication will strongly appeal to computer-savvy kids.

The key is to stay in touch with kids on an ongoing basis. If kids' clubs do not maintain personal contact of some kind with their members, the children will lose interest and drift away.

FIGURE 15-1

Use of Communications Vehicles by Kids' Clubs	
COMMUNICATIONS VEHICLE	EXTENT OF USE
Contests	95%
Coupons	70
Direct mail	65
Magazine (editorial/ads)	39
Major events	78
Newsletter	74
Premiums	70
Radio (programs/ads)	10
Television (programs/ads)	83

- Each club has one or more **communication vehicles** to inform children of club activities and benefits. The table in **Figure 15-1** shows various communication devices and the extent to which kids' clubs use them. They include letters, newsletters, magazines, advertising, catalogues, events, broadcast programming, publicity, and promotion (contests, coupons, and premiums) that target children and perhaps their parents and schools.

These communications form the link between children and clubs that give children a sense of attachment and identity. Because these functions account for a large share of operation costs, they receive most of club management's time and energy. For example, the Desert Kids' club of the Desert Schools Federal Credit Union in Phoenix, Arizona, issues a quarterly newsletter. It also offers joint promotions with Baskin-Robbins on members' birthdays, the local zoo for an annual visit, as well as occasional outings to the theater, circus or other special events. These are major undertakings for a small club, but they have an important purpose—to grow potentially lifelong customers for the credit union.

- Most kids' clubs have a **spokesperson**, whether it be a live person or cartoon character. Delta's Dusty, Orbill, and Phee characters greet and talk with children through the pages of *Fantastic Flyer* magazine. At the Fox Kids' club at KCPQ-TV in Seattle, Q-Bird does the talking, while at the Sailor Sams Club of the Navy Orlando Federal Credit Union, it's Sailor Sam himself, a cartoon mouse in a sailor uniform.

These mascots personalize their clubs and they are warm, fun, and engaging. A mascot can be a good friend, someone who is in charge, so to speak, and yet not bossy and critical like parents and other adults can be. Consequently, they are good representatives of their clubs, they usually teach good values to children, and they help bond children to the club and its sponsor(s). Kids' clubs also use real spokespeople, but characters offer the advantage of being fully controllable.

When a 3rd-grader in Beijing, China, was asked to "Draw what comes to mind when you think about watching TV." He drew an excellent likeness of Mickey Mouse filling the screen. Even if he hadn't labeled the drawing with the words, Mickey Mouse, it would have been quite apparent what he was thinking. Unfortunately, The Disney Company's strict rules concerning the use of the image of Mickey Mouse do not allow us to show you this child's drawing.

Mickey Mouse is perhaps the ultimate example of a character around which to build a kids' club. Mickey is not very gender-specific so both boys and girls are comfortable with him. He is friendly, warm, simple, non-threatening, someone a kid would want to play with. Characters with these qualities make good representatives for a club, and can be created specifically for that purpose. Of course, it takes time to imbue characters with character, but the investment may be worth it. With that kind of charm, you can build more than a kids' club. You can build an empire.

- Kids' clubs wouldn't get too far without membership rosters. At the minimum, a club **database** has to have names and addresses. It may also contain other information such as birthday. Acknowledging a 7-year-old's birthday with a funny and thoughtful card is a great way to deepen the kid-club relationship. Adding a coupon for a free kids' meal or other promotion will prompt direct contact. If the mission of the sponsoring organization is to sell to children and their families, the database should also contain purchase history, interests, and some measure of the member's value as a customer.

Databases permit kids' clubs to develop and maintain relationships with members. They are also very expensive and labor-intensive to maintain, requiring constant attention. Add to this the costs of producing and mailing communications and it's easy to understand why top management requires cost/benefit analysis to justify databases and prevent them from being a drain on resources. The reality is that databases make clubs feasible operations.

Acknowledging a 7-year-old's birthday with a funny and thoughtful card is a great way to deepen the kid-club relationship.

Basic Activities of a Kids' Club

Three basic activities of kids' clubs consume most of their resources. They are communications, distribution, and research. The chart in **Figure 15-2** illustrates the approximate allocation of funds to these activities among a sample of kids' clubs. All maintain databases to facilitate these functions. The chart shows that most dollars go to communications, then to distribution and research, in that order.

Communications

Kids' clubs often begin life as marketing communications efforts intended to build and maintain relationships with children as future consumers. Through communications, they attract members, develop members into potentially loyal customers, and direct them to the sponsoring firm's offering at the appropriate time in their lives.

The major communications tools usually consist of a mix of advertising, promotion, and publicity wrapped around a mail-based newsletter or magazine. Local clubs tend to use event publicity more, while larger regional and national clubs do relatively more advertising and promotion, although heavy use of promotion is common to most clubs. For example, the Topanga Plaza

Kids' club, a shopping mall club in Canoga Park, California, puts on events at least once a week, mostly for preschoolers and their parents, including elaborate puppet shows twice a month. It also conducts a number of joint promotion with mall tenants. Its birthday program sends members greetings they can use to obtain gifts and coupons from center merchants. Club management reports that balloons given to kids at events can be seen throughout the mall for hours afterward and provide a barometer of the effectiveness of club events—i.e., getting families to the mall and into stores.

Managers of kids' clubs—they tend to be called coordinators and directors—are typically skilled in one or more fields of marketing communications. If a club has a magazine or newsletter, it often receives the greatest share of the manager's time and attention since it is usually the principal medium of communications. Through a magazine, for example, the club can advertise benefits and activities, conduct contests and sweepstakes, offer coupons, and present publicity pieces about the sponsor.

Distribution

Kids' clubs place different degrees of emphasis on the distribution function. Some clubs are designed almost solely as a channel of distribution through which products and services are sold to members. Essentially, these are in the catalog or direct-marketing business. For some clubs, the distribution function is only incidental with an occasional offering of coupons and premiums.

Clubs whose primary function is distribution have selected kids (and usually their parents) as a current primary sales target. They are not very "clubbish," but database marketing in the most fundamental sense. Kool-Aid's Wacky Warehouse is an example. Bob Horne of Kid Think Inc., a subsidiary of Griffin Bacal advertising agency, described it this way in an issue of *Marketing News*: "(Kool-Aid's Wacky Warehouse) isn't really a club, it's more like, 'Here's all this neat stuff you can send for.'"

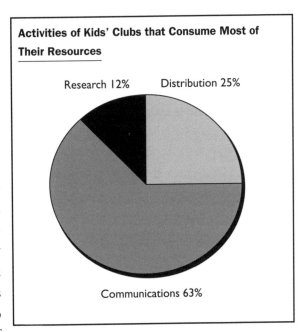

Activities of Kids' Clubs that Consume Most of Their Resources

Research 12%   Distribution 25%

Communications 63%

FIGURE 15-2

Club KidSoft is another sales-oriented kids' "club" from an educational software producer. It has about 40,000 members to whom it distributes a quarterly magazine and catalog. Young recipients are expected to ask their parents to order educational software from the catalog, and software is also featured in the magazine.

Kids' clubs commonly distribute coupons and paper premiums such as stickers and printed games. These items are relatively low cost, and have made the large lists of national kids' clubs, such as Burger King and Fox, attractive to major consumer-goods manufacturers.

Research

Kids' clubs as a market research source is a relatively new but rapidly expanding idea. Done right, collecting information from members can improve club offerings, even suggest product concepts and marketing strategies for the business as a whole. As a side benefit, seeking children's opinions can make them feel important and closer to the sponsoring firm. This warm feeling in turn can increase response rates well above industry norms.

Some research is conducted automatically as a normal part of club operations, as when updating a member database that includes names, addresses, birthdays, and so on. Sometimes it's a matter of analyzing existing information. For example, a club whose primary function is product distribution will naturally examine sales records to better understand what its members like and don't like. Clubs might also routinely gather information about members who attend club events, send for special offerings, and redeem coupons. Submitting questionnaires to members is also increasingly common, often to obtain lifestyle information.

Club KidSoft regularly conducts research among members to obtain information about their demographic characteristics, interests, opinions, and suggestions. Club management has spent much time perfecting questionnaires that speak children's language. It reports that participation has been building, and it expects a dramatic increase in response rates when the club goes online.

Managing a Kids' Club—Some Dos and Don'ts

Financial fears and resistance to long-term commitment has fostered the myth that kids' clubs are a burden on the bottom line. The number of failures and shutdowns in the kids' club business have created additional apprehension. A cursory examination of the facts, however, suggests that the concept of kids' clubs is not to blame; it's the way they are managed.

Our research shows that three in four new kids' club startups were managed by people with no previous experience in this admittedly specialized endeavor. Moreover, in many cases managers were selected using such criteria as: "likes kids," "likes to work with children," and "has kids of her own."

Perhaps even more debilitating to kids' clubs has been their lack of purpose. During the latter half of the 1980s, many clubs started with no more of a mission than to copy competition. Nickelodeon, for instance, started a kids' club and grew membership to a seemingly respectable 3 million, then discontinued it—according to Nickelodeon management, because it wasn't distinctive from the competition. Overall, the failure rate among kids' clubs has probably approximated that of kids' products in general; at least two-thirds don't make it.

Research among a sample of current clubs, however, shows a high degree of optimism. **Figure 15-3** summarizes responses to questions about the positive and negative impact of kids' clubs on their sponsoring companies. Over three-fourths of reporting club managers say they would do it again and do it the same way because they had met their major goals. They have contributed substantially to sales and profits, improved product and company image, and increased the visibility of their firms among targeted groups.

From these club managers, we can discern some dos and don'ts that may not guarantee success, but will hopefully avert utter failure:

FIGURE 15-3

What Club Managers Say about the Impact of Kids' Club on their Sponsoring Companies	
CLUB MANAGERS' RESPONSES	**EXTENT**
Visibility of firm increased	98%
Sales increased	90
Corporate or product image improved	85
Profits increased	83
Said they would do it again	77
Marketing research improved	54

Do have clear goals. Kids' clubs are a great way to compete for the kids market, but just being competitive is not the right reason to start one. The most logical goal is to grow future customers—that is, to develop a steady stream of new customers when they reach market age for a business. Targeting kids as an influence market may make better sense, depending on the product offering. But if growing future customers is truly the main goal, it may be wise to stick to it, but to select a partner who targets kids as a current market and can share operations costs.

Don't forget parents. Since the club will be making various offers to children—products, contests, coupons, questionnaires—and these offers will most likely go to the home through the mail or via the Internet, parental approval is very important. At a minimum, conduct focus groups to gauge parental response to all offers. At the other extreme, send offers to parents to give to kids themselves.

Kids want and expect to socialize in a club.

Don't share members' names and addresses. Nothing will anger parents more than this. Privacy is a giant-size issue in database marketing, and understandably so. The database marketing industry is shot through with sleaze and disregard for privacy. Don't add to it. It is tempting to share the list, as some clubs do, because of its attractive revenue, but doing so will also attract trouble. This doesn't apply to partners, of course.

Don't offer shabby merchandise and premiums. Hawking "25 colorful Christmas ornaments for $5 just in time for the holidays" that are all printed on a single sheet of paper is no way to grow customers, just enemies. If the offer is a play item, test it for playability. If it is a snack item, test it for taste and nutrition. And test everything for parental acceptance. The point is that this is a chance to grow customers for years to come, so don't blow it. Offering high quality will have them coming back for more and telling others about it. It may be tempting to use a kids' club membership as a channel of distribution and pump it full of worthless merchandise with the support of deceptive sales messages. Don't do it. Children don't forget; parents don't forgive.

Do make a club "clubbish." It may not be called a club, but if it is presented and marketed as a club—if it asks children to join, if it refers to participants as members or fellows and similar terms— it should be gregarious. It should help members associate with one another through mechanisms such as letters to the editor of a magazine or newsletter, as pen pals and e-mail friends. Develop a spokescharacter and put him or her (better if it is neither) at the social center of the club. Kids want and expect to socialize in a club. Don't seek and accept their membership and then treat them as individual islands.

Do go with experienced management. Getting a club up and running is hard work. Maintaining it and growing it is even harder work. None of it is for the faint-hearted. Kids are a very special group. Clubs are a very special kind of marketing. Most likely the future customers for a firm are the focus. It doesn't get any more important than that. Go with a pro. There are firms that specialize in relationship programs, including database management. For example, Frequency Marketing, Inc, Milford, Ohio, designs, manages, and maintains frequency programs of various kinds including all the direct marketing and database work, and has done this work for years.

● ● ● ● ● ● ● ●
Children don't forget; parents don't forgive.

A Final Note

Kids' club surely offer lots of benefits for the businesses that are clear on the costs and risks attached. This doesn't mean they are for everyone. There seems to be a "If you don't have a kids' club, get one" mentality in the kids marketing business. This is probably bad advice. Kids' clubs are costly, troublesome, and will absorb all the money and manpower put into them and want more. That said, they are a terrific way to grow future customers.

Keep in mind that a kids' club is probably not the best way to sell to children as a current market. So don't start a club, get kids signed up, give them a great T-shirt with the club's logo on it, and then pound them with sales mail. In particular, don't do this with the kind of negative-option programs that adults' book and music clubs use. This annoys parents, causes difficulties between parents and children, hurts the image of kids' clubs in general, and of course, ultimately creates a piranha-like reputation for the sponsoring firm.

Finally, whatever kind of club you develop, whatever goals you set, and whatever communications and marketing strategy you pursue, remember it is for kids. Getting mail, having fun, and being acknowledged as bona fide consumers—this is what matters to kids. Do these things and do them well, and you will satisfy the kids, their parents, and even the bottom line.

CHAPTER 16

Kids' Packaging: Overlooking the End User

MYTH: "In the milk industry, we have been targeting kids for years, but they are still reluctant to make it their favorite snack beverage."

REALITY: A kid can't snack out of a gallon jug.

Playful white mustaches notwithstanding, kids won't perceive milk as a snack item as long as it is in those monstrous gallon jugs. I believe that if the milk people were designing a car to accommodate a large family, they wouldn't think of a minivan with three rows of seats; they'd start with a coupe and put one big seat in it!

If you have kids, your household probably consumes a fair amount of milk. You may actively encourage your children to drink milk. But you probably buy it in gallon or half-gallon containers. By the time they are 10, most kids have learned firsthand that nothing goes further or covers better than a gallon of milk spilled on a kitchen floor. Ditto for two- and three-liter soft-drink bottles with equal spreading power and additional sticking power.

Good kids' packaging is hard to find. On the A-K scale (adult to kid), the design of most packaging for kids' products skews toward the A end. Milk in a gallon jug is just one example among hundreds. Look at ready-to-eat cereal boxes and compare the brands primarily targeted to kids with those primarily targeted to adults. What's the difference? There isn't any. Kids' cereal boxes might be decorated in a different way—i.e., funned up—but they're function-ally identical. This is also the case for kid versions of most adult products—toothpaste, facial tissue, frozen desserts, software, etc.

Why are kids' products in adult packages? Essentially, it's because pack-aging is not a very consumer-oriented industry. To the extent it is, it views its customer as the producer rather than the end user. Another reason is that it doesn't understand the world of children and its role in that world. Through no inherent fault of their own, children get in trouble when they spill the very milk their parents urge them to drink. This isn't serving the end user; it's also not serving the packager's perceived customer, the dairy industry.

Let's look more closely at why kid products come in adult packaging, why this is wrong, and what to do about it.

Packaging for Kids Should Be Different

There's probably not a packaged-goods industry that doesn't target kids in some way or other, but marketing's "4Ps" to kids too often ends when it comes to the "fifth P"—packaging. It's not really clear why this disconnect occurs. Maybe it's because no one is in charge of packaging, or perhaps because just about everyone seems to be in charge of packaging. It is one of those activities that production believes it should control, retailing knows it should control, and marketing should control. The net result is that responsibility for the package goes where the power is or becomes a compromise. In any case, it frequently ignores the consumer, particularly the young consumer.

Let's break out the old textbook on packaging, define its tasks, functions, duties, responsibilities, and see how they respond to kids and how they should respond to kids. We'll call these functions and try to indicate how to "kidize" them. A good kids' package is one that appropriately performs its functions within the constraints of kids' language, lifestyle and physical limitations.

> *A good kids' package is one that appropriately performs its functions within the constraints of kids' language, lifestyle and physical limitations.*

Contain and Release the Product

If you have ever watched a kid fill a balloon with water and try to carry it, you have witnessed poor packaging for kids from a containment standpoint—fun but bad. A package should appropriately contain the product with respect to the end user. The contents shouldn't leak from the package when it is handled, yet should easily release the product when wanted. A tube of kids' toothpaste, for instance, shouldn't emit toothpaste when kids lay it on the bathroom counter with the cap off.

As a case in point, the typical catsup bottle is not an especially good package because its narrow neck doesn't easily and smoothly release its contents. For kids, it's worse. Easy-open, single-serving packs of catsup would be better for kids—they even connote that much-loved fast-food atmosphere. But like the milk industry, the catsup industry recommends the large economy size for households with kids.

Protect the Product

A good package protects its contents from moisture, light, and temperature changes as appropriate for the product and its consumer. I am old enough to remember when a loaf of bread came in a package that one couldn't close well enough to keep the bread from drying out. Some bread still does. It took a century of consumer complaints and the simple wire twist to revolutionize that package.

It will probably take that long and something that simple to improve a really bad package concept like the chip bag. Even more than the gallon milk container, the un-closeable, guaranteed-crushable chip bag deserves the antisocial award of the century for its contribution to poor mother-child relationships. The attitude of chip producers such as Frito-Lay suggests they are oblivious to the basic protection function a package is supposed to perform.

These kinds of packages have helped boost the repackaging industry—resealable containers such as those from Rubbermaid and Tupperware, along with the many various plastic and aluminum wraps, and of course, clamps for chip bags. As useful as these are for adults, they are not necessarily a good answer to bad kids' packaging. In the grand scheme of things, the investment in developing and producing improved packaging would be well worth it. Look at Pringles. Its innovative package design is a selling point, and Procter & Gamble probably gives it credit for much of the brand's market share growth.

Protect the User and the Environment

All packaging should be safe for consumers during purchase, use, and for re-use where appropriate. For children, this requires extra care. It means avoiding sharp edges exposed during opening and closing, such as those on some metal packages. Glass containers are also inherently dangerous to children. Microwaveable products targeted to kids should have easy-to-see, easy-to-read directions that safely guide them through the preparation process. Liberal use of clear illustrations will assist children who think visually.

Packagers should also be sensitive to protecting the environment. Children are environmentally sensitive people. Sometimes they learn about it

Microwaveable products targeted to kids should have easy-to-see, easy-to-read directions that safely guide them through the preparation process. Liberal use of clear illustrations will assist children who think visually.

from their parents, but they also pick up environmental information from school, media, and other sources. In fact, children often teach their parents about environmentally friendly behaviors and may urge them to recycle. Packagers should strive to make their products recyclable and to convey this information to young consumers.

Packages should be environmentally efficient, too. Overpackaging, especially common in the software business and the toy industry, should be avoided. Kids and parents alike can readily see how it can harm the environment. Kids may not be as aware as adults that overpackaging also costs them more, not only because it adds to the product cost but because it costs to dispose of it all—many Americans pay by the bag for nonrecyclable garbage.

Kids may not be as aware as adults that overpackaging costs them more. Kids and parents alike can readily see how it can harm the environment.

Identify Seller, Contents, and Directions for Use

Here we're talking mainly about the communications function of packaging. Each of the thousands of different packages of kids' products on store shelves in the U.S. is an opportunity to "talk" with young consumers about their contents and producer. Kids know when a package is for them.

Kids generally perceive and treat a properly designed kids' package as special for a number of reasons:

1. It identifies products they desire;

2. It explains (shows) how kids can easily use its contents;

3. It announces a premium (in-pak) or an offer (on-pak) in nondeceptive terms;

4. It uses words and symbols that speak their language;

5. It emphasizes the brand name, which is usually important to them;

6. It provides necessary descriptions of the product inside and often of companion products;

7. It tells how to convert the package into after-consumption use;

8. It meets parents' imposed communications requirements; and

9. All of this is typically offered in a self-service, satisfying, and fun format.

A series of studies we did of children's ready-to-eat cereal packaging provides strong evidence of the importance of packaging communications. We twice replicated a study done in the 1970s to understand the perceptions children have of packaging. In the mid-1980s, we asked first- and third-grade children to "Draw a cereal package." The first graders did a pretty good job. About half supplied a brand name and some brand-specific graphics on the front panel. Virtually all of the third graders provided front panels with brand names, usually exactly the way the packages illustrated them, including many graphic features such as colors and slogans. The children showed us very vividly that a package is not just a package; it's a Cheerios package, for example, with very specific graphics, a detailed picture they carry in their heads.

In 1996, we repeated the study and found one major difference. Half of the children provided a side panel showing in great detail the required nutritional information of the specific cereal, as shown in **Figure 16-1**. In this particular case, the child acknowledges "Nutrition Facts," and lists them such as "calories," "fat," "vitim (vitamin) C," and "sodim (sodium)." It would appear that the health and fitness emphasis of the 1990s has reached children loud and clear. They have watched their mothers look at and explain this nutritional information to them, and they have picked up on its importance.

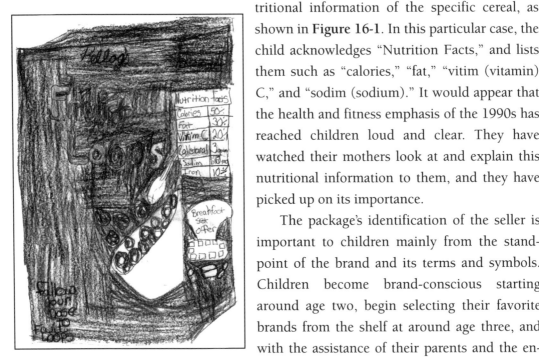

FIGURE 16-1

The package's identification of the seller is important to children mainly from the standpoint of the brand and its terms and symbols. Children become brand-conscious starting around age two, begin selecting their favorite brands from the shelf at around age three, and with the assistance of their parents and the encouragement of advertising, arrive in elementary school keenly aware of hundreds of brands.

Since children buy by brand most of the time, packages should clearly present the brand and its identifying symbols. For example, General Mills has created a rabbit as a symbol of its Trix cereal. Most children need only a glimpse of that rabbit and they know the cereal. Such identification—easy recall of the product and its attributes—makes shopping easier for kids in what is mainly an adult environment. This may sound simple and logical, but with all the copy-cat efforts of many supermarkets to imitate packages of leading sellers, confusion abounds.

When presenting brands within a family brand—General Mills Cheerios, Post Alpha-Bits—packages should signal attributes of both brands. Kraft Foods, for example, has begun a major push to give meaning to the Kraft name along with its many well-known brands such as Jell-O, Kool-Aid, and Oscar Mayer. If a producer imbues a parent brand with special meaning among children, it can extend this to packages of new products and give kids confidence in making additional satisfying purchases. On the other hand, multiple brand names can be confusing to kids (adults, too!), so this may be an uphill battle.

Identifying the contents of the package means children and their parents know what they are getting. As a rule, entire contents are important to children and parents and probably should be presented in the language of both. Verification of contents may be done graphically for the children, alphanumerically for parents. Ready-to-eat cereal, for instance, usually shows a picture of a bowl of cereal on its front panel (often exaggerated, unfortunately), along with pictures of in- or on-pak premiums. Most text appears on the sides and back panels, including ingredients and nutrition facts. A combination of graphics and text on the back may further describe premiums, offer games and puzzles, or explain other "fun" attributes. Such pictorial identification is very important to kids, who often generalize. For example, they may see bottles of liquid detergent and bottles of shampoo as similar.

Describing directions for use is an important package function—for the contents and for the package itself. Children need to know how to use a package—how to open and close it, how to use it in the product's preparation or use—and need instructions for any secondary purpose. All this needs to be communicated in kids' language—a combination of graphics and words is probably best. Placement should also be considered. For example, the typical board game should have directions on the box in which it comes and is stored, not on a separate piece of paper that is apt to get ruined or lost.

Packagers should also bear in mind that parents will see instructions directed at kids, so they had better meet with approval. Mom may be the one who decides if the product will be bought again, and her decision may be made on the basis of how well the package is designed with her kid in mind, not some ergonomically contrived kid.

Provide Convenience in Purchase and Use

In China, soft drinks are sold in the supermarket only one bottle or can at a time. That's convenient for the typical Chinese kid who expects to buy them this way. It would be inconvenient for American kids who also expect to buy them in a 6- or 12-pack. The gallon bottle of milk mentioned earlier is inconvenient for a kid to purchase anywhere and equally inconvenient to use.

A package for a product targeted primarily to kids should be convenient to purchase—to retrieve from the display fixture, transport in a shopping cart, take through the checkout, and carry to school, home, or tree house—and convenient to use. A typical box of ready-to-eat cereal, package of cookies, or bag of chips meets all of the requirements of being convenient to purchase, in that it is not too bulky, heavy or delicate, but these packages are not necessarily convenient to use. Some packages need to hold up through multiple use and storage, such as those for board games.

Ironically, the ice-cream industry has some of the most convenient kid packages but hasn't capitalized on them. Its pint and quart containers have been around for a long time, and their quality has been improved in recent years. Yet the industry does a poor job of merchandising these packages for kids. It usually doesn't place appropriate graphics on containers and usually doesn't display them appropriately for kids. Instead ice-cream makers and sellers try to push half-gallon and gallon containers to families, generally the same error its milk-producing colleagues make.

Provide Additional Uses

The typical kid, like the typical adult, can never have enough "things" and "stuff." The difference is that kids can get a lot of play value out of packages themselves, including those for adult products, after they have fulfilled their primary functions. Keeping packages and reusing them is environmentally friendly. It's also fun. Kids have a wonderful way of creatively converting bags and boxes into play things. Moreover, many magazines for kids, such as *Crayola Kids*, offer great ideas for converting leftover packaging into things for kids.

Some packages might require modest modifications to be converted into kids' stuff. For example, a jar lid might need a slot punched out to become a bank. The point is that many packages have one or more reuses that can add kid appeal. Cereal boxes have done a lot of package reuse throughout the years, but wouldn't it be nice if chip bags or cookie packages could turn into toy boats or hats! Pringles packages already function really well, but by offering suggestions to turn them into telephones, telescopes, kaleidoscopes and other play things, Procter & Gamble could enhance their value to consumers, and their competitive value to the producer.

So Where's All the Good Kids' Packaging?

The functions of consumer packaging set out above have been well established for years. The packaging industry conducts ongoing research to make products more useful to consumers. For example, *Packaging* magazine conducts annual surveys that ask consumers what packaging features are important to them. At the top of the packaging priority list is "value for the money," meaning convenient storage, easy-opening, resealability, and tamper-evidence. As we move through supermarkets, superstores, fast-food outlets, and malls, we can see good examples of these functions applied to kids' products. So, all that is needed for good kids' packaging that meets their requirements and those of their parents is to integrate these functions. Well, maybe.

Figure 16-2 illustrates a half-dozen major sources of various requirements placed on consumer packaging. The sources include young consumers and their parents, of course, but also package designers, package suppliers, producers, retailers, and regulators. Other possible inputs to the design of kids packaging not shown include transportation and storage providers and various types of wholesalers. **Figure 16-2** also shows second and even third layers of package requirements within major categories, such as marketing and production managers at the producer level and department managers and buyers at the retail level. It's obviously a complex process to bring all these players together in agreement.

FIGURE 16-2

Major Sources of Requirements Placed on Packaging for Kids

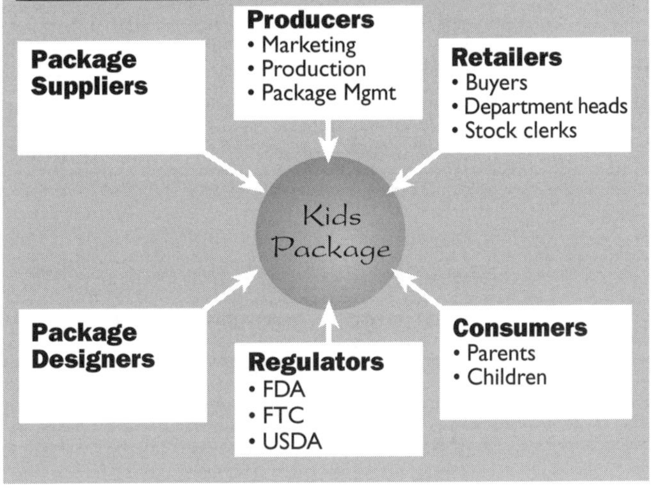

- Package Suppliers
- **Producers**
  - Marketing
  - Production
  - Package Mgmt
- **Retailers**
  - Buyers
  - Department heads
  - Stock clerks
- Package Designers
- **Regulators**
  - FDA
  - FTC
  - USDA
- **Consumers**
  - Parents
  - Children
- Kids Package

Logically, producers should be responsible for the final design of the package and that decision should be based on what best satisfies the consumer—kids and their parents. But in the case of most consumer goods primarily targeted to kids, reality indicates that the producer does not research the entire design in accordance with the needs and requirements of kids and their parents. And the final vote is more often than not the retailer's, whose wishes may or may not coincide with the wishes of the primary consumer or even the producer of the product. The retailer will apply various S tests to most packaging either before, or worse yet, after it has been designed—is it "shelvable, stackable, storable, sellable, steal-able"—and most likely show only passing regard for the kid consumer.

Within the producer's organization, at any point in time, there may be turf wars among several factions claiming power over the package. For example, a three-way contest may ensue among production, whose main concern is probably the package's compatibility with the production line; marketing, whose principal concern is probably the promotional ability of the package and secondarily retailers' requirements; and a packaging department likely to deal with the details of costs and protecting the product. Of course, this internal struggle does not include external players such as package suppliers, package design groups, ad agencies, and promotion agencies that may have a lot of influence on the final package.

At the retail level, a number of people may impose package requirements, again, both before and after the final package design. Manufacturers may consult with retailers about package features. Even when they don't, they often give retailers' requirements much consideration since retail buyers may reject a product outright based on its package, or reject certain sizes or styles of packages. Some supermarketers are concerned with taking on additional toiletries for kids, and packages may play a role in whether or not they agree to stock them. For example, Procter and Gamble's Crest Kid's Sparkle Fun toothpaste doesn't have a very eye-catching package, and some supermarkets might be reluctant to take on another version of it in a similar package. On the other hand, the high kid appeal built into packages of Johnson & Johnson kids' toiletries may make additions more welcome.

Regardless of package design and intent, individual store personnel—department managers, assistant department managers, stock clerks—may receive a product for kids and shelve it in inappropriate ways that do not serve the goals of the producer, retailer, or young consumer. Dannon has a line of yogurts for kids called D'Animals. They are offered to supermarkets in 6-packs with the primary panel on top presenting attractive appeals to children, if they can see them. In a Kroger supermarket, I observed this product on chiller shelves stacked so high that neither kids nor adults could see the top panel. In contrast, a P&C store correctly shelved them in low open refrigerated bins so even a 3-year-old could pick out the package with the sticker of her choice on its top panel.

Why do retailers appear to thwart the sales of kids' products by inappropriate shelving? There are probably three reasons: slotting fees, slotting fees, slotting fees. When retailers get paid up front to stock a product, they may get a bit careless when it is time to nurture its sales.

Regulators are mainly concerned with packages' protective features and potential deception in graphics and structure. We need to bear in mind that kids are a special case. They often do not have the ability to assess the protective qualities of a package. For example, they are not aware that packaging material might interact with contents to produce spoilage. Further, kids may not pick up on deceptive graphics, for example, the cereal box whose front panel illustration exaggerates the size of the flakes to make the product more appetizing. In both cases, regulators should be sensitive to the limited abilities of children and set stricter standards for kids' packaging.

Consider a Kellogg's package. One version of its Frosted Flakes package shows the familiar Tony Tiger on the front panel along with a photo of Dale Earnhardt with both presenting the front cover of *Racing for Kids* magazine. Splashed over the magazine cover in multiple colors is, "3 Free Issues." Below it, much smaller white print reads, "with a 1-year subscription." To summarize, parents can order a year's subscription to the magazine for $19.95 and get 3 issues free. Kids are likely to request the cereal because they believe they are getting 3 free issues, unaware this may commit their parents to a modest expense. Parents might not notice until they get the box home at which point they either have to spend the money or disappoint the kids. This is not a pleasant position to be put in and one that won't endear parents to the producer whose package made the offer less than clear. In this case, both parents and children might feel deceived.

The Federal Trade Commission is concerned with "unfair or deceptive acts or practices in commerce," but how deceptive do a package's graphics have to be to attract the attention of this regulator? Regrettably, there is no Children's Packaging Review Unit, as there is a Children's Advertising Review Unit, to monitor kids' packaging and encourage a higher degree of honesty among packagers of kids' products.

Conclusions: Less and Better Kids' Packaging Needed

When it comes to packaging for kids there appears to be an abundance of relatively poor packaging. It's not that producers of consumer goods don't see the package as important in the marketing mix, and it's not that they don't realize a properly designed package will add to the bottom line. They do. Manufacturers frequently attempt to give new life to flagging products by redesigning the package; thus suggesting that an effective package may even be the heartbeat of a successful product. Snapple beverages is a case in point. It recently redesigned its containers by adopting a woodcut style that plays up the beverage's natural ingredients.

This discussion of packaging for children's products—which is also packaging for parents in most cases—may have obscured the fact that good packages do exist. Which ones are good, great, or outstanding is naturally debatable since packaging has to meet the requirements of several players—producers, channel members, and consumers—and perform several functions. The net result, though, is that a good deal of kids packaging ends up being a compromise that isn't very satisfying to anyone.

For sure, licensed characters, building-block lettering, bright colors, and premium offers do not make a kids' package, although these attributes may certainly make a package more inviting to kids. Graphics also offer a convenient opportunity to provide children with play features such as on-pack games and cut-out toys—but a "one-need" package doesn't cut it. **Infavoidance**—the need to avoid humiliation—and **harmavoidance**—the need to avoid pain—are also important to children, and packaging that isn't easy for little hands to handle or open and close is sure to produce parent/child conflicts.

All the play satisfaction does not have to come from graphics. Packages that convert to play items after their contents are depleted can do a great job of satisfying the play need. And of course, a premium inside a package is treasure most kids seek. The Fun Feast line of frozen kids' meals offers various premiums, such as a set of stickers kids can put in a notebook to produce a "flip" cartoon. Finally, the product itself can be a source of play—fun to eat, fun to drink, fun to use.

A package with "kidized" graphics and lots of play value may still receive low marks if it not easy to open, easy to close. In this era of Post-It notes that stick to virtually anything over and over, surely packagers can add resealability to a kids' package—parents insist on it, according to industry research noted earlier. Nabisco's Oreo package would not receive passing marks because it cannot be opened or closed effectively in spite of the rapid deterioration of this particular product that occurs when exposed to humid air. Yet, this same company places another favorite kid's

> *The terms **Infavoidance** and **Harmavoidance** are contrivances of Henry Murray, the noted motivational psychologist of the 1930s and 40s. Because of his popularity, these terms are commonly use in psychology literature and can be found in marketing literature, as well.*

cookie, Chips Ahoy!, in a package that is easy to open, easy to close, and even possesses an easy open-close inner package. With additional kid-oriented graphics and play value, the Chips Ahoy! package could be even more of a kid-pleaser.

The salty snack people could take some lessons from the Chips Ahoy! package. A recent Chee-tos cheese snacks bag from Frito-Lay was dressed up in an eye-catching orange, red, and black color combination with Chester Cheetah beckoning. Disney's Dalmatian puppies surrounded the package window revealing the yummy, crunchy, cheese snacks inside. The bag was also blanketed by an ad for Disney's *101 Dalmatians* movie and an offer for a free *Disney Adventures* magazine. Wow! All that "kidized" graphics on a single bag, but regrettably a bag that was an open-at-risk-of-spoiling-because-you-can't-close-it bag. What a letdown for little kids and their moms who pay more than $3.50/pound for this very perishable product. And what a great kids' bag it could be with all those fun graphics if it only had a simple open/close feature.

Look at ready-to-eat cereal boxes and compare the brands primarily targeted to kids with those primarily targeted to adults. What's the difference? There isn't any.

Perhaps some of the best packages around that target kids are the boxes some fast-food restaurants use for their kids' meals. Their graphics are typically very eye-catching, the box usually has games such as mazes or word puzzles, not to mention the treasured premium inside. The boxes can be re-used, seem to open and close easily, and usually come equipped with a handle suitable for little hands. They may also contain coupons and contests. But not all fast-food firms use these packages. Some opt for bags with little or no kid appeal, and the food they carry is often wrapped in plain paper instead of "kidized" paper. A couple of years ago, one fast-food executive responded to comments like these by saying, "You gotta watch the costs. Packaging can kill you." It must be true. That chain appears to be dying.

It doesn't take a category leader to come up with a solution. Tropicana put a screw-cap on its half-gallon juice cartons that makes them easier for kids to use compared with its previous typical coated paperboard spouts. The original leader in frozen and chilled juices, Minute Maid, somehow ignored Tropicana's easy-use package for a long time, but finally introduced a similar package. While neither package has much kid-appeal graphics, both moms and kids appreciate the easy-pour, easy-close spouts. Who knows, maybe milk packagers will take notice of these juice packages.

In closing, lest it be thought no one in the dairy industry is paying attention to the gallon-jug dilemma, the American Dairy Association & Dairy Council Mid East has recently developed, licensed, and shown a new milk package for kids. If milk processors adopt it, it will be a giant step forward in the milk industry's efforts to target and satisfy kids. It is an attractively labeled 12-ounce, fit-a-kid's-hand, resealable plastic container of various flavored lowfat milks under the brand, Moo Koolers, available in 4-packs. It is an all-around good example of what a kid package can be, and I hope retailers and parents will see it as I do, as the greatest thing from the industry since pasteurized milk. Maybe, just maybe, the milk industry will become the leader rather than the laggard in kids' packaging.

CHAPTER 17

Brands: Kids' Best Friends

MYTH: "Children change brands often and show little brand loyalty."

REALITY: Children find security in attaching themselves to an object—a pillow, a blanket, a store, a brand—that enhances their well-being. But children's curiosity has not yet been suppressed as ours often has, so they do turn their attention to other objects including other brands.

A recent issue of *Advertising Age* magazine featured the headline: "Hardees debuts $100 mil in ads to rebuild brand." The article describes how Hardees Food Systems, the fourth-largest burger chain behind Wendy's, Burger King, and McDonald's, is reinventing its brand name by spending a fortune on associating the name with "hometown values." In effect, giving itself an identity.

The problem for Hardees, and many other major brands, is that it got so caught up in the race that it forgot the name on its jersey. It just kept fighting harder, running faster, and constantly keeping its eyes on the runners around it, and rarely on itself. Therefore, it did not realize the name on its jersey was obscured—by the many sponsors' names worn on it, by the many product names worn on it, and by the mud kicked up by other runners—and becoming unclear to the cheering fans in the stand. In fact, Hardees did not seem to understand that many cheers were for the little gifts it and other runners threw to the crowd in Mardi Gras fashion, and not for the runners themselves. Most of all, it forgot that consumers, and particularly those millions of kids just learning to be consumers, relate to a firm through its name—through the meanings associated with its brand name.

The name is fame. Burger King has its Burger King Kids Club that constantly keeps it name before kids, and McDonald's playgrounds are a natural part of the restaurants that associates the firm with kids. Hardees has nothing comparable. Through many promotions, it identifies itself with popular names in the entertainment field—just as Burger King and McDonald's do—but without something meaningful for kids to hold on to, and the kids never learn who it really is. Hardees is an acquaintance rather than a friend.

What Hardees has been doing is reminiscent of what Burger King did in the 1970s and 1980s—varying management, varying products, varying messages and obscuring its name, its identity. But it is clear that Burger King today has a handle on its problems and is doing a great job of growing customers from childhood with relationships it builds through its kids club. Hardees should take a cue before it spends $100 million to buy an identity, and carefully plan to spend a portion forming a brand relationship with kids.

When Do Relationships with Brands Begin and How Do They Grow?

When do children start relationships with brands? My research suggests that children begin to relate to brands—names, symbols, characters, colors—during infancy when parents introduce them to the concept. Hence, when children begin talking, they begin asking for things by brand name; when they begin walking, they begin taking things from store shelves by brand name.

It's understandable. By the time babies' eyes can follow their drool down to their chest, they find a brand name there such as Baby B'gosh. That's how they begin to identify themselves. When mom feeds them prepared baby food, she is almost sure to show them the baby picture on the Gerber jar. When toddlers receive their first transition food, from soft to solid, there's a good chance it will come out of a big yellow box of Cheerios. Mom may even take her baby's fingers, move them over the lettering on the box, and say soothingly, "Cheeeeriooos." And when junior heads for his first day of school, Mom is likely to make sure his new crayons are in that familiar yellow and green Crayola box, just like hers were. Brands marketers have a lot to thank mothers for.

By the median age of 24 months, most children are treating brands as objects. They can be heard to say, "I want my Trix." Thus, brands become an identification tool for children just as the names of their brothers and sisters do. Somewhere around this time, parents begin placing their little ones in front of the TV set at cartoon time, which nowadays is just about anytime. To their amazement, their 2-year-old is likely to shout with glee when she spots a favorite brand in a commercial. She is likely to do the same thing in the supermarket when in the presence of the product's package, particularly if it is at her eye-level.

Such connections confirm brands as a familiar part of the children's personal world and allow them to expand their world to include TV programs and commercials. Understanding the ad as an ad is too abstract at this age, but seeing the yellow Cheerios box in another context is actually comforting—"there's my Cheerios," they are likely to sense.

Somewhere between 3 and 4 years of age, children begin evaluating brands—seeing one brand of cereal or soft drink as better than another. The locus of these standards usually lies outside the individual child, but they are claimed as his or hers. However, some of the value assigned to a brand by children seems related to the length of their association with the brand. The longer the child has known about and experienced the brand, the more favorable the evaluations attached to it. This sounds like brand loyalty, and may very well be, but it may also be a part of children's egotism that shows up around this time. That is, it may be, "I use this brand; therefore, it must be better than the brands I don't use." Swiss child psychologist Jean Piaget might describe this behavior as: "The moon follows me around." Do you remember thinking that?

● ● ● ● ● ● ● ●
By the median age of 24 months, most children are treating brands as objects. They can be heard to say, "I want my Trix."

By the time a child enters school, brands take on an additional attribute—i.e., objects in the domain of other people. Hence, another person can be identified with a brand and a brand can be identified with a person, which may make the person and/or brand good, even great. For example, if friend P likes brand O, such as Nintendo games, and our subject, Q, likes P, this automatically enhances brand O in Q's eyes. We don't know if this is exactly the reasoning process that takes place, but it looks that way from a research standpoint. What is apparent, however, is that children may associate brands with significant persons and exchange attributes between the two.

Brands can also take on certain meanings through their association with particular individuals—Michael Jordan can enhance and expand the meaning of the Nike or Wheaties brand to children. Brands also give additional meanings to the people who have or consume them—children see other children who wear Nike's or eat Wheaties as exceedingly athletic. This pattern speaks to the power of brands, a power children understand and reflect in their brand consumption behavior.

In a proprietary study of elementary school children's attitudes towards athletic shoes, one part asked the children to: "Draw what comes to your mind when you think about running shoes." A typical result was a drawing of a shoe with a brand name on it, and in almost two-thirds of cases, a number representing a professional athlete. (We thought at first the numbers, such as 77 and 88, might be prices, but what do adults know?!) Thus, the children paired the two in their minds—brands and athletes—probably, in this case, as television advertising and sports programming taught them.

The meanings a brand user receives from a brand cannot be overstated when it comes to children. Remember, they are 3-footers in a 6-foot world and are looking for opportunities to "grow six inches in six months" as an old comic book ad used to promise. Brands that make them cool, make them stand out in a crowd, and give them definition may be sought at almost any price, including the willingness to offend their parents.

These abilities (attributes) of brands are important to children because of their "double whammy" effect, illustrated in **Figure 17-1**. The consumption of certain brands can intrinsically and extrinsically enhance self-concept. By wearing, eating, drinking, playing with brand X, an individual communicates with himself and transfers the socially attributed meanings of brand X to himself. For example, owning a Barbie doll, or even several, can confirm to a little girl that she is what Barbie is—cool, knowing, on her way up, attractive. By showing Barbie to others, to an audience of peers, she is communicating with that audience that she and the Barbie brand are associated with the standard of cool. Of course, this only works if the meaning of the Barbie brand is common knowledge, so the audience will transfer that socially attributed meaning to the person who displays it. When they are, however, they enhance the self-concept. No wonder children wear brand names like a badge.

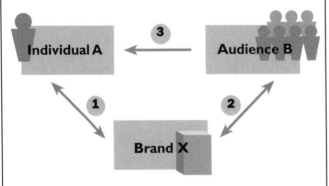

How Consumption of Brands by Children Intrinsically and Extrinsically Enhance the Self-Concept

1. By use of Brand X, an individual communicates with himself and transfers the socially attributed meanings of Brand X to himself.

2. By presenting Brand X to Audience B, the individual is communicating with them that he and Brand X are associated.

3. If Brand X has a commonly understood meaning, Audience B will transfer the socially attributed meanings of it to person A who displayed it. Thus, the self-concept of Individual A is enhanced again.

FIGURE 17-1

Whether as objects, identifiers, or standards, brands play a major role in children's lives. At any point in time, a number of brands have high value to them. Consequently, kids will try to hold on to them, call them "my" and "mine," and appear to be brand-loyal to them. In effect, brands become good friends. Frequently during their doodling, children may draw certain brand names, their symbols, or parts of them. Many even decorate their rooms with brands —NFL, Pepsi-Cola, Tony Tiger. Whatever we call this— brand loyalty, brand preference, brand affinity, brand fixation, or just simply brand consciousness—the businesses that own those brands should be elated, for such responses could mark the birth of a lifetime customer.

Licensed brands—characters, persons, and products that a firm may lease or buy—have taken on a life of their own as instant brands. Buying or licensing a brand permits a producer of a product to get instant recognition for it. What once was mainly a way of selling one more T-shirt is now a $70 billion-a-year business with at least 30 percent in the kids market.

Probably no licensed brands have more recognition among children than those of Disney, and they just keep coming because Disney and its licensees know they can make a product an overnight success. Disney movie characters such as The Lion King and Pocahontas have helped Burger King sell countless kids' meals and action figures. Fred Flintstone, from Turner Home Entertainment, has pleased children with vitamins, hotel rooms at Days Inn, all kinds of toys, and of course television programs, and he is now on the hoods of NASCAR racing cars. Interestingly, ordinary product brands such as Crayola, Barbie, and Hershey also generate sales when applied to clothing and bedding, for instance.

The drawing in **Figure 17-2** indicates how preoccupied children can be with brands. When asked to, "Draw what comes to your mind when you think about going shopping," a 9-year-old girl penciled this shopping setting. Notice the prominence of a brand name, Esprit. Not once, not twice, but three times she displays this rather complicated word, for a 9-year-old, on store offerings, and then she even wraps it around her own shirt. Moreover, she illustrates it exactly as the brand owner does! And then, bless her heart, she misspells "shirts" and "skirts" and writes "shrits" and "skrits." (If only her teacher could be an advertiser!) A researcher cannot avoid viewing these errors as significant from an information processing standpoint. They clearly suggest that a brand name may get more emotional treatment in children's minds than common words such as the generic name of the product that the brand name represents.

• • • • • • • •
A brand name may get more emotional treatment in children's minds than common words such as the generic name of the product that the brand name represents.

FIGURE 17-2

Some Theoretical Considerations of Brand Consciousness

Consumer behavior theory provides some concepts related to the storage and retrieval of brands and how the resulting cognition ultimately determines what brands consumers buy, including children. These constructs help explain young consumers' responses to brands—brand names and brand-related symbols, terms, colors, and sounds. Let me briefly describe these notions because they have major implications for brand marketers, producers, and retailers who might choose to target kids with products and stores.

• • • • • •
By the time children enter first grade, they appear to carry around 200 brands in their repertoire.

Brand Repertoire. The brand repertoire consists of all brands of all products with which a consumer is familiar.

Brand Awareness Set. This concept embraces all brands that the consumer is aware of within a product category.

Evoked Set. The evoked set consists of the few brands a consumer will consider when making a purchase within a product category.

Inept Set. This group is made up of the brands a consumer rejects from purchase consideration.

Inert Set. This set is all the brands in a particular product category a consumer is unsure whether to consider for purchase.

It is believed the **brand repertoire** of an average adult consumer holds about 1500 brands, while that of a 10-year-old may hold 300-400 brands. Most of the early entries are put there by promotion by parents who first introduce their children to brands of foods and beverages, then to play items and clothing items, describing them with positive adjectives not unlike an effective advertisement. By the time children enter first grade, they appear to carry around 200 brands in their repertoire—learned from parents, promotions, and peers—and at this point the curve turns up fast.

As with any mentally stored collection, the majority of brands is held in the subconscious while only a small percent is held at-ready. This skill of storing away "unneeded" things develops so early in childhood that it appears instinctive. The theory is that brands are organized in the mind according to product categories, and numerous studies bear this out. Therefore, when a child considers a purchase request for a soft drink, for example, the mental machinery goes to the soft-drink group and chooses among the most favored brands—those in the **evoked set**—those worthy of consideration at purchase time. "Be sure and get some Cokes when you go to the store," we may hear a young consumer say to her mother, "They're my favorite."

Brands deemed unworthy of consideration when making a purchase—those in the **inept set**—are familiar, but usually receive no attention. They get no consideration because they were at one time given consideration and did not prove satisfying. Thus, experience directs the mind to place certain brands in the "recycle bin." In a focus group, children were asked how they would describe a brand of canned meat product, and one youngster quickly shouted, "Yuck!"—a good one-word description of brands in children's inept set.

There is another set of brands within the brand awareness set of children, the **inert set**, that also receive little or no consideration. This isn't because children don't like them, but because they know little about them and are unsure about them. Often, these are brands irregularly promoted to children, perhaps because of limited budgets. Children may have heard of them or seen them, but have few feelings about them—"Don't like it; don't dislike it," is how they might describe a member of this brand set.

A purchase, then, almost always comes from the set of brands in the evoked set, probably two or three in each product category. There is little reason to buy brands in the inept set. Likewise, there is not much motivation to buy a virtually unknown brand in the inert set except out of curiosity or when evoked-set brands aren't available.

Consumer-behavior theory holds that a measurable distance exists among the few brands in an evoked set. This is often called **psychological distance**, and represents differences in liking for brands as might be determined on an attitudinal scale. For example, a particular young consumer may rate Pepsi-Cola number one in her evoked set, and Coca-Cola may be a close number two, while number three, Dr. Pepper, falls farther down the list. This ranking suggests that Pepsi-Cola always gets first consideration and is purchased most of the time by this young consumer. Coke typically receives quite a bit of consideration and some purchase, perhaps depending on value-added promotions or premiums, such as a trading card with each unit purchase, which serve to narrow the distance between number one and number two. Dr. Pepper receives occasional consideration and purchase, maybe in response to an ad targeting children that suggests Dr. Pepper is fun for a change, which may temporarily reduce the distance between number two and number three.

As children switch among brands in their evoked sets, they may give the impression they are not very brand loyal. Also, their natural curiosity may cause them to explore brands in their inert sets more than adults do.

> • • • • • •
> *As with any mentally stored collection, the majority of brands is held in the subconscious.*

This activity may further suggest a lack of brand loyalty to the uninformed. It is important to note, however, that most brands outside the evoked set—the vast majority of brands—get relatively little consideration. Therefore, it is imperative for marketers to position their brands in the evoked set, preferably in the number one or two position.

While we know relatively little about the way children store and retrieve brand sets, we believe that locating a brand in a favorable location in a child's mind works the same way as it does among adults. The child must hold a favorable view of the brand. They must like it because of a satisfying experience—not necessarily their own, but perhaps that of their parents or best friends. They must be frequently reminded of the brand since they are easily distracted by messages about any potentially satisfying product.

Adults and children alike give brands favorable positions in their minds (evoked sets) according to the brand's beneficial attributes, but what is beneficial to children and to adults are two different things. For example, the sugar content of a soft drink may be very important to children, but a negative attribute to adults. The play need is more important to children, whereas the affiliation need may be equally important to kids and adults. Both groups may give more favorable ratings to brands endorsed by role models, but who these role models are is likely to differ.

It is logically difficult to successfully market an adult-associated brand to children, e.g., *Newsweek* magazine, Citibank, or Buick, and expect them to welcome it into their evoked sets. The brand should clearly have at least the appearance of being for kids, for example, *Newsweek for Kids* or KidVisa—neither of which exist to my knowledge. In fact, it is theoretically easier to market a kid-oriented brand to adults, e.g., Disney or Frosted Flakes, than an adult brand to kids, since adults were kids, but kids have not been adults.

Once children place a brand in their evoked set, it is likely to stay there for life. Even if they do not purchase it in adulthood—although they probably will for their own children—they still have fond memories of it, and it will remain in their evoked set, providing the same sense of security and belonging that it did in their childhood.

Perhaps equally important to marketers, the brands in kids' evoked sets also tend to enter parents' evoked sets. These are brands parents have bought for children, brands children buy with their own money, and brands children proclaim as good and preferred. Theorists may not want to call the mind cell where parents hold their children's preferred brands an evoked set

● ● ● ● ● ● ● ●
Once children place a brand in their evoked set, it is likely to stay there, for life.

since this term is intended to refer specifically to parents' own preferred brands. But it seems appropriate since most parents know their kids' favorite brands, want to buy them for their kids, and usually enjoy doing it. For example, parents tell us they often buy for home the soft-drink brands their children most prefer.

We noted in an earlier myth-reality discussion that parents spend somewhere around $300 billion annually based on the indirect influence of their children. Much of this spending goes for brands that parents know children like. Since the notion of evoked set is only a hypothetical construct anyway, it seems useful to think of a sub-evoked set in parents' minds that contains their children's preferred brands. Perhaps we could term it the "evokked" set, with the extra "k" representing kids. If this is the case, the products might not only be requested by children, they will get a warmer response from parents.

When children make requests for things from the supermarket, slightly over 90 percent are by brand name.

Store Brands vs. National Brands

Store brands have gained in popularity during recent recessional years due to their economic appeal and to retailers' improved merchandising. Since children learn a lot of consumer behavior from their parents, we figured that children would possess some likes/dislikes regarding store brands. So we went into supermarkets and asked mothers with children aged 14 and under about their purchases of national and store brands and the influence of their children on these purchases. We assumed that asking questions in the supermarket about branded products would help to stimulate consumers' thoughts about them.

The first question qualified moms as store brand buyers—65 percent were willing store-brand buyers. Next, we asked, "When your children make requests for things from the supermarket, how often do they do it by brand name?" Answer: Slightly over 90 percent of children's requests are by brand name.

The concepts of national brand and store brand were explained briefly, and we asked, "When your children request things from the supermarket by brand name, how often do they ask for national brands?" Response: The children requested national brands 82 percent of the time. The other 18 percent consisted of requests for products without mentioning brand names, such as "Get some strawberries," or requests for store brands.

Last, we asked, "When your children request things from the super-market by brand name, how often do they request store brands?" Answer:

The most common response was "almost never," but about 7 percent of requests were for store brands, usually snack items.

To get beyond image and into actual use of store brands, we asked mothers two more questions. "When foods and beverages are served at home, do brands make a difference to children? If so, how much difference?" "Definitely," was a frequent response. Overall, 70 percent of moms told us brands are very important to their children's consumption of foods and beverages at home. Another 20 percent said they were somewhat important.

Mothers' reports indicate that 43 percent of children complained when store brands were served at home.

Then we asked, "If you serve store brands of foods and beverages at home, are there any complaints from your children? If so, what are they?" Mothers' reports indicated that 43 percent of children complained when store brands were served at home. One-fourth complained of a difference from national brands while actually consuming store brands; 18 percent complained even before they were served.

However, nearly half of children reportedly did not notice a difference, and 11 percent said they did not care. These figures suggest store brands are acceptable in some product categories, or at least that children don't detect differences.

Regarding the nature of children's complaints about store brands, 75 percent said in various ways that store brands were poor quality compared with national brands, while the rest said they did not like particular store brands because others, peers or role models, did not like them. "He wants his sandwiches made out of a good brand of bread just like his father does," was one mother's remark.

Sometimes national brands vs. store brands result in mother vs. child debates. One single mom told us, " I buy three or four kinds of cereal. Most of it's for my son, Wayne. I don't buy store brands much, but I've started buying two kinds of Kroger cereal because it's a lot cheaper. I don't think there's much of a difference between it and the big brands. For instance, Kroger sells a cereal that's just like Cheerios. I can't tell the difference. But Wayne says he can, and says he doesn't like to eat the Kroger cereal. I told him maybe he ought to go hungry once in a while. He'd eat it then."

This particular research effort was conducted among parents rather than children in the belief we would get a truer measure of children's influence on parental purchases of supermarket brands. It does not prove children understand the concept of store brands; only that they generally do not respond as positively to them as they do national brands. What seems clear is that children hold preferences for brands that are advertised and brands that significant others own and use. The notion of store brands vs. national brands may not even exist in children's minds; only brands in general.

Is the opposite true? That is, if store brands regularly advertised and promoted to children, would children be more aware of them and demonstrate greater preference for them—particularly since their parents probably like and buy some store brands? The answer is not in the study presented here, yet it does seem apparent. If store brands were more visible in children's world, some would likely become more desirable. After all, parents in this study reported that 46 percent of children did not detect a difference between store and national brands served at home. Another 11 percent did not care.

If many consumer behavior patterns are set in childhood as we believe they are, store brands could easily benefit in the future by targeting more marketing communications to children today. Supermarkets are the first stores most children visit. They are the place most children make their first in-store requests to parents and first independent product selections. Such a relationship certainly would facilitate a marketing strategy targeted to kids. In-school marketing programs, for example, in which supermarket personnel introduce children to store brands and their benefits—low price, good quality—seem logical. Few supermarkets, however, exhibit any signs of making a strategic push for the youth market through their own brands. National brands that are increasingly concerned about the incursion of store labels can take solace in the fact that they still own the kids.

Few supermarkets exhibit any signs of making a strategic push for the youth market through their own brands.

A Closing Note Regarding the Value of Developing Brand Loyalty in Childhood

Research offers mixed signals regarding brand loyalty today. Whether it is suffering a general decline or on the increase, almost every marketer thinks it is desirable and something to cultivate. Specifically, a firm should attempt to develop brand loyalty among its customers to get a greater "share of the customer" and greater "lifetime revenue" from each customer.

By targeting kids, brand marketers increase their chances for a greater share of each customer's business later in life. Brand preference is more foundational when formed in childhood—resulting in greater lifetime revenue. It has been suggested, for example, that lifetime revenue from one customer for a pizza company—retailer or producer—might be $8,000. Since it is relatively easy for a pizza marketer to develop a relationship with children, this target of $8,000 should be manageable.

Also, as noted, when a firm develops a brand loyal relationship with kids, there is a good chance the brand will enter parents' evoked set, too. Parents may complain that the brands their children prefer are too expensive, too fattening, or contain too much sugar, for example, but they probably buy those brands for their children, and only those brands, to please them. That's the way most parents are.

In a recent issue of *Brandweek*, Jacques Chevron, who has his own brand development firm, ponders the development of brands and how they come about. He notes: "After many decades of marketing, of academic papers and of smart thinking on the subject of branding, we still do not have an agreed upon recipe for creating a brand." I agree with him in principle, particularly when he defines a brand as he does. He says a brand is "a covenant with the customer." In other words, a brand is a promise of performance, a statement of reliability. It is what facilitates the shopping experience by trusting that brands selected last time will be of the same nature and quality this time.

> **● ● ● ● ●**
> *Brand is a common concept among children, and they rely on it implicitly to deliver a product as described in marketing communications and interpersonal communications with parents and peers.*

Where I disagree somewhat with Chevron, recognizing he is the branding expert, is his belief that we still do not have a recipe for creating a brand—creating covenants between customer and company. I think we have at least a general recipe, and these past few pages describe it. Brand is a common concept among children, and they rely on it implicitly to deliver a product as described in marketing communications and interpersonal communications with parents and peers. It is not unlike a child's best friend. When the child hears its name, he knows what to expect. These expectations and this trust is the foundation of a brand.

To accomplish this covenant, brand marketing must start with children. Even if, the child does not buy the product and will not for many years— AT&T services, IBM computers, Sears appliances—the marketing must begin in childhood to reach the critical level of relationship necessary for a brand to survive. This is what Coca Cola and McDonald's, for example, have been doing throughout their histories. They survive today despite the torrential competition from Pepsi Cola, Burger King and many others because their covenants are well established with their once and future customers. That is a recipe for successful branding.

CHAPTER 18

Successful Kids' Products and Services: Satisfying Kids and Their Parents

MYTH: "Kids love products that are just like Mom's and Dad's."

REALITY: Kids love products that are just like Mom's and Dad's, but not as much as they love products just for kids.

MYTH: "If your kid's product can only satisfy one need, let it be the need for play."

REALITY: If your product for kids can only satisfy one need, shoot it and put it out of its misery.

MYTH: "Satisfy the kids, and you satisfy the parents."

REALITY: Children loved their free Mystic Magic Magnifiers, but parents hated the burned holes in their curtains and tablecloths.

When we think of products for kids, we usually think of sweet things and play things. These two categories make up the largest expenditures kids make with their own money, but constitute only a small portion of the total number of products kids buy or want to buy. Today, virtually every adult consumer good from seeds to soap has been scaled down and funned up to suit children.

Figure 18-1 was drawn by a fourth-grader asked to: "Draw what comes to your mind when you think about going shopping." In effect, what the child is saying in the drawing is this: "I like to go shopping Saturday mornings at the

FIGURE 18-1

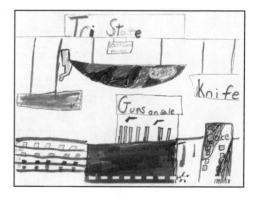

local sporting-goods store, get a Coke from the machine, and look at hunting and fishing equipment. I can either buy things with my own money, such as a knife or some shotgun shells, or ask my dad to buy something for me such as a rod-and-reel combination or a rifle." This youngster is keenly aware of the adult products he can buy or ask his parents to buy. He knows, too, from reading his own magazines, for example, that many of these products are just for him.

• • • • • •
Businesses appear to follow a pattern of sorts when they enter the kid market.

Businesses appear to follow a pattern of sorts when they enter the kid market. First, one or more executives of a firm hear about the increasingly attractive market potential of the children's market and investigate it. In quest of more revenue, they extend an existing product to this market by scaling it down and adding fun to its package and/or brand name. Often the "new" product or brand targeted to children is only a slight variation of the original, and the brand name is modified simply by adding the words, "for kids," and putting them in building-block lettering or other type face that suggests "kidness"—for example, Kleenex for Kids or Pert Plus for Kids. Some firms go so far as to make the word "kid" a more integral part of the brand name, such as Duncan Hines Kids Cups (cupcake mix) and Hormel Kid's Kitchen (microwave meals). There. They're in the kid market with a kid product.

Many initial forays into the kid market are merely superficial changes in adult products made by decision makers with no experience in this market except, perhaps, that they are marents—marketers who are also parents and therefore feel they have special insights. Consequently, of the thousands of new products introduced in the past decade, most have not succeeded. It appears, in fact, that the failure rate of new products for kids is much greater than that for adult products. That is, a greater number of products for kids fail to meet their stated financial goals such as revenue, market share, and return on investment.

The three myths stated above are probably responsible for most of the product failures or near failures in the kid market. We will examine each in detail, for they are preventing success, costing businesses millions of dollars every year, and most important, creating much dissatisfaction among children and parents.

Scaled-Down, Funned-Up Adult Products are Risky

There probably is not a little girl who hasn't tried on her mother's dresses or little boy who hasn't put on his father's shirts or trousers. Kids are role players, imitators, dreamers. They frequently make probes into the adult world by trying out available adult products. Parents encourage their children to play "grown-up," as long as it doesn't hurt anyone or anything.

Toy tools, child-sized furniture, and press-on earrings are ways for children to be like adults without the unpleasant repercussions of getting into Mom's nail polish. Fisher-Price and Playskool are just two of the many companies making a living from adult-like products for kids. In fact, the long-term success of toy replicas of adult products has probably inspired many other producers of adult products to jump into the kids market with various diminutive analogs. This doesn't mean it's always the easiest or best way to go.

Whether it is lack of experience in the children's market, lack of appropriate research, or the fact that some adult products are simply unappealing to kids when scaled down for them, the plain fact of the matter is that many adult-to-kid products—toys, foods, newspapers, toiletries, clothing—have failed. This is ironic since marketers usually perceive this route as a low-risk way to enter the kid market.

I think a major problem with these products is that they tend to be highly discretionary items. They have a novelty appeal to children and parents. As long as times are good, parents indulge their kids. But if economic conditions get a bit gloomy, parents stop buying products labeled "for kids" except maybe on sale. Instead, they buy only the regular products—the ones for adults, so to speak—often at a lower unit cost.

For example, back in the late 1980s, major producers of frozen meals spun off scaled-down versions for kids. ConAgra introduced Kid Cuisine, Tyson Foods had Looney Tunes kids meals, and Campbell offered Swanson Fun Feast meals. But during the recession that followed, most households cut back on all buying and products like these didn't stay on shopping lists. Tyson got out, while others tried to hang on to a not-too-profitable, not-too-distinctive, "peas in a pod" kid category. These $2 meals were essentially copies of $2 adult frozen meals that most kids did not scream for and most parents did not look for. Other adult-to-kids products that fall into the discretionary category and are vulnerable to changes in economic conditions include toiletries such as toothpaste, shampoo, and soap, as well as facial tissue, bottled water, garden seeds, and computer hardware.

Now that the economy has recovered, we might expect these types of products for kids to fare better. But Americans came out of the last recession with a more permanent sense of value-consciousness, which doesn't bode

● ● ● ● ● ● ● ● ●
The failure rate of new products for kids is much greater than that for adult products.

well for "kidized" products. Also, adults somehow feel kids' products should cost less than their adult counterparts. To the extent this is not true, producers should be prepared to demonstrate their products have added value for kids. Saying a bar soap smells good to kids and makes them wash more is not likely to justify a unit cost as high as or even higher than that of adult analogs.

Some industries face an even greater uphill battle than toiletries do. The health industry is beginning to target children with a wide range of "products" ranging from healthy lifestyles to specific medicines. But health is an evasive concept to most children; it's not something they are looking for or hounding Mom to buy. For example, several nonprofit (as well as for-profit) organizations have been trying without much success to "sell" children on the notion of eating five servings of fruits and vegetables every day. So far the results indicate this task is five times as difficult as "selling" them on the idea of eating one serving a day—that is, in many cases, a practically impossible job. The health industry seems to feel children will do something that's good for them if they understand its benefits, like ask their parents to take them to get shots. Sure. It's hard enough to get adults to do things that are good for them.

Over-the-counter medicines, which receive more marketing expertise, do a better job of designing some products for kids, mostly because they take advantage of their ability to mimic candy forms. Dimetapp has introduced Get Better Bear Sore Throat Pops, which look promising. They are essentially bear-shaped lollipops that incorporate symptom relief for sore throats. A similar product, Cough Pops from CoughCo, offers children zinc-based suckers to deal with cold symptoms, while Quigley Corporation puts cold symptom relief in Cold-Eeze Bubble Gum. Such products go far beyond "for kids" remedies that have been around for years by adding play and sentience to their offerings. Yet they are only baby steps for this sleeping giant.

The "Kidness" Scale

The biggest problem with many adult products for kids is that they don't do much for kids. In fact, they may offer a higher degree of satisfaction to parents than children. Parents usually are delighted when their preschoolers emulate them by wanting tools like Dad has in his workshop or makeup like Mom wears. These actions signify maturity to parents who usually like children to act older than they are. It's a salute to parenthood.

> • • • • • •
> **The health industry seems to feel children will do something that's good for them if they understand its benefits, like ask their parents to take them to get shots.**

Parents also view such products as something beyond play items. They see them as teaching tools by introducing children to adult activities such as cooking and housecleaning. Children are well aware that "helping" behavior makes their parents happy. Consequently, some of the oohs and aahs children express when they receive them as gifts may be intended to patronize parents, rather than just demonstrate their own happiness with the gifts. This isn't to say kids don't truly enjoy their "lawn mowers" and "vacuum cleaners." Indeed, very young children are often adamant about helping Mom around the house to the extent they get in the way. Often, by the time they are big enough to really help, they've lost interest.

I often view products for kids on a scale from A to K, from adultness to kidness, like that shown in **Figure 18-2**. At the A end of the scale are products strictly for adults such as life insurance and tobacco. One notch away from the A end are banking, newspapers, eye glasses, prunes, and garden tools, as examples. As we move a bit more along the scale toward the K end, we might find clothing, luggage and computer hardware, among other things.

Somewhere around the middle of the scale are all the scaled-down, funned-up adult products—miniature power tools, washing machines, and telephones that make satisfying sounds but do not actually work—as well

• • • • • •
The biggest problem with many adult products for kids is that they don't do much for kids.

A Continuum Scale of Products Ranging from Adults-Only to Kids-Only

ADULTS ONLY		MOST PRODUCTS FOR KIDS			KIDS ONLY
A					K
Life Insurance	Banking	Clothing	Toy Tools	Dolls	Bubble Gum
Automobiles	Newspapers	Computer	Magazines	Candy Bars	Novelty Candy
Tobacco	Garden Tools	Luggage	Toiletries	Fruit Drinks	Toys

FIGURE 18-2

---

as toiletries, magazines, fresh fruits, and many hobby items. Further along toward the K end are traditional kids' products such as dolls, candy bars, and fruit-flavored soft drinks—things that still retain a vestige of appeal to adults. At the very K end of the scale are bubble gum, novelty candy, and the most uniquely kid-oriented toys, including the gross and grotesque. One way to "test" how far along something is on the K end of the scale is to gauge the extent to which adults are described as "childish" when they buy, use or consume them.

Generally speaking, the closer a product is to the K end of the scale, the more children will desire it. Naturally, the exact spot a product occupies on the scale varies by children's age, gender, cultural background, and so on. Research efforts such as sorting techniques and perceptual mapping can determine scale locations fairly accurately.

Moving From Adult Toward Kid

• • • • • • • •

Parents want to see their kids happy, having fun, being silly, laughing, but they also want them safe, healthy, learning, and not squandering money.

Taking the first steps of scaling down and funning up can move an extremely adult product such as a power tool or a bank account as much as halfway along the scale to a point where kids and parents are likely to desire it to some extent. Additional creative efforts can move the product even further toward the K end. For example, the Fox Kids Club might start its own bank savings accounts for kids and integrate them into its nationwide programming for kids. This bank account would be much more for kids than for adults. Kids and adults alike would acknowledge it as a product for kids. While such efforts require more investment, they are more likely to succeed with a greater return on that investment.

As another example, consider licensed characters from the perspective of the A-K scale. When we look at an array of licensed characters, we judge some to be more kid-oriented than others, although all may target kids. For example, one might sense that a tie-in with Disney's *The Lion King* or *Toy Story* possesses more kid appeal than a tie-in with Disney's *Hunchback of Notre Dame*. It would not be very difficult to test such a hypothesis, and the results could be worth a lot of money. Burger King's management appears to have perceived all offerings from Disney as equally appealing to children, but reportedly, and not surprisingly, the promotion did not do nearly as well with Hunchback as it did with Lion King.

Marketers seem to sense that a product can move toward the K end of the scale by adding what we might call "kidness," but sensing it and doing it are two different things. Jell-O gelatin, for instance, has done a good job of taking a product traditionally positioned as an inexpensive adult dessert and turned it into a product kids like and request. The canned-pasta industry has excelled in redesigning and repositioning for kids to the point that the products are viewed more as kids' products than adults'. Originally these products were directed at "working men."

Some products require more creative redesigning and repositioning. Fresh fruits such as apples, oranges, and bananas have inherent appeal to kids due to their colors and flavors and even their potential messiness, so kids accept them to some extent without much positioning effort. Dried fruits, on the other hand, tend to look unappealing. They have not succeeded in overcoming this obstacle to draw in the kid market. Sun-Maid raisins, for instance, has made various efforts to target families and kids, but has accomplished little to overcome kids' resistance to the product. In fact, most marketers in the fruit and vegetable category take the nutrition approach and rely on parents to make kids eat the stuff. Such efforts won't move these products closer to the K end of the scale.

One shining exception breaks this rule. Fruit snacks completely redesign the raw product into a new, more desirable form for children. General Mills has led the way in showing a better way to market fruit to kids with its Fruit Roll-Ups and Fruit By The Foot. It has moved this product and subsequent spin-offs close to the K end of the scale. The number of me-too products from competitors is testimony to the success of the concept, a concept that should have originated with the fruit industry. Similarly, the raisin people now know a good way to sell raisins to kids is to produce and promote them in more palatable transitional forms such as candy and chocolate coatings. By pairing them with more acceptable objects such as chocolate, they move them toward the K classification. Children who like these products may grow to be more receptive to raisins in other forms.

A little of the gross and grotesque for kids goes a long way with parents.

Pleasing Kids May Mean Losing Parents

One danger of moving a product concept nearer the K end of the scale is that it may or may not please parents more. Parents want to see their kids happy, having fun, being silly, laughing, but they also want them safe, healthy, learning, and not squandering money. A little of the gross and grotesque for kids goes a long way with parents—e.g., slimy toys such as Gak, Smud, and Floam from Mattel. Likewise, adding $20 to the cost of a $10 plush animal by adding sound effects, such as Tickle Me Elmo or Sing And Snore Ernie, may please kids more with its silliness than parents who see it as a waste of money and annoying to hear over and over.

Conflicts often arise between parents and children over K products. Kids want them, but parents don't see the appeal, especially if the price tag is high. A frequent outcome is that parents agree children can buy them, but with their own money. This can obviously hamper sales, unless producers do something to create some parent appeal.

Sometimes it's possible to have a kids' product at more than one location on the A-K scale as a market segmentation strategy. Barbie dolls come to mind. Over the years, fine tuning has moved this product closer and closer to the K end of the scale. But other adjustments have moved Barbie closer and closer to the A end, too. Lots of serious doll collectors buy $150 limited-edition designer Barbies.

Another factor that helps Barbie maintain her two-tiered appeal is nostalgia. As the price of Barbie dolls and related accessories rise, parents might resist. But because it's Barbie, they might not resist as much as for similarly priced products. In the same way, parents may complain about the time their children spend glued to TV screens watching cartoons. But they may be more receptive to "The Flintstones" and "Scooby-Doo," shows they fondly remember from their youth. They may even get glued to the screen on occasion themselves.

A new approach has emerged to address the parent-child balance. "Edutainment" products educate and entertain. These learn-and-play products are often media-based, including magazines, books, video games, board games, and computer software. The question is how much education (adultness) and how much entertainment (kidness) is the right balance. In general, edutainment product features should aim toward the K end of the scale, but promotion should be directed to both parents and kids. These products are often more expensive than other K-type products, so parental approval is crucial.

I would emphasize, or re-emphasize, one more fact regarding the location of products on the A-K scale. Most parents do try very hard to please their children, to give their children most of the things they request, and in general, to try to make their children happy. Further, most parents recognize products toward the K end of the scale are most satisfying to children. Consequently, parents often bite their tongues a bit when children ask for seemingly disgusting or ridiculous things and allow the purchase to take place. In fact, when economic times are tough, these are the products that best endure. Parents seem to feel kids deserve a few moments of happiness in a not-so-happy world. So, as a rule, K- bound products provide the most satisfaction for kids' needs and the most satisfaction for parents' needs for their kids.

Kidizing Stores

Finally, while we have been concentrating on products, stores also fall on the A-K scale. This does not mean "adult" stores are automatically located on the A end of the scale and toy stores are on the K end. The opposite may be true. An auto dealership that offers premiums to kids or a bank with a play area may be positioned near the K end, while toy stores that stock

• • • • • • • •

An auto dealership that offers premiums to kids or a bank with a play area may be positioned near the K end, while toy stores that stock items out of kids' reach and display intimidating signs such as, "If you break it you buy it," may be on the A end.

items out of kids' reach and display intimidating signs such as, "If you break it you buy it," may be on the A end.

McDonald's rates highly with kids, probably much higher than say Taco Bell, but not because of its food. Kids like both burgers and tacos. McDonald's higher K rating is because it has playgrounds. In Chapter 10, we discussed what kids like about stores. The more features a store offers, the closer it will be to the K end of the scale. They include:

- Kid-friendly atmosphere;
- Offers kids products in depth;
- Eye-level accessible displays;
- Communicates with kids; and
- Others like it, namely, parents and peers.

• • • • • •
McDonald's higher K rating is because it has playgrounds.

Does it make a difference if a store places high on the K end of the A-K scale since stores are mainly for adults? It does indeed, because parents bring children with them on all kinds of errands. This is obviously even more true for stores that sell any kid-oriented products. Parents tend to choose the fast-food restaurants and mass merchandisers, for instance, that please their children.

McDonald's has been tinkering with its offerings to make its establishments more appealing to adults. It introduced new sandwiches such as the Arch Deluxe. It also gave Ronald McDonald a more adult-like personality. This shift in focus surely seems like a big mistake. The fast-food giant already has a wonderful position toward the K end of the scale as a place for kids to come with their parents. It should be taking advantage of its kid position in today's new era of the family and moving the restaurant up a notch as a family restaurant—not to the A end of the scale for dad and his golfing buddies.

Kids' Products Must Satisfy Kids' Needs

The myth that a kids' product must mainly satisfy the play need has, in part, been attributed to me. I can understand this since I have often said that children's single most important need is play. But children possess all the needs held by adults.

It is generally held that all humans harbor the same needs, although they prioritize them and express them differently depending on their age, gender, cultural background, and other individual characteristics. For the most part, children first learn to express their needs from their parents. This is one of the major reasons why children are often said to look and act "just like" their mothers or fathers. Young children imitate the need expression of adults and older kids, but often prioritize them differently.

Play—the tendency to act for fun without further purpose—probably does rank as kids' single most important need, but to say this can be very misleading to marketers whose job it is to satisfy young consumers. Children, just like adults, practice "need fusion"—that is, they are continually trying to satisfy as many needs as they can. A product that satisfies only the play need will quickly lose out compared with a product that offers more. Take, for example, a box of Crayola crayons. This one simple product can satisfy kids' needs for play, sentience, achievement, novelty, and affiliation.

FIGURE 18-3

Six most important needs of children. Ranked by age.		
0–4 YEARS	**4–8 YEARS**	**8–12 YEARS**
Sentience	Play	Affiliation
Play	Sentience	Play
Succorance	Affiliation	Achievement
Change	Achievement	Autonomy
Affiliation	Change	Sentience
Exhibition	Exhibition	Exhibition

The table in **Figure 18-3** attempts to list the half-dozen most important needs of American kids of different ages. Warning: This list is not complete and is unlikely to describe correctly the need prioritization for any individual child, particularly the child of a "marent." Furthermore, it may not apply in a general way to kids outside of the United States. But it is based on many years of studying children, and, of course, this author's willingness to stick his neck out. Brief definitions follow:

Achievement: To accomplish something difficult, something adult-like.

Affiliation: To have cooperative relationships with others such as family and peers.

Autonomy: To act independently, particularly of parents and guardians.

Change: To do new and different things.

Exhibition: To make an impression, to be seen or heard.

Play: To act strictly for fun, to be entertained, amused.

Sentience: To seek and enjoy sensuous impressions.

Succorance: To have care and sympathy from others.

The six needs listed under each age group in **Figure 18-3** have various scholarly synonyms, but I have used the descriptors here for many years; they originated with psychologist Henry Murray and his associates. The ranking here doesn't necessarily indicate the magnitude of overall need, but the frequency of need. A psychologist might say that the most important needs are those with the highest frequency of periodicity, that is, those needs that regularly repeat themselves the most.

An understanding of children's needs will provide the answers to age-old questions such as: "Why do children like to play with their food?" "Why do they prefer to shop in mass merchandisers rather than department stores?" "Why do they like Disney animated movies best?" "Why won't they come in for dinner when I repeatedly call them?" A brief description of each need from a childhood context follows in alphabetical order.

In the case of kids, doing something grown-ups do is an achievement

Achievement: This is the need to accomplish something significant, to do a difficult task well, to do things better than others, to overcome obstacles. In the case of kids, doing something grown-ups do is an achievement—for example, negotiating the checkout at Kmart, making your own Slurpee at a 7-Eleven, or preparing your own breakfast of microwaveable pancakes. Also, competing with peers and siblings is an achievement. This need usually takes on great importance when children enter elementary school, and continues to be important for the rest of their lives. We can see it in action when children fuse it with the play need and participate in sports and music, and when they enter contests. According to several studies I conducted, it is probably the most important need for Chinese children compared with number three or four for American children. The achievement need appears to be slowly growing in importance among U.S. children, as parents who worry about their children's future encourage achievement more than they did in the 1980s.

Affiliation: This is the need to have a cooperative relationship with others, to be loyal to friends, to do things with friends, to form attachments. For kids, the need to form bonds with others—with parents and peers, with brands and stores—appears early in life and continues to grow in importance. At some point, usually around age 10 or 11, it is perhaps the most important need for kids. It is the need for affiliation, often in fusion with the achievement and play needs, that causes boys and girls to group together and take on activities such as touch football.

Autonomy: This is the need to act independently, to do unconventional things, to criticize those in positions of authority, to say what one thinks, to resist restrictions. The autonomy need becomes particularly significant at around age 8 or 9 as children attempt to free themselves from the restraints of parents. The autonomy need fuses with the achievement need to produce independent achievements such as winning a one-on-one game. Together with the need for change, the autonomy need may push children to run away from home and school.

Change: The need for change is the need to explore, experiment, move from place to place, seek adventure, novelty, enjoy new sights, sounds, ideas, and things. This need is noticeable in very young children who enjoy exploring new surroundings—another child's room, another store, another brand. It fuses with the sentience need to cause children to try new flavors, sounds, sights. As noted above, it also fuses with the autonomy need in later years to cause children to avoid their home, their room, their parents.

> It is the need for affiliation, often in fusion with the achievement and play needs, that causes boys and girls to group together and take on activities such as touch football.

Exhibition: The need for exhibition is the need to be the center of attention, to ask questions others cannot answer, to have others comment about one's appearance and acts, to say witty things. This need seems important to children of all ages, toddlers to teens. At young ages, it is: "Daddy, look what I can do;" at later ages, it is: "Look at my new shirt." Advertisements that shout, "Hey kids" get attention because of this need. The exhibition need fuses with the affiliation need to produce look-alike clothing among group members, and with the autonomy and achievement needs to produce shouts of joy from winning a game or some other accomplishment.

Play: The need for play is the need to act for fun without further purpose. It is the need for make-believe, for fantasy behavior. Unlike most needs, it achieves no external effect; it is strictly for fun. Even though all people need some level of play, this is the need most identified with childhood, probably because it has no apparent purpose or goal except self-pleasure. It seems to almost have a biological or tissue source, but no scientist to my knowledge has ever advanced such a hypothesis. It also appears to be a built-in stress reducer, as children can be observed turning to play when faced with serious adult situations. In infancy, the play need manifests itself by repetitious behavior such as touching one's fingers and making bubbling utterances. Later, watching TV, listening to music, and motor efforts such as jumping and bicycling become play activities. In tween years, play includes sports and dancing. The play need fuses with affiliation to produce play with others, playing of sports with others, watching TV with others. Play is surely the highest priority need of children, at least until the teen years when authority figures such as parents and teachers begin to suppress it. Parents recognize the play need as important to their children, but do not understand it well, as demonstrated by their expectations that kids will combine it with education but not somehow with eating.

Sentience: The sentience need is the need to enjoy sensuous impressions, to touch and be touched, to smell pleasurable scents, to taste delicious foods, hear beautiful sounds, see beautiful sights. It is noticeable in infancy when babies can be observed rubbing the fabric in Mom's blouse between their thumb and forefinger. It later manifests itself in the oohs and aahs made when a child walks into a bakery. It combines with play to produce drawing, coloring, and playing with food. It fuses with exhibition to produce dancing and singing, and with affiliation to produce pairing with others. Interestingly, it fuses with autonomy to cause children to want candies whose flavors are repugnant to adults. It drives children to develop more vocabulary to describe their pleasurable sensory experiences. Its expression helps explain why children like a certain store, a certain food, a certain color, even a certain person, including parents.

Play is surely the highest priority need of children, at least until the teen years when authority figures such as parents and teachers begin to suppress it.

Succorance: The need for succorance is a need we all possess, but its manifestations are most noticeable in early childhood. It is the need for care, sympathy, and support from others and from objects. It is looking to parents for the fulfillment of one's needs, relying on a Linus blanket for security, trusting a pet as a protector, and depending on teachers and other adults for help and encouragement. As small and new people, children often feel insecure and helpless and must rely on others for protection and support. When little children talk about their favorite things, they may mention a lamp in their room, "my light;" their pillow, "my pibby;" and pretend friends such as dolls and plush animals, "my Pluto." All of these items give them comfort and a feeling of protection.

These needs are important to children in different degrees at different times in their lives. They have physical needs such as hunger and sleep, and learned needs such as aggression and nurturing that direct their behavior. The needs in **Table 18-3**, however, give the most direction to their behavior.

These needs most commonly guide them in the marketplace, and these needs typically cause them to pay close attention to some advertisements and ignore others.

What about other needs such as the acquisition need, the need to own a lot of things, to "collect all six?" To the extent we can call this a need, compared with an attitude, it appears to result from a fusion of the achievement and exhibition needs. Thus, owning many action figures is an accomplishment that can attract attention from others. Fast-food restaurants are right on the money when they suggest children "collect all five" of some kind of toy. Such an appeal informs the children they can meet the combined achievement and exhibition need called acquisition, while also meeting the needs for play and sentience with some tasty food prepared with kids' needs in mind.

Of all the human needs a psychologist might posit, the play need seems most important to children. It often appears to be more important than eating and sleeping, and usually more important than important adult needs such as worshiping and working. The play need is the one marketers who target kids should almost always focus on, particularly for kids under age 8 or 9. But play is also somewhat perplexing and complex. It might better be classified as an emotional need compared with affiliation and achievement, which have apparent and visible external goals.

Play Should Never be the Only Need Marketers Target

Children have other important needs and often fuse them with play. Marketers ought to try to satisfy play along with at least one other need more readily understandable to adults (i.e., marketers and parents), such as affiliation or achievement. Thinking this way about a firm's offerings to children will meet parents' need for children, too.

Measuring Needs

Market research to identify which needs are most important to children; which needs they try to meet most with specific products and brands of products; which needs particular products meet; and which features, models, or brands of a product or retail store best satisfy certain needs is critical to the success of any kids' product. But such measurements are difficult to obtain, which may explain their rarity as well as the high failure rate among products for kids.

I have no simple answers or directions for obtaining these assessments even though it is something I have done, in one form or another, for many years. Generally researchers utilize the "why" question one-on-one or in small groups, and follow with probes—"Which other dolls do you like besides Barbie?" "What is it you like most about that store?" "How often do you watch that program?"—as they do with adults. With children under 12, however, such procedures often are empty efforts.

I will suggest that qualitative measurements seem to serve best, at least as initial inquiries, for uncovering relationships between marketing objectives and children's needs. I pay a lot of attention to the "I wantta's," believing that wants are manifestations of unmet needs. Wants can be elicited in many ways. For example, ask children how they would spend an unexpected windfall of $100.

Parents want their children free of worry, contented, smiling, and in general, in a happy state of mind.

Asking children to compare two similar items is often asking too much of them, particularly if the two similar items are both desirable. But giving children situations in which they choose between the two items will help them verbalize the differences. Asking third-person questions may be useful for obtaining perceptions of children about certain products. For example, asking what type of child uses a particular product, what do friends like in specific product categories, and what do parents prefer are ways of getting the children to articulate beyond the "It's fun" and "It's cool" level. Asking parents about children's requests when they are actually in the shopping setting makes such inquiries more specific and top-of-mind.

I like to use drawing studies to ascertain information about the products and stores children want or like, particularly with kids aged 7 or older. If not restricted, and if properly instructed, children draw what they value (want, like), and will give clues to what best satisfies them. In turn, findings from the drawings can provide the foundation for more extensive and more structured studies.

Satisfy the Kids and Their Parents, Too

The myth that suggests that if a firm satisfies kids, it automatically satisfies the parents, is high risk and probably wrong most of the time. The notion assumes that as long as kids are happy with a product or service, the parents are also happy because they value their children's happiness and well-being. It also assumes that children hold great sway over parents. The two assumptions are closely related in the sense that parents do want to see their children happy, and fulfilling their requests is a normal means of providing that happiness. So, the latter assumption is a valid one in general. The former assumption is deficient. Parents practice need fusion too, and they need more for their children than just happiness, however we might define this concept.

As a result of thousands of interviews with parents over the years, it appears that parents possess three fundamental needs for their children. They are:

• • • • • • • •
Parents gener-
ally are willing
to pay more for
products and
services that
promote the
health of their
children.

Happiness. Parents want their children free of worry, contented, smiling, and in general, in a happy state of mind. Parents worry their children will be depressed by world events—rampant crime, AIDS, corruption in government—and by family problems such as divorce and financial difficulties. To a great extent, parents believe they can protect their children from depression and worry by providing them with the things that make them happy.

Healthiness. Parents have become very health-conscious for both themselves and their kids. They have learned a healthy body contributes directly to a happy person. They want to see their children with sound bodies and minds. They fret even more than they used to about the nutritional value of the foods kids consume, perhaps prompted by personal experiences and many media reports on this subject, not to mention school-based and other outreach programs. They worry also about communicable diseases among children, and about the mental health of their children. Parents generally are willing to pay more for products and services that promote the health of their children. For example, they understand their children like sweets and play, and tend to be attracted to fun-to-eat sweets that also offer some nutritional benefits such as General Mills' Fruit Roll-Ups.

Preparation for life. Parents want their children ready to cope with daily events, and to cope as well or even better than other children. Parents see the walls of basic institutions—church, school, government—crumbling around their children, and they need their children to function well in these dire circumstances. So, healthy and happy aren't enough; parents want their children smarter, cleverer, more competitive than other children. Parents who at one time scoffed at the Asian model of education in which children receive various kinds of education around the clock are increasingly buying into it—piano lessons after school, investment camps in summer, and travel to other countries.

Parents attempt to fuse these three needs when they are buying for their children and when they are considering whether or not to approve of children's requests or purchases. Consequently, meeting the three needs for their children may produce conflicts not easily reconciled. For example, promotions by fast-food restaurants that target children often present problems. Parents view much fast food as less than optimally nutritious for their kids. When kids say they want to go to a particular restaurant to obtain a free gift, parents may experience cognitive dissonance. They want their kids to receive the gifts that will make them happy, but they don't want them eating unwholesome foods. They may take the kids to the restaurant, but try to make sure the food they eat there is as healthy as possible. Parents may also be very critical of these restaurants and more vocal about their marketing strategies.

Kids marketers have two sets of constituents to please.

The messages to marketers seem clear. Satisfy the kids and their parents. Market products that have benefits apparent to parents, too. Test market strategies on parents as well as kids. Meeting parents' needs for kids also offers a huge opportunity—the chance to market to children more expensive, more complex products and services that parents see as beneficial.

A Concluding Note: Innovative Products for Kids Needed

In theory, if a business produces a product that satisfies the needs of a body of consumers, it will also satisfy its financial needs. Kids are unique as a market because they are parents' responsibility, so marketers have two sets of constituents to please. No big problem, really. It just takes well-thought-out new product development strategies supported by good research.

But as I look at the product planning and development process as it relates to kids products, I am a bit confused and concerned. It appears to be driven, in great part, not by kids but by competitors; not by markets, but by marketers. Let me explain.

Probably half of revenues in the toy industry are derived from licensed concepts. That is, of the toys made by Mattel, Hasbro, Applause and others, about half are based on concepts developed by other firms for them, such as Disney, Warner, and Saban. Most of the premium concepts offered to kids and families by fast-food chains are not developed by them or their agencies, but by the likes of—that's right—Disney, Warner, and Saban.

McDonald's, for instance, recently made a ten-year deal with Disney for such concepts. Now, if I were McDonald's looking for a kids marketing partner, I couldn't do better than Disney, particularly if I didn't want to create my own premiums. That's the point. Originality in product planning and development for the kids market seems minimal.

Businesses can pursue two new product development strategies—innovation and imitation. Either a business creates its own concepts (innovation) or it copies them (imitation) from its existing products or those of other companies. Today, imitation rules in the kids market. As described in the preceding pages, many firms are entering with scaled-down, funned-up copies of existing products. This strategy often results in superficial products and meager sales. It is not unlike the fresh-fruit industry targeting kids with small apples and oranges. Businesses also copy lots of things from other companies. Just look at the "clones" of General Mills' noncarbonated fruit drinks for kids, Squeeze-It.

All in all, the strategy of innovation in developing kids' products is not common. I think it is only alive and well in the software industry and maybe in the confection industry. The net result is lots of products that only slightly satisfy or do not satisfy at all. Both situations result in product failure. The companies lose money and lose confidence in functioning in the kids market. The kids, and their parents too, lose the joy that comes from innovative products.

Kids' meals don't have to be copies of adults' meals, and Barbie as a doctor doesn't have to become Barbie as a lawyer. For example, Mattel is beginning an online business through which children can design their own Barbie—color of skin, eyes, hair. While this custom manufacturing is more expensive, its success rate theoretically should be greater. Letting the child design the product is a step closer to innovation and a big step away from imitation. But Mattel and others need to take the additional step of interpreting children's needs and parents' needs for children, and originating products and services that will really satisfy them.

Finally, products such as Barbie and McDonald's have intergenerational acceptance—grandparents, parents, and children all like them as products for children. They have become woven into the fabric of our culture. They are unusual and unusually successful, and appear to owe their success to truly satisfying both children and parents. Calling such items "products for kids" may not do them justice, but perhaps all the attempts to copy them do.

• • • • • • • •
Products such as Barbie and McDonald's have intergenerational acceptance—grandparents, parents, and children all like them.

CHAPTER 19

Researching the Kids Market: Hard Work, Questionable Results

MYTH: "We must always utilize good market research principles regardless of the market."

REALITY: Market research principles and practices were developed by adults for adults. They don't always produce the right results with kids, and we are not sure when they do and when they don't.

The fact that children are directly and indirectly responsible for almost $500 billion a year in household spending has captured the attention of most consumer goods industries. The result is that companies in these industries are either developing entirely new products for children, or more commonly, modifying current lines of products for them. In total, thousands of producers are targeting kids with products. The available inventory of television advertising to kids is growing far faster than its adult counterpart to satisfy the marketing communication needs of these firms. Selling this multitude of products, in turn, is the responsibility of thousands of retailers, many of whom are new to the kids market. Some retailers are adding kids products to their existing lines, some are setting up separate departments for kids, and a few are spinning off entirely new stores to serve kids and their parents.

All this kid-targeted marketing activity requires enormous amounts of kid-targeted market research to provide solutions to its many new problems and questions, placing demands on an industry that essentially did not do this kind of work just two decades ago. Most of the early comers conducted their own market research on kids instead of farming it out. This happened for several reasons: Partly, it was because they wanted to save money and maintain competitive secrecy; but mostly, they did their own work because few market research firms were equipped to do this kind of research. Today, 10 to 20 U.S. market research firms specialize in the kids market, many more claim some skill in doing it, and most market research departments in companies with an investment in the kids market are now actively engaged in some kind of kid research.

All of this growth in kids market research has not been without a lot of groping and stumbling. No one know how many product missteps can be attributed to hit-or-miss research, but it certainly shares the responsibility along with the other marketing functions. The prevailing attitude of those earlier days is summarized in one seemingly innocuous sentence in a 1990 issue of *Marketing News* that reviewed the research going on in the kids marketing field: "Researchers are realizing that with a few modifications, they can tap into this group (kids) with the same techniques they've been using on adults."

I would suggest that by 1990, many researchers were beginning to realize just the opposite, that shoving adult research techniques down to the child level "with a few modifications" is even less effective and more error-prone than pushing scaled-down adult products to kids. Both thoughts are based on the assumption that children are simply mini-adults, an assumption fraught with fallacies. This kind of thinking is surely at the foundation of the myth that standard market research techniques are sufficient. Of course we should use good market research principles regardless of the market, but we should not disregard the nature of the market. We should use the right tools for the right job. One size does not fit all. Planning and designing a market research undertaking should begin with the market in mind just as planning and designing a new product should.

When George Carey set up Just Kid Inc., an integrated marketing firm that specializes in the children's market, his years of experience at Saatchi & Saatchi convinced him that all marketing activities directed to kids must be adjusted accordingly, including products, brands, advertising and publicity, as well as market research. The JKI group set about rethinking and modifying current market research techniques and procedures. Today, the firm enjoys worldwide distinction for its innovations in this special field of research.

Use Adult Research Techniques Among Kids?

Market research techniques and procedures are not normally designated as being appropriate for adults or children. When Burke Research Institute,

- - - - - - -
Shoving adult research techniques down to the child level "with a few modifications" is even less effective and more error-prone than pushing scaled-down adult products to kids.

for example, advertises its many workshops that teach market research principles and procedures, it doesn't label some as intended for use in the adult market and some for the kid market. Its messages imply the tools will serve for all market segments.

Of course, this is rarely true. Research tools usually must be age-graded in some way for both chronological age and level of maturity. An examination of the history of scientific research in human behavior reveals an adaptive process when applying new research methods to children. First, people conceive a research method through various creative efforts based on a theoretical notion. Subsequently, they develop the method into a system of study, usually consisting of a set of steps or an instrument, and test it for workability and validity. Following the testing period, it goes through a period of use and reexamination until it becomes an accepted constituent of a discipline's research tools.

● ● ● ● ● ● ●
Planning and designing a market research undertaking should begin with the market in mind.

In most cases, this developmental flow involves adult subjects—adult researchers researching adults. When it involves children, it quickly becomes apparent that the process can't be applied without creating questions concerning its validity. Thus, research methods developed to assess cognitive concepts such as intelligence, personality, motives, and attitudes require alterations before they will elicit appropriate information from children. Some market researchers have opted to devote their talents and energies to adapting popular adult-based measuring instruments to children, and in a few cases, to originate methods strictly for use among children, often within a narrow age range.

The point is that market researchers can rarely examine some behavioral aspect of children using existing research tools and expect results commensurate to those obtained with adults for whom they were intended. But that is what they often do. Even the market research firms that specialize in children usually have not developed their own research methods or other methods intended exclusively for children. Instead, they tend to work on and hone their individual skills to the point that they feel confident about applying the adult-based applications with which they "grew up." For example, one research house uses adolescents to moderate focus groups of children. While such a modification sounds logical—kids talking to kids is less intimidating than adults talking to kids—it may be "sending a boy to do a man's job" in the sense that even though kids talk kidtalk, they lack certain skills and maturity.

Myth-Made Market Research Errors and How to Avoid Them

It is obvious that market research mistakes in the children's market will produce marketing mistakes—improperly designed products, inappropriately chosen brand names, incorrectly developed advertising and promotion programs. Therefore, reducing the number and kinds of research mistakes is imperative. Many articles talk about the problems and mistakes in kids market research (KMR), and offer guidelines for overcoming them. Such writings surely help those interested in improving their KMR, but I fear they don't change the attitudes of many decision makers who use market research support.

• • • • • •
Unqualified researchers can be worse than no researchers at all.

Not Enoughs

I think three "not enoughs" lie at the heart of the problems; specifically, not enough kids research is done, not enough is done by qualified researchers, and not enough of the right kind is done. Let me explain.

1. **Not enough kids market research is done.** Many businesses have trouble allocating adequate funds for research, but in the case of kids, a market we don't understand very well, we should be prepared to spend lavishly. Yet in my opinion, lack of funds usually isn't the major reason for a lack of KMR. It is more likely to be due to a bad attitude or set of attitudes: children do not constitute a very important market; they are easy to understand if you have children of your own; all they like is sweet things and play things (or some other stereotype).

   Together, these fallacious thoughts discourage and reduce research on kids' consumer behavior. For example, a food producer I worked with decided to copy a successful kids' product and bring it to market under one of its current brands. The only research it conducted was a set of focus groups with kids. The product has been struggling in the marketplace for nearly two years, and those in charge seem to feel the product was given all the research support it deserves. When the product fails, and I think it surely will, who will accept the responsibility? And what reasons will she or he give? Faulty product? Faulty market research? Faulty management? Probably none of these. Instead, as often the case, it probably will be blamed on a poor economy or on the capriciousness of kids.

2. **Not enough research is done by qualified researchers.** When companies conduct research related to kids, they are not likely to have an experienced staff on hand. In fact, such research may not

even be done by a research group at all, but by decision makers who feel comfortable working with kids because they have kids of their own or, again, because they perceive the kids market as not very significant. For instance, a manager in a major fast-food chain was curious about how children mentally classified the main players in the industry. So he simply undertook some focus groups with the aid of an assistant "to get an idea about it." As far as I can tell, everything was done perfectly wrong.

Unqualified researchers can be worse than no researchers at all. A typical scenario is for a firm to enter the children's market using the research group it has always used in the adult market. Chances are it will also use the same ad agency and promotion group, too. If the entry succeeds against the odds, it will have "proven" that research is research is research and skill in the kids market is unnecessary.

> *Children are a unique market that requires specialized market research, and may require a new partner.*

It may be comfortable and expeditious for a company to go with the research group that has always done its research work, just as it is to go with the ad agency that has been faithfully serving the firm, but it may not always be the most effective. We have a saying in my part of the country: "You ought to dance with him that brung you," but "you may have to sneak a new partner if you want to learn a new step." Children are a unique market that requires specialized market research, and may require a new partner.

3. **Not enough of the right kind of research is done.** Some KMR is "quick and dirty," some is inadequate, and some is just downright bad. For instance, the kneejerk reaction to, "We need some research" is too often, "Let's get some focus groups going." Focus groups are good research tools for certain purposes, but their results do not stand alone. Yet many major decisions are based solely on the outcomes of focus groups. That's not the right way to use research to support decision making.

The Tickle Me Elmo doll was the smash toy hit of the 1996 holiday season. What should its producer and competitors have done next to capitalize on its success? Look at the options:

A. Produce Variations—larger, smaller, different clothing, different sounds;

B. Produce Spinoffs—e.g., Hug Me Elmo, Bounce Me Elmo;

C. Apply the same concept to other characters—e.g., Tickle Me Garfield.

Which of these options is likely to be most profitable? The question requires all the research skills a firm can muster. It requires sophisticated techniques and the most experienced children researchers. Yet I'm guessing that some firms took on this task with a few focus groups and a few Tickle Me Elmo dolls as cues. (The producer chose B.)

Avoiding Some of the Mistakes

Let me offer some **do's** and **don'ts** that address some common mistakes in researching the kids market.

Do speak in pictures whenever possible.

In general, probably two-thirds of all stimuli reach the brain through the visual system, and for children the percentage is even higher. Thus, children, particularly those under age 9, possess a relatively large visual as well as a verbal vocabulary—their heads are full of pictures. Research techniques that elicit these visual codes can be just as effective as those that elicit verbal codes while avoiding some of the language problems that come with researching kids.

So, do use visuals whenever possible. Give kids pictures of store interiors, print ads, packages, brands, products to respond to, or just to think about as they answer related questions. Scale options can be in the form of smiley and sad faces or sunshine and rain. "Who" questions—who is likely to shop at this store?—can employ sketched options as answers such as a rich person or a smart person. Whenever logical, seek children's responses in visual form. Get them involved in drawing studies such as the ones illustrating this book. Drawing exercises really provide a good idea of children's perceptions of marketing objects such as brands, prices, and stores.

Don't work beyond their knowledge limits.

Children really do not know much about Kmart stores, only about the one in their city; or about the ingredients in peanut butter, but about its flavor and appearance; or about their parents' finances, but about their own. An 8-year-old may be able to hold a good conversation, but only on a relatively small number of topics drawn from his or her relatively small world. On the other hand, children strive to be members of our adult society and may pretend to know something about a topic.

Every word and topic of a questionnaire must be pretested on kids of a certain age range. Reading ability and knowledge are related, too. Age-inappropriate questionnaire wording may not only lose its meaning for children but drastically slow the research process. Remember, there may be a lot of difference in the cognitive makeup of a kid who has just completed first grade and one who has started second. Kids have an impact on the world, but their world is their perspective.

Don't ask kids to do much reasoning—particularly those under age 9 or 10.

Asking them to think about the pollution of our rivers and streams, for example, is usually asking too much in spite of the fact that this may be a topic in their classrooms and homes. When people ask children if they are concerned about environmental pollution, they often answer yes because they know it's the right thing to say, but they don't truly understand why. In fact, this question requires reasoning that goes beyond most kids' abilities. They may have the vocabulary in the sense that they can parrot their parents and teachers, but they process few of the factors and implications of pollution.

Yet, we persist in asking kids about pollution, world hunger, AIDS, and other very adult topics, and kids often respond without much conviction behind their answers. For example, kids love animals, particularly dinosaurs. So, when asked about their interest in protecting animals from extinction, they may show much enthusiasm but possibly for the wrong reasons. If extinct animals are as "good" as dinosaurs, kids may want more extinct animals.

Thus, we can put words in kids' mouths but not reasoning in their minds. The latter has to develop over time. Abstract thought questions such as, "Imagine what the world would be like if . . ." cannot be expected to be fruitful with most pre-teens. In fact, a good research rule is: don't ask them to reason but to respond. It is probably better to ask, "Which best describes what the world would be like if kids were our national leaders," followed by a list of well-researched choices. Asking children to state their favorite brands of various products or their favorite stores might be better accomplished by utilizing a word association test that seeks their responses to a set of cue words. As a rule, soliciting kids' responses rather than reasons will provide higher-quality research results.

Don't be afraid to be creative with market research techniques.

This suggestion may sound a bit unscientific, but we still don't know what works best with kids. For example, one of the problems often encountered when researching kids is shyness. Around half of kids between the ages of 5 and 10 will be shy, even to the point of thwarting most standard research efforts and introducing a good deal of nonresponse error. Questions about personal matters usually elicit more shyness than questions about play or eating, particularly when asked by an unfamiliar adult.

We have never figured out how to overcome shyness, but it does beg for some creative market research techniques. One possibility is to depersonalize an interview by placing questions on a tape and asking children to respond to them when they are alone. A similar method is used by the British Household Panel Study among children as a means of giving them more privacy, and also to overcome the problem of literacy. Similarly, some research firms use online interviews to overcome some of the shyness elicited by in-person interviews.

Getting children to talk about topics that provoke inhibitory resistance needs much research development. More picture tests might be appropriate. In the 1950s, psychologist G. S. Blum created a special set of drawings of a dog and his family called The Blacky Pictures; the purpose was to get children to talk about sexual topics. The premise behind this picture test is that children will talk about animal sexual behavior more easily than human sexual behavior.

Don't be afraid to substitute parents for kids.

It's a way of overcoming many of the problems inherent in researching kids. Researching parents may introduce some problems of its own, of course, but they seem less insurmountable than many of those we experience with kids. Parents add another link to the communications chain between researcher and child, and therefore more opportunity for communications errors, but they also can speak on behalf of timid youngsters who might otherwise be reluctant or unwilling to participate. Parents may also introduce errors in the sense that they don't necessarily understand their children's inner thoughts any better than anyone else.

Normally, however, parents possess a lot of detailed information about their kids such as their money management habits, their favorite brands of cereals, and how often children ask them for products. When using parents as surrogates for their children, researchers should be aware of the social desirability variable (SD); that is, parents may say things about their children to make themselves look good. I sometimes describe the mom who does this as Mrs. McImmaty, the term standing for my child is more mature

· · · · · · · · ·

Parents possess a lot of detailed information about their kids such as their money management habits, their favorite brands of cereals, and how often children ask them for products.

than yours. Moms have a tendency to brag about their kids simply because their kids are extensions of them. But this problem is not ordinarily severe and can be dealt with, first, by avoiding asking parents for characterizations of their kids, and second, by developing a measure of the SD factor to adjust suspect data. Otherwise, parents are good sources of information about their children, and researching them can circumvent typical KMR problems, increase research accuracy, and consequently reduce some costs.

Do speak to children in a language they understand.

When I conducted my first focus group work among some kindergartners in the early 1960s—we called them group depth interviews then—I tended to use what I would call babytalk to communicate with them. That was wrong, but I thought somehow I was speaking their language. Instead I was speaking down to them.

At the other extreme, **don't** expect kids to talk like adults. They will try, just as they do for their school teachers, but they often will not succeed. In their desire to please, they will say things they don't mean or that don't make sense. With rare exceptions, kids just cannot articulate like adults can. Besides the fact that they are shy and usually intimidated by adults, they do not possess the verbal vocabulary and syntax.

Therefore, **do** keep it simple, keep it short (as in short words), keep it in their language. Keep in mind the age of the kids to whom you're speaking. If they're not actually infants in arms, don't baby talk; that's talking down to them. Consult an elementary school teacher if there is doubt or if there appears to be opportunity for verbal mistakes.

The way to learn kids' language is to listen to them. Their vocabulary tends to mirror their interests, and their interests mirror their needs and wants, in the following order:

VOCABULARY → INTERESTS → NEEDS/WANTS

Listening carefully to children's choice of words can provide an interviewer with samplings of their language that may improve the communications process between child and researcher. Incidentally, part of their language are the utterances, uh-huh and mmh-hmm. An interviewer who uses these may elicit more conversation from children.

This doesn't mean interviewers should resort to slang in an effort to "relate" to kids, by using words as "cool" or "bad" (meaning good). Such language is likely to produce mistrust if children view it as patronizing.

• • • • • • • • •
Children will talk about animal sexual behavior more easily than human sexual behavior.

What I am suggesting here is the use of familiar words. One way to ascertain kids' vocabulary is to consult books written for the age range of interest. Researchers should also avoid vague (to a kid) words, such as "according," "opinion," and "consider."

Which Research Techniques Work Best with Kids?

The way to learn kids' language is to listen to them.

The notion that "we must always utilize good market research principles regardless of the market" is misleading when applied to kids because what researchers think are "good market research principles" usually are adult-based. For example, when sampling age groups, chronological age works fine with most adults for most purposes. But children of the same chronological age may vary tremendously in maturity and ability. Studies among 10-year-olds may have more variance than a study of adults in one age group. Hence, it is wise to use larger sample sizes when maturity is an important factor as it is in children's understanding of an advertisement, opening/closing a package, or playing a new video game.

This book is not the place to detail research rules about concepts such as sampling, reliability, or validity, but it is important to mention them as possible areas of errors when studying the kids market, errors that can misdirect a marketing strategy all the way to failure. Most of these errors probably occur as a result of an inappropriate choice or use of data collection methods. I would like to offer some assessments about four basic techniques most commonly used in the investigations of children's consumer behavior.

Observational Research

Unobtrusively monitoring and recording behavior to obtain primary data is one of the oldest research tools for studying children's behavior. The technique can be virtually foolproof by avoiding many of the problems associated with researching children. It involves no exchange of words so it does not produce any communications errors. It requires no reasoning from the subjects. It avoids errors due to intimidation, unintentional as it may be, by adult interviewers. All in all, observational research is the technique of choice for those who seriously study children's behavior.

Observational research has its downside, too, of course. Its most serious shortcoming is its inability to accurately assess any cognitive activity—attitudes, perceptions, motives. It strictly measures behavior. Of course, a skilled observer can infer cognitions with a substantial degree of accuracy, but this inferring can naturally introduce errors, possibly serious ones, into the research process and consequently into marketing strategy.

But as long as the objective is to assess concrete behavior—use of products, frequency of store visits, shopping with and without supervision, use of media, use of packaging, as examples—observation is the way to go. For example, monitoring devices can reveal the number of hours children watch TV at home, although not at friends' homes; the number of times they try a video game on display at a store; and the ways they mix beverages at a self-serve soft-drink display. Mechanical, electronic, audio, and video monitors, along with a bit of creativity, can provide an endless variety of objective measures of children's consumer behavior. Add kid-qualified people to the mix, and the variety and quality increase even more.

• • • • • • •
The observational method eliminates many sources of potential errors.

Because the observational method eliminates many sources of potential errors, I strongly recommend it, particularly to the researcher who is new to researching kids. It is especially useful in researching young children, a group less amenable to many research techniques. It is, perhaps, less satisfactory with older children, who may discover they are being observed and not behave spontaneously. When observation is one of a set of options, go with it. In fact, researchers should carefully determine if this method can be substituted for others and use it whenever possible. For example, use it to determine how often children perform certain shopping activities instead of asking them or their parents. As long as the technique is applied systematically with specific goals in mind, it is near or at the top of the list of what is often termed scientific research.

Focus Groups

I'm not sure if a lot of focus group research preceded the growth of KMR or if KMR caused focus group research to flourish. But wherever you find research efforts targeting the kids market, you'll find focus groups. I understand this. I even agree with the use of focus groups as a basic research technique. But I view it primarily as an exploratory technique, a way to produce information that will guide more formal efforts. Too often I have heard businesspeople talk along the following lines: "We need to find out for sure what kids think about this before we give it a go. Let's get MR to work up some focus groups." Focus groups have probably received too much attention for the wrong reasons.

Focus groups should not be viewed as a necessity that always precedes a major marketing effort in the kids market. Survey research is expensive, and marketing to kids requires a lot of it. There is no cheap way out. Focus groups can reduce these costs while making survey research more effective. But focus group research isn't cheap either, often costing several thousand dollars per group. They should be as deliberate a tool as any other.

One of the best reasons to use a focus group is to lay the groundwork for other survey research. For example, focus groups can guide question wording. When researching kids, we may be unsure what terms to use, what terms kids understand, what questioning style to use, how many questions are appropriate, and the exact makeup of the sample to which the questions will be directed. Properly designed focus group discussions will answer these questions, substantially enhancing the value of further survey work.

Another popular, though risky, use of focus groups is to assist in product design. Focus groups can test alternatives along the development route, such as different sizes, colors, weights, or shapes. Carefully controlled samples of six to eight kids per group can act as sounding boards for alternatives in a sequential sampling scheme. In other words, use different samples until sufficient evidence validates a preference for one of the alternatives. Similar procedures can test other important elements of the marketing mix such as advertising formats and messages, package designs, and prices. While this procedure is quick, and the small number of respondents helps maintain security needed for competitive marketing strategies, making decisions based solely on such small samples is high risk.

One feature of typical focus groups may be a detriment to kid research—the facilities in which they are normally conducted. The one-way mirrors, protruding-out-of-the-ceiling microphones, and sterile furniture may intimidate and inhibit kids. On the other hand, these physical features may cause some children to talk almost in puppet form simply because they feel they should. This is particularly true for those who are regularly recruited and paid to be talkative. Focus groups probably will produce more valid results when conducted in familiar surroundings such as schools, homes, and children's clubs. Familiar settings may encourage shy children to talk more freely.

Experimental Method

The experimental method is considered the most accurate and most reliable method of market research. It has even been referred to as the "scientific method" in research. The experimental method may not always be applied

. . . .
Focus groups probably will produce more valid results when conducted in familiar surroundings such as schools, homes, and children's clubs.

in a very scientific fashion to kid research, but it is popular due to its wide range of applications, maintenance of competitive secrecy, and relatively low cost. Also, it seems to suit kids because it often uses visual stimuli.

The primary use of experimentation, which is wide ranging, is to test the effects of the marketing mix on children's consumer behavior. That is, to what extent do product designs, package designs, advertising formats, point-of-purchase displays, and prices (the independent variables), cause children to like, want, and purchase (the dependent variables). Virtually all marketing variables can be presented to children in visual form. And the tests can be conducted in the secrecy and control of a laboratory setting, as opposed to test marketing a product in the public arena.

Legitimate questions arise about the validity of results obtained in an artificial setting. But they remain a reasonable alternative to revealing activities to competitors. The results, in turn, can accelerate a standard test market where time favors the competition.

Projective Techniques

According to a classic article by Mason Haire that appeared in the *Journal of Marketing* in 1950, "Basically, a projective test involves presenting the subject with an ambiguous stimulus—one that does not quite make sense in itself—and asking him to make sense of it." Haire goes on to explain that to make sense out of a stimulus, subjects project a part of themselves into it. Thus, projective methods provide researchers with a lot more information about a child than he or she can or may be willing to tell them. This is a very significant benefit. Youth researchers often report that it is difficult to get children to talk freely, to respond satisfactorily to straightforward questions. Either they are intimidated by adult researchers or by the research situation, or they simply have difficulty expressing themselves.

Projective techniques—there are hundreds of them—work well with children because many are in pictorial or play forms that engage children's interest. On the other hand, because of these same characteristics, these research tools usually produce less than objective results. Therefore, like focus group research, researchers should ordinarily use them as exploratory devices whose results are to be tested using more structured methods.

While psychologists developed most projective techniques, market researchers have adapted many of them to consumer scenarios. Projective techniques can be classified as connection, completion, or construction tests. Let's look briefly at some examples of each.

Connection Tests. Market researchers often want to know the connections that exist in kids' minds, such as the stores that come to mind when kids think of buying a certain product, the brand that comes to mind when they think about a certain product, or the ad slogans they think of when they think of a particular brand. Marketers know these connections occur, but children have trouble articulating them.

Various connection, or association, tests attempt to duplicate and elicit these links in kids' minds. In a traditional word association test, when an experimenter says "salt," the respondent might be expected to reply "pepper." When this technique is conducted in rapid-fire fashion, it is believed to tap inner-mind connections. For example, a researcher might ask children to say the first word that comes to their mind when they hear a list of brand names, revealing the products or concepts connected to these brand names.

The stimuli do not have to be words. They can be sounds—the clicking of a computer keyboard, the muffled shouts of a crowd, the bells and whistles of a video game. They can be pictures—stimulus cards containing brand names, store fronts, cartoon characters, sandwiches. They can be simply colors, such as the color combinations in brand logos.

Completion Tests. Completion tests reveal the way people approach and solve problems or questions. Designed with kids in mind, completion techniques can be fun and evocative. The most popular type of completion test is the sentence completion test. For example, a set of incomplete sentences designed to study kids' play habits might include statements such as:

"On weekends I look forward to playing with _____."
"The game I like to play best is _____."
"When I play with my friend I like to play _____."

This method can be presented in either written or verbal format, depending on children's reading and writing ability.

A variation of the completion technique is to ask respondents to complete conversations between two people drawn in comic-strip form. It is vital that the drawings be slightly ambiguous to avoid "leading" the respondent in a particular direction. For example, a drawing might show a mother standing at the door of her home saying to a child, "Robert, it's time to come in and eat," with the respondent asked to describe the child's possible response. Another might show one child

> • • • • • •
> *To children, drawing is a very engaging activity that permits them to truly express themselves and their wisdom.*

saying to another, "Let's go to my house and watch TV," with the subject asked to write in the response of the other child.

One benefit of this technique is that the situation is that of a third person, and does not require subjects to speak directly about themselves. Thus, market researchers can use the completion projection technique to gather information from children about embarrassing or sensitive topics.

Figure 19-1 illustrates a completion test that was part of a study among Chinese children to determine their likes and interests regarding TV viewing. The characters are children drawn by children. Their faces are not visible, and the picture on the TV set is vague to reduce directive bias. In this scenario, a girl is asking a boy what program he wants to watch next. Male respondents are asked to write in the empty balloon over the boy's head what they believe he will answer. Girls responded to a reverse scenario.

FIGURE 19-1

Construction Tests. In this technique, subjects create things such as drawings, collages or stories. In the process, the subject projects his or her feelings, beliefs, perceptions, and motives into the product. For example, in the Thematic Apperception Test (TAT), subjects look at vague pictures and tell or write stories about what is happening. In so doing, they reveal personal cognitions about a particular situation. The concept of the TAT has been adapted to market research for many years, and its pictorial nature lends itself to studies among children. Pictures that show children and adults in various vague shopping situations, e.g., standing in a checkout line or entering a store, can elicit information about children's feelings about shopping alone and with others.

I have used drawing studies among children for many years to learn about their perceptions of the shopping setting. A number of illustrations throughout this book are based on the question: "Draw what comes to your mind when you think about going shopping," intended to tap into a wide range of knowledge and feelings related to shopping. Children hold many pictures in their heads that their words cannot describe. Asking them for pictures is simply asking them to reproduce the pictures in their heads.

To children, drawing is a very engaging activity that permits them to truly express themselves and their wisdom. It is also a wonderful way to circumvent language problems and has been a blessing when I conduct research in other countries. The drawings scattered throughout this book attest to the benefits of this technique. It is a research procedure that works well in all cultures, is acceptable to teachers and parents, and has a long history to support its use. Though difficult to score in a quantitative fashion, I am reminded over and over that a picture really is worth a thousand words.

• • • • • • •
It is also possible to research this market as well as possible and still have inadequate information.

Final Note: Marents Mar Much Research

Throughout the book, I have mentioned the effects marents may have on marketing efforts that involve children. Marents are marketers who are also parents and feel that their dual roles give them special insights into children's consumer behavior. Marents can certainly contribute to research on children, but they can also create misunderstandings and mistakes because their opinions rest on a sample of one or two—their own kids. They may not rely on research because they feel they already know the answer. They may also avoid the directions implicit in research results because the results are inconsistent with their thinking.

These are probably errors we have all made, whether or not we are parents. Marents are not the only ones who think they can save the company money and time by not doing research, or by doing a minimum amount and relying on their intuition. Marents are also not the only ones ignoring the results of research and going with their gut instincts. And marents are not the only ones misled by researchers who don't clearly present their results. Yet marents may convince others that they know what they are doing, which makes them potentially more dangerous.

As suggested in these pages, not doing research, not doing enough research, or not doing the right kind of research is high risk when it comes to the kids market. It is also possible to research this market as well as possible and still have inadequate information. I'm not sure we can ever completely correct this situation, but we should try. And we should not be misled into thinking that the research tools and procedures we use are the right ones. We need to compare notes with other youth researchers and keep upgrading our own methods until we get it right. The price we pay in errors is too high not to do this.

CHAPTER 20

The Kids Market Doesn't End at U.S. Borders

Myth: "Children in the U.S. represent enormous market potential."

Reality: True, but there is ten times as much market potential among children in the rest of the developed and developing world.

Worldwide Market Potential of Kids

Unless you have been away for a while you know the rallying cry during the past decade among U.S. businesses that target kids has been "Go global." And they have. Cross-border alliances are now commonplace in most industries that market to children.

There are several good reasons for this. Most of the world's population and wealth is outside of the U.S., and both are increasing more rapidly than they are domestically. Most of the real growth potential in consumption of typical consumer goods such as ready-to-eat cereal, shoes, and toys lies outside U.S. borders. Competition is intense in virtually every consumer goods industry here. American goods are also in great demand overseas, even to the point that people spend big money on *used* Nike shoes and Levi's jeans. The U.S. model of consumption, in general, has become the guiding model of new consumers the world over, suggesting great market opportunity for many existing U.S. products and brands.

More specifically, the overseas potential of the youth market for U.S. consumer goods is many times greater than that of its counterpart in the United States. The world population overall is substantially younger than that of the U.S. Children under age 15 account for about 32 percent of the world population, compared with 22 percent in the U.S. Including the 59.4 million children in the U.S., that's nearly 2 billion children, according to Population Reference Bureau estimates.

• • • • • •
The 4-to-14 urban population of the world amounts to around 626 million—more than 14 times the youth population in the U.S.

Recognizing that children in rural areas of many countries have meager market potential, let us look more closely at the world's urban population. Of the world population in 1996, 43 percent, or 2.5 billion, was considered urban. Thus, of the under-15 population, 0.8 billion were urban. To get a rough approximation of this population's market potential, we shall focus only on children aged 4 and up—the age at which children may begin to spend money. Thus, the 4-to-14 urban population of the world amounts to around 626 million—more than 14 times the youth population in the U.S.

To put this into money terms, consider first how much of their own money (in U.S. dollars) children spend on their own wants and needs. To approximate this figure, let us average the amount spent by kids in the U.S., one of the highest in the world, and for kids in the Philippines, one of the lowest. These figures are conservatively around $10/week or $520/year for kids in the U.S., and around $1.50/week or $78/year for kids in the Philippines, or an average for the two countries of $5.75 per week and about $300 per year. My research in a dozen countries suggests this is a fair estimate. Multiplying this average by the approximate number of urban kids aged 4 to 14 yields a primary global market of $188 billion, almost eight times the amount spent by all children in the U.S.

Now, let us estimate kids' worldwide potential as an influence market. We know children in the U.S. influence around ten times more than they spend themselves. Since American children spend so much more of their own money than children elsewhere, this 10:1 ratio is not the highest in the world. In China and several European countries, for instance, the ratio is roughly 15:1. This influence-to-spending ratio reflects not only the generosity of parents—Chinese parents are relatively more generous than U.S. parents with household monies—it also takes into consideration the relative income of each. If we use the lower ratio of 10:1 of the U.S. and apply it to urban children, we get a measure of approximately $1.88 trillion ($188 billion times ten). Combined with their personal spending, it appears that the world's urban children have a current market potential as primary and influence markets of almost $1.9 trillion. And this does not even include the greatest part of their market potential and the most important reason to target them—they are a future market for all goods and services.

Let me narrow these world estimates to a more manageable regional level. Consider the case of Asia-Pacific countries where I have conducted a good deal of market research among children and their families. The table in **Figure 20-1** lists major countries in this region (it does not include

• • • • • • • •
Combined with their personal spending, it appears that the world's urban children have a current market potential as primary and influence markets of almost $1.9 trillion.

Brunei, Laos, Macau, Mongolia, Myanmar, North Korea, or the smaller Oceania islands), urban population, and youth population aged 0 to 4, 5 to 9, and 10 to 14. The total population of this region is around 1.9 billion, dominated by China, which accounts for two-thirds of the total. The urban population aged 4 to 14 is approximately 150 million.

Children in the Asia-Pacific Region (population numbers in thousands)

COUNTRY	TOTAL POPULATION	URBAN	UNDER 15	AGE 0-4	AGE 5-9	AGE10-14
Australia	18,077	85%	22%	1,304	1,339	1,276
Cambodia	10,600	13	46	1,895	1,533	1,228
China	1,210,000	28	26	96,443	102,932	115,459
Hong Kong	6,000	95	20	330	349	392
Indonesia	192,543	31	34	21,388	20,327	22,773
Japan	125,213	77	16	6,298	6,821	7,431
Malaysia	20,000	51	38	2,719	2,616	2,429
New Zealand	3,531	85	23	291	268	248
Philippines	69,209	49	39	9,822	8,837	8,227
Singapore	2,943	100	24	238	250	213
South Korea	45,083	74	24	3,365	3,634	3,997
Taiwan	20,879	75	26	1,680	1,736	2,021
Thailand	59,510	19	29	5,687	5,778	6,088
Vietnam	74,108	21	37	9,947	9,077	8,681
Total	**1,857,696**	—	—	**161,407**	**165,497**	**180,463**

Note: The 1995 data reported in this table show population distribution by age groups. Summary estimates for 1998 show a regional increase of 16.4 million children under age 15 and a total population increase of 68 million for the region.

source: *Population Reference Bureau*

If we apply the rough global average estimate of $300/year to represent kids' personal spending, which might be a bit high for this area, Asian and Pacific children spend around $45 billion on their own wants and needs. Further, if we apply the 10:1 ratio to measure the influence they have on parental spending, which appears very conservative for this population, it will amount to $450 billion. Thus, total market potential for kids as primary and influence markets in the Asia-Pacific region is somewhere around $495 billion.

FIGURE 20-1

China: The World's Largest Market

To narrow our estimates of children's market potential even more, consider China, the largest country in the world. China is a country that conjures up many superlatives. "China has to be the most exciting emerging market in the world," is how Richard Burkholder Jr., director of worldwide operations at Gallup, Inc. puts it. China has the world's largest population, the fastest-growing economy among large nations, and its advertising expenditures are growing faster than anywhere else. Furthermore, no country may enjoy a greater level of discretionary income—only about 20 percent of the average family's income goes toward necessities, the rest is covered by subsidized housing, education, and health care.

• • • • • • • •
China has the world's largest population, the fastest-growing economy among large nations, and its advertising expenditures are growing faster than anywhere else.

Superlatives also apply to China's children who constitute the largest youth population in the world—90 million under age 15 in its urban areas alone, compared with 60 million in the entire U.S. These children already have a substantial amount of money of their own to spend, and are spending it, even though China is still developing. Even more significant, they have a great deal of influence on family spending—probably around 68 percent compared with perhaps 45 percent for U.S. kids.

Chinese children seem very aware of their multi-tiered role as primary, influence, and future consumers. This is succinctly demonstrated in **Figure 20-2**, drawn by a 9-year-old after being instructed to draw what comes to his mind when he thinks about going shopping. He shows himself among other young shoppers in a department store spending his own money on toys at a toy counter. Another child is buying clothing, a third is leading his mom by the hand to items he wants her to buy, and a fourth child is looking at appliances she will someday purchase. The sign above the appliance area states that appliances are on sale, while the sign above the clothing counter says, "Welcome, hello customers."

FIGURE 20-2

China adopted a one-child per family policy in 1979 that has fundamentally become reality in urban areas. These only children receive a large amount of love and attention from both parents as well as four grandparents. In effect, a "4-2-1 indulgence factor" operates in China—four grandparents and two parents indulging one child. These pampered children have been described as "spoiled brats" and "little emperors." Studies I have conducted in China indicate such titles may be all too apt.

Studying Chinese Kids As Consumers

To produce what was apparently the first description of the nature and extent of Chinese children's consumer behavior, I joined with a group of academic researchers at China's Peking University. We administered two pre-tested questionnaires to 1,496 families whose children attended five elementary schools in Beijing and Tianjin selected to be as representative as possible of China's urban children.

Chinese children have three main sources of regular income.

We gave kids in Kindergarten through fifth grade two questionnaires to take home so their parents could complete and return them. One questionnaire covered children's spending behavior, the other, their influence on parents' spending. We received 870 completed questionnaires regarding children's spending and 626 regarding their influence on parental spending. About 45 percent were from girls and 55 percent from boys. (This is in line with the overall proportion of boys to girls in China of approximately 119 to 100.) Mothers completed all the questionnaires. Of these, 99.2 percent had only one child.

The spending questionnaire attempted to determine the amount and sources of children's income, how much they spent and saved, where they shopped, and what they bought. The influence questionnaire asked parents to estimate the degree of children's influence on their purchases in 25 product categories. The survey also collected information about children's gender, age, and some family characteristics. Some study findings follow:

Income. The table in **Figure 20-3** reveals that Chinese children have money to spend beginning at age 4, and that their income increases throughout their elementary school years. They have two equally important types of income—regular and special.

Chinese children have three main sources of regular income. The primary source, accounting for 40 percent, consists of frequent small money gifts from parents, provided to children of all ages on an as-needed basis. The amount is somewhat related to the number of requests children make. An allowance—what we described to parents as periodic distribution of money to children, usually without specific conditions attached—is the second most important source of regular income and averages 32 percent of the total. Children of all ages may receive an allowance, but is more common for children aged 8 and up. Money gifts from others, mainly grandparents who live in the children's households, make up 22 percent of children's regular income. Children, mainly older ones, earn just 6 percent of their regular income—

3 percent for work in the home and 3 percent for work outside the home.

Chinese children also receive what we call special income from parents and grandparents on special occasions—namely, Chinese New Year, Children's Day, Moon Festival, and on birthdays. *Hong bau* money given during the two weeks of Chinese New Year celebration is by far the largest gift. Sixty percent of mothers indicated they expect children to save this money.

* * * * * * * * *
Chinese children save about 60 percent of their total income.

The table in **Figure 20-3** shows that children's average weekly income—including regular and special income—increases significantly with age. It ranges from 3.2 yuan for 4-year-olds to 21.1 yuan for 12-year-olds. At the time of the study one yuan was equivalent to about 15 cents U.S. Because both grandparents and parents provide special income, this type almost always exceeds regular income primarily given by parents. For example, around 70 percent of an average 4-year-old's income is special; for 12-year-olds, it is roughly 50 percent.

While all children receive special income, younger ones are less likely to have regular income: just 21 percent of 4-year-olds do. The share rises steadily to age 9, at which point all children receive regular income. Boys and girls have similar regular incomes, but girls receive significantly more special income at all ages. We expected the opposite because of the emphasis given the male child as future head of the household. It may be that parents in fact give equal special gifts to boys and girls, but grandparents give more money to girls, perhaps in sympathy for girls' continued second-class standing.

Savings. Chinese children are savers. According to this study, they save about 60 percent of their total income. **Figure 20-3** shows how saving rates decline from 75 percent for 4-year-olds to 51 percent for 12-year-olds. As noted above, parents expect children to save special income, and since this is a greater share of younger children's total income, it drives up their saving rate. Around 15 percent of parents

Weekly income, spending, saving, and saving rate of urban Chinese children, by age.				
AGE	INCOME	SPENDING	SAVING	RATE
4	3.2 yuan	0.8 yuan	2.4 yuan	75%
5	4.8	1.4	3.4	71
6	6.5	2.2	4.3	66
7	8.2	3.1	5.1	62
8	12.0	5.3	7.7	64
9	14.5	5.5	9.0	62
10	16.3	6.1	10.2	63
11	18.4	7.8	10.6	57
12	21.1	10.3	10.8	51

Note: *One yuan is roughly equivalent to 15 cents US.*

FIGURE 20-3

report that their children, usually the older ones, spend some of their special income. Of regular income, children save about 30 percent on a weekly basis, similar to their counterparts in the U.S. Most of children's savings are kept in commercial depositories with only small amounts kept at home. Boys and girls exhibit no significant differences in average weekly savings rates.

Spending. Chinese children spend about 40 percent of their total income, most of it regular income kept on hand as cash at home. **Figure 20-3** shows how spending rises steadily with age, from one yuan per week for the youngest to ten times that by age 12. Boys aged 11 and 12 spend significantly more than girls, mainly by taking some out of savings. In fact, based on remarks from some respondents, it appears that parents may be more flexible about allowing boys to tap savings than allowing girls to do so.

> *Boys aged 11 and 12 spend significantly more than girls, mainly by taking some out of savings.*

Purchases made by urban Chinese children, with parents and independently, by age.

AGE	PURCHASES W/PARENTS	WEEKLY TRIPS	NUMBER OF STORES	PURCHASES ALONE	WEEKLY TRIPS	NUMBER OF STORES
4	67%	1.2	1.0	5.1%	0.6	1.0
5	69	1.2	1.0	12.0	0.9	1.0
6	70	1.7	1.0	38.0	1.5	1.0
7	89	2.1	1.0	68.0	1.6	1.0
8	100	2.1	1.0	98.0	1.7	1.7
9	100	2.4	1.2	100.0	2.4	1.8
10	100	2.5	1.2	100.0	2.8	1.9
11	76	1.9	1.3	100.0	2.9	1.7
12	62	1.2	1.2	100.0	1.5	1.6

FIGURE 20-4

Independent Purchases. Parents were asked to what extent children go to the marketplace with them, as well as on their own. The term "marketplace" embraces retail stores and street vendors, both of which are major shopping outlets in China. **Figure 20-4** shows a summary of the parents' responses. Most children of all ages make some independent purchases while shopping with their parents or grandparents. Approximately two-thirds of children aged 4 to 6, 89 percent of 7-year-olds, and practically all children aged 8 and older make some independent purchases with parents.

One of every six responding mothers volunteered that 11- and

12-year-olds usually do not go shopping with parents because they have to study for middle-school entrance exams. Column three of **Figure 20-4** shows that, on average, Chinese children make two shopping trips per week with parents during which they make a purchase. The youngest and oldest children make slightly fewer trips.

From age 8 on, virtually all children make some purchase visits independently. It should be noted that retailers and residences are located together in urban China, which makes it easier for young children to shop on their own. Also, Chinese children typically walk to and from school, which provides them with additional opportunities to shop. Once they get older, they are likely to do this with other children of the same sex. In general, gender is not a significant influence on average number of store visits with or without parents, although there is a tendency for girls to shop more frequently with parents.

Store Visits. Children visit an average of slightly less than three store types per week, one with their parents and nearly two without. Street vendors are considered one type of store even though many sell a wide range of products.

We asked parents what kinds of stores their children visit. Children under age 10 frequent food stores most, whereas those aged 10 and older are most likely to visit book stores. Toy stores rank second with the young set, whereas food stores are second with the older children. Stationery stores, where children buy many of their school supplies, rank third among all children. Street merchants, where children can conveniently buy almost any product they desire, rank fourth among all children. Department stores rank last, and are frequented almost solely by the 10-and-older group. Store visit frequencies do not differ by gender, although girls tend to patronize food stores and book stores slightly more than boys do.

Purchases. Parents also were asked to estimate how their children allocate money among eight product categories: snacks (food and beverages), books and magazines, school supplies, play items (including pay-to-play video games), clothing, sporting goods, recorded music, and electronic items. We tested the questionnaire to come up with this list of culture-appropriate categories. The results are as follows: snacks, 21 percent; books and magazines, 31 percent; school supplies, 25 percent; play items, 8 percent; clothing, 10 percent; music, 2 percent; sporting goods, 2 percent; and electronics, 1 percent. In

● ● ● ● ● ● ● ● ● ●
Chinese children typically walk to and from school, which provides them with additional opportunities to shop.

total, slightly more than half of Chinese kids' spending goes to school-related items—books, magazines, and school supplies. Children under age 9 allocate significantly more of their money to snacks and play items, while older children allocate significantly more to books, clothing, and electronics. Boys and girls spend their money in approximately the same ways.

Children's Influence on Parents' and Grandparents' Spending. Parents were given a predetermined list of 25 items Chinese households commonly purchase and asked to estimate to what extent, if any, their children influence purchases. **Figure 20-5** displays these items alphabetically and shows the average percent of child influence for each. Children's influence is clearly high, especially for items we might normally associate with children; 75 percent or more for parental purchases of bakery items, candy, clothing, fruits, fruit juices, gum, ice cream, imported candy, movies, nuts, shoes, stationery, toys, and video games. Their influence is predictably lower for deli items, meats, sea foods, and vegetables. As children get older, they are less likely to be involved with purchases of bakery items, gum, ice cream, milk, and toys, but significantly more involved in purchases of toothpaste and toothbrushes. Girls and boys have equal influence on most items, but girls have significantly more influence on bakery items, fruit juices, ice cream, and toys.

Actually, children often exert more influence on parental purchases than these figures disclose. One-fourth of the parents voluntarily reported they usually have their children's likes in mind when they make most purchases. This is what we earlier called children's indirect influence. Therefore, the measures of influence shown here are conservative.

Grandparents are also a significant target of influence, because around 25 percent of Chinese children live with grandparents. We asked parents if children request things from grandparents in the household, and if so, to check off these items on the list of 25 products. According to parents, 43 percent of children who have grandparents living with them ask grandparents for books, 35 percent for toys, 28 percent for vegetables, and 23 percent for school supplies. The youngest make significantly more requests for candy and soft drinks. Boys are significantly more likely to ask grandparents for books, toys, and video games, while girls seek more clothing.

One-fourth of the parents voluntarily reported they usually have their children's likes in mind when they make most purchases.

Chinese children's influence on parent's purchases, shown as percentage by age.

ITEM	AGE 4	AGE 5	AGE 6	AGE 7	AGE 8	AGE 9	AGE 10	AGE 11	AGE 12
Bakery items*	95%	95%	95%	95%	94%	94%	92%	89%	84%
Books	58	59	63	57	57	84	59	71	59
Bread	65	76	61	61	58	61	59	56	65
Candy	88	82	79	79	74	76	70	78	79
Clothing	80	82	84	88	88	88	89	90	90
Cookies	72	68	58	56	60	71	59	58	69
Deli items	35	45	46	48	48	46	48	43	43
Fruits	89	91	91	92	92	93	93	93	93
Fruit juices	89	89	91	92	92	93	93	93	93
Gum*	91	93	90	91	91	88	76	83	84
Hair care items	59	59	61	29	30	46	43	53	55
Ice cream*	93	94	95	95	95	93	90	88	88
Imported candy	98	98	97	97	96	95	95	94	93
Meats	48	28	37	35	35	38	36	39	35
Milk	71	74	64	70	74	71	60	62	63
Movies	71	98	94	92	90	95	93	93	90
Nuts	92	92	90	90	90	91	91	90	88
Seafood	52	48	51	39	39	60	51	53	50
Soft drinks	71	72	74	73	73	76	68	73	76
Shoes	79	81	60	74	74	82	78	83	75
Stationary	66	62	80	82	88	87	86	85	86
Toothpaste/brush**	63	63	61	64	64	75	75	75	76
Toys*	93	93	92	92	90	91	90	86	86
Vegetables	38	28	28	18	18	26	28	27	26
Video games	73	98	94	92	90	95	93	93	94

*influence declines significantly with age
**influence increases significantly with age

FIGURE 20-5 **Overview of Chinese Children's Consumer Development**

This initial study suggests the consumer role is an important element in urban family life in spite of China's socialist structure. Children are typically assisted into the consumer role before they begin elementary school. They receive money to buy things as early as age 4, and visit the marketplace as co-purchasers which soon turns into independent purchase behavior. During preschool years, Chinese children learn to obtain products from the marketplace by requesting them from parents who apparently cede substantial consumer decision-making power as soon as children seek it. Indeed, by the time the children in this study become acclimated to school, they are also fully participating consumers. It would appear, then, that the consumer socialization behavior of Chinese parents toward children is very much like that found in U.S. families, although perhaps a half click slower.

While Chinese children spend their money on a relatively wide range of items, it is surely their expenditures on reading material and school-related items that distinguish them from U.S. children. Chinese children spend over half of their own money on school-related items, while American children spend virtually none. Children also have strong influence on parental spending in this category. It appears that the paramount importance of education is instilled very early in childhood by Chinese parents. Education is rationed in China, so doing well on entrance exams at each educational level is absolutely necessary in order to get a seat in a good school. Chinese parents and children consider the best educational materials a necessary but small price to pay for a bright future. There is a possibility that American families will head in the same direction as Chinese parents, increasingly viewing education as the only way for their children to keep up in a globally competitive economy. But at this point, this attitude does not extend to American children's school-related purchases.

Chinese children spend over half of their own money on school-related items, while American children spend virtually none.

Chinese children's overall index of influence on family spending on 25 items is around 68 percent, easily surpassing the approximately 45 percent for U.S. children on similar items, and warranting such often used descriptors as "spoiled brats" and "little emperors." This high level of influence on family spending suggest a "filiarchy" in Chinese households that determines consumer behavior patterns at least as much as the patriarchy for which China is known.

It is important to note that young children in this study learn about saving as well as spending. To oversimplify somewhat, they receive regular income to spend and special gift money to save. We must look beyond China's socialist economy to its ancient culture to understand the strong emphasis on saving money. The early saving of money in Chinese childhood contributes to the development of one's prestige or face, what the Chinese call *mien tsu*. Saving is also a way to learn balance, not give in entirely to one's impulses, or what Confucius termed "the mean." So saving, like spending, satisfies several important needs. It permits planned spending, probably for relatively expensive items, and it enhances one's dignity and one's feelings of security and contentment. Thus, Chinese children save their regular income at around the same rate as U.S. kids and for the same reason—to buy high-ticket items at a later date. But Chinese children have a second important reason to save—to save face.

Grandparents are an important element of Chinese children's consumer development. In this study, grandparents who live in children's households provide money to children, favoring girls somewhat more than boys. They also fill some of children's requests for a number of products, particularly books, toys, and foods.

When one steps back and looks at the overall pattern of consumer socialization of urban Chinese children in this study, similarities to Western children are more apparent than differences. Chinese toddlers of both genders, like those in the U.S., learn the basics of the exchange process from their parents through encouragement and practice, and by the time the kids are comfortably situated in elementary school, they also routinely perform in the consumer role by making a number of independent shopping trips to stores. They receive money from family members, they spend some on their own wants and needs, save some, and they make purchase requests to parents and grandparents.

China also exerts culture-specific influences on children, however, in its effect on saving rates, for example. The ritualistic large money gifts on special occasions are unusual, particularly in a relatively poor economy. China's male dominance appears to be declining, but it is still prevalent and manifests itself in several ways in consumer behavior. Boys are more readily able to access money from their precious savings accounts. They usually get to go shopping on their own a bit earlier than girls. At the same time, grandparents tend to give more special money to girls than boys, perhaps in an effort to make up for this cultural bias. China's glorification of education is apparent in the products children buy with their own money, the kinds of stores they like to visit, and in the requests they make to parents.

The economic impact of China's urban children is substantial and, based on my best estimate, growing at least 10 percent a year. Using some household expenditures obtained from the Beijing Statistical Bureau, we can get some idea of Chinese children's market potential in U.S. dollars. For example, children aged 4 to 12 in only the big cities of China conservatively influence $44.8 billion of annual food purchases; $4.1 billion in children's clothing purchases; $2.7 billion for school supplies, not including text-

• • • • • • •
Chinese toddlers, like those in the U.S., learn the basics of the exchange process from their parents through encouragement and practice.

books or computers; and $2.7 billion for toys. In addition, these children annually spend $6 billion of their own.

If western marketers can persuade Chinese children to spend much of their savings on high-ticket items such as computer software and athletic shoes, as they do in the U.S., this $6 billion could easily double. Furthermore, household spending is increasing dramatically in China, probably at double-digit rates in most major cities. And even though China's government severely limits the number of children per family, the country is so huge that it has roughly 28 million births each year—approximately the total population of Canada. It is reasonable to assume that the economic prowess of Chinese children will reach that of U.S. children by 2010.

Final Note

Today, the United States is both the world's largest exporter and importer. Thus, whether or not they wish to be, and whether or not they acknowledge it, most U.S. marketers are now part of the international marketing system. The number that wants to be on the export side of the equation is rapidly growing.

What I have attempted to do briefly in these few pages about children as a potential global market is what a firm ordinarily does when it is considering overseas markets. I started out looking at children as a world market using the standard People x Dollars = Markets approach. I then identified the market with the most concentration of population and dollars and greatest potential for virtually any U.S. marketer—China.

Yet, I know, and research confirms, that such facts and figures will not tempt most U.S. kids marketers. It is hard to explain, but most U.S. marketers are very nationalistic. In a way, they are as much convenience shoppers as the consumers they target in the U.S. It is these marketers who perpetuate the myth that children in the U.S. represent an enormous market. It is kids in other nations who represent a truly enormous market! The U.S. is an attractive market, but it is highly competitive and highly saturated. The future of the kids market is the world—a daunting but exciting prospect.

Kids in other nations represent a truly enormous market. The future of the kids market is the world.

Index

About the Author

DR. JAMES U. MCNEAL is Professor of Marketing at Texas A&M University where he teaches courses in marketing and consumer behavior. He is the author of more than 80 articles and five books. His earlier books include *Children as Consumers* (1987), *A Bibliography of Research and Writings in Marketing* and *Advertising to Children* (1991), and *Kids as Customers* (1992). His many articles describe children's consumer behavior from both a domestic and global perspective, and the appropriate marketing strategies for effectively targeting this market segment.

Dr. James U. McNeal and friends

During the past ten years, he has conducted studies of children's consumer behavior in China, Hong Kong, Japan, New Zealand, North Korea, and Taiwan. He recently completed his sixth study in China and is an advisor to a research consortium that is attempting to describe the consumer behavior of children worldwide.

Dr. McNeal's consulting clients include the following organizations: AT&T, Audience Research & Development, Best Western International, Boy Scouts of America, Binney & Smith (Crayola), Coca-Cola, Campbell Soup, Delta Airlines, Consumer Unions, Fiesta Texas amusement park, Fox Broadcasting, General Mills, Howard Johnson, Holiday Inns, International Apple Institute, Just Kid Inc. (an integrated marketing firm), Johnson &

Johnson, Kodak, Kraft Foods, Limited Too Stores, M&M Mars, Nike, Marvel Entertainment, PepsiCo, Procter & Gamble, Sears, ShowBiz Restaurants, Sive/Young & Rubicam advertising agency, Strottman International promotion agency, Time Warner, Tracy-Locke, Universal Family Entertainment, USAA, Walt Disney, White House Office on National Drug Control Policy, and World Health Organization.

About the Publisher

Paramount Market Publishing (PMP) publishes books and reports about markets and market segments. In addition, PMP offers a carefully chosen selection of marketing sources from other publishers. To find out more about PMP and how to earn discounts on future publications, visit our Web site at **www.paramountbooks.com** or call us at 888-787-8100.